Awful Disclosures
by
Maria Monk
of the Hotel Dieu Nunnery of Montreal

Maria Monk

Awful Disclosures by Maria Monk of the Hotel Dieu Nunnery of Montreal

The present edition is a reproduction of previous publication of this classic work. Minor typographical errors may have been corrected without note; however, for an authentic reading experience the spelling, punctuation, and capitalization have been retained from the original text.

ISBN: 978-1-64799-632-1

CONTENTS

PREFACE

Here is the reprint of one of the most formidable books against Nunneries ever published. It has produced powerful impressions abroad, as well as in the United States, and appears destined to have still greater results. It is the simple narrative of an uneducated and unprotected female, who escaped from the old Black Nunnery of Montreal, or Hotel Dieu, and told her tale of sufferings and horrors, without exaggeration or embellishment. Though assailed by all the powers of the Romish priesthood, whom she accused, and by the united influence of the North American press, which, with very small exceptions, was then unenlightened by the discoveries of the present day, the book remains unimpeached, and still challenges the test of fair and open examination.

Many an American female, no doubt, is now living, who might justly acknowledge that she was saved from exposure to the suffering, or even the ruin, often the consequences of a Convent education, by the disinterested warning given in this book; while its author, disheartened at length by the powerful combination of Protestants and Papists against her, led to distrust even the few who remained her friends, destitute of the means of living, and alternately persecuted and tempted by her ever watchful and insidious enemies, died some years since, under condemnation (whether just or unjust) for one of the slightest of the crimes which she had charged against them—thus falling at last their victim.

American parents have here a book written for the salvation of their daughters; American patriots, one designed to secure society against one of the most destructive but insidious institutions of popery; American females, an appeal to them of the most solemn kind, to beware of Convents, and all who attempt to inveigle our unsuspecting daughters into them, by the secret apparatus of Jesuit schools. The author of this book was a small, slender, uneducated, and persecuted young woman, who sought refuge in our country without a protector; but she showed the resolution and boldness of a heroine, in confronting her powerful enemies in their strong hold, and proved, by the simple force of truth, victorious in the violent conflicts which were waged against her by the Romish hierarchy of America and the popular press of the United States.

The publishers have thought the present an opportune period to place this work again in the hands of American readers, with such information, in a preface, as is necessary to acquaint readers of the present day with the leading circumstances attending and succeeding its original publication. They have examined most of the evidence supporting the truth of the narrative, of which the public can judge as well as themselves. The details would be voluminous, even of those portions which have been collected since the heat of the controversy which the book long ago excited. Suffice it to say, that undesigned and collateral evidence in corroboration of it has been increasing to the present day; and that the following brief review of some of the early events will afford a fair specimen of the whole.

In the year 1835, Maria Monk was found alone, and in a wretched and feeble condition, on the outskirts of New York city, by a humane man, who got her admitted into the hospital at Bellevue. She then first told the story in outline, which she afterwards and uniformly repeated in detail, and which was carefully written down and published in the following form:—she said she was a fugitive nun from the Hotel Dieu of Montreal, whence she had effected her escape, in consequence of cruelty which she had suffered, and crimes which were there committed by the Romish priests, who had the control of the institution, and to which they had access, by private as well as public entrances. Having expressed a willingness to go to that city, make public accusations, and point out evidences of their truth in the convent itself, she was taken thither by a resolute man, who afterwards suffered for an act of great merit; but she was unable to obtain a fair hearing, apparently through the secret opposition of the priests. She returned to New York, where her story was thought worthy of publication; and it was proposed to have it carefully written down from her lips, and published in a small pamphlet. Everything she communicated was, therefore, accurately written down, and, when copied out, read to her for correction. But the amount of important material in her possession, proved to be far greater than had been supposed, and many pages of notes were accumulated on numerous topics brought up to her attention in the course of conversation and inquiry. All those were submitted to persons fully competent to decide as to the reliability of the evidence, and the strictest and most conscientious care was taken to ascertain the truth.

There were but very few Protestants in the United States acquainted with the condition or history of convents in different countries, the characters of those who control and direct them, the motives they have for keeping them secret, the occupations often pursued within their walls, in short, the shameful practices and atrocious crimes of which they have been proved to be the theatres, in modern and ancient times, by Romish ecclesiastics and even popes themselves. The public were, therefore, quite unprepared to believe such accusations against men professing sanctity of life, and a divine commission to the world, although Miss Harrison and Miss Reed of Boston had published startling reports respecting the character of the priests and nuns in that vicinity.

The following were some of the considerations which were kept in view by those who proposed the publication of the narrative:—

"If the story is false, it must have been forged by the narrator or some other party. There must have been a motive in either case; and that may be either to obtain notoriety or money, to injure the reputation of the priests accused, or ultimately to remove the unfavorable impressions thrown upon them by their former accusers, by first making charges of atrocious crimes, and then disproving them. On the other hand, the story may perhaps be true; and if so, the world ought to know it. In the meantime, here is an unprotected, and evidently unfortunate young woman, of an interesting appearance, who asks to be allowed to make her complaint, voluntarily consenting to submit to punishment if she does not speak the truth. She must be allowed a hearing."

It is but justice to say that the investigation was undertaken with strong suspicions of imposture somewhere, and with a fixed resolution to expose it if discovered. As the investigation proceeded, opinions at first fluctuated, sometimes from day to day; but it became evident, ere long, that if the story had been fabricated, it was not the work of the narrator, as she had not the capacity to invent one so complex and consistent with itself and with many historical facts entirely beyond the limited scope of her knowledge. It was also soon perceived that she could never have been taught it by others, as no part of it was systematically arranged in her mind, and she communicated it in the incidental manner common to uneducated persons, who recount past scenes in successive conversations.

As she declared from the first that she had been trained to habits of deception in the Convent, and accustomed to witness deceit and criminality, no confidence could be claimed for her mere unsupported declarations; and therefore a course of thorough cross-questioning was pursued, every effort being made to lead her to contradict herself, but without success. She told the same things over and over again in a natural and consistent manner, when brought back to the same point after intervals of weeks or months. In several instances it was thought that contradictions had been traced, but when called on to reconcile her statements, she cleared up all doubt by easy and satisfactory explanations. The course pursued by the priests of Canada and their advocates, was such as greatly to confirm the opinion that she spoke the truth, and that they were exceedingly afraid of it. The following were some of the contradictory grounds which they at different times assumed in their bitter attacks upon her, her friends, and her books:

That she had never been in the nunnery.

That she had been expelled from it.

That she had fabricated everything that she published.

That several pages from her book, published in the New York "Sun," were copied verbatim et literatim from a work published in Portugal above a hundred years before, entitled "The Gates of Hell Opened."

That there never was a subterranean passage from the seminary to the nunnery.

That there was such a passage in that direction, but that it led to the River St. Lawrence.

That the drawings and descriptions of the nunnery, and especially of the veiled department, were wholly unlike the reality, but applied to the Magdalen Asylum of Montreal.

That several objects described by her were in the nunnery, but not in those parts of it where she had placed them. (This was said by a person who admitted that he had been lost amidst the numerous and extensive apartments when he made his observations.)

That the book was fabricated by certain persons in New York who were named, they being gentlemen of the highest character.

That the book was her own production, but written under the instigation of the devil.

That the author was a layman, and ought to be hung on the first lamp-post.

That the nunnery was a sacred place, and ought not to be profaned by the admission of enemies of the church.

After a committee had been appointed to examine the nunnery and report, and their demand for admission had been published a year or more, the editor of L'Ami du Peuple, a Montreal newspaper, devoted to the priests' cause, offered to admit persons informally, and did admit several Americans, who had been strong partisans against the "Disclosures." Their letters on the subject, though very indefinite, contained several important, though undesigned admissions, strongly corroborating the book.

One of the most common charges against the book was, that it had been written merely for the purpose of obtaining money. Of the falseness of this there is decisive evidence. It was intended to secure to the poor and persecuted young female, any profits which might arise from the publication; but most of the labor and time devoted to the work were gratuitously bestowed. Besides this they devoted much time to efforts necessary to guard against the numerous and insidious attempts made by friends of the priests, who by various arts endeavored to produce dissention and delay, as well as to pervert public opinion.

The book was published, and had an almost unprecedented sale, impressing deep convictions, wherever it went, by its simple and consistent statements. In Canada, especially, it was extensively received as true; but as the American newspapers were soon enlisted against it, the country was filled with misrepresentations, which it was impossible through those channels to follow with refutations. Her noble sacrifices for the good of others were misunderstood, she withdrew from her few remaining friends, and at length died in poverty and prison, a victim of the priests of Rome. Various evidences in favor of its truth afterwards appeared, with which the public have never been generally made acquainted. Some of these were afforded during an interview held in New York, August 17th, 1836, with Messrs. Jones and Le Clerc, who had came from Montreal with a work in reply to "Awful Disclosures," which was afterwards published. They had offered to confront Maria Monk, and prove her an impostor, and make her confess it in the presence of her friends. She promptly appeared; and the first exclamation of Mr. Jones proved that she was not the person he had supposed her to be: "This is not Fawny Johnson!" said he; and he afterwards said, "There must be two Maria Monks!" Indeed, several persons were at different times represented to bear that name; and much confusion was caused in the testimony by that artifice. The interview continued about two hours, during which the Canadians made a very sorry figure, entirely failing to gain any advantage, and exposing their own weakness. At the close, an Episcopal clergyman from Canada, one of the company, said: "Miss Monk, if I had had any doubts of your truth before this interview, they would now have been entirely removed."

The book of Mr. Jones was published, and consisted of affidavits, &c., obtained in Canada, including those which had previously been published, and which are contained in the Appendix to this volume. Many of them were signed by names unknown, or those of low persons of no credit, or devoted to the service of the priests. Evidence was afterwards obtained that Mr. Jones was paid by the Canadian ecclesiastics, of which there had been strong indications. What rendered his defeat highly important was, that he was the editor of L'Ami du Peuple, the priests' newspaper, in Montreal, and he was "the author of everything which had been written there against Maria Monk," and had collected all "the affidavits and testimony." These were his own declarations. An accurate report of the interview was published, and had its proper effect, especially his exclamation—"This is not Fanny Johnson!"

The exciting controversy has long passed, but the authentic records of it are imperishable, and will ever be regarded as an instructive study. The corruptions and crimes of nunneries, and the hypocrisy and chicanery of those who control them, with the varied and powerful means at their command, are there displayed to an attentive reader, in colors as dark and appalling as other features of the popish system are among us, by the recent exposures of the impudent arrogance of the murderer Bedini, and the ambitious and miserly spirit of his particular friend, the Romish Archbishop of New York.

Among the recent corroborates of the "Awful Disclosures," may be particularly mentioned the two narratives entitled "Coralla," and "Confessions of a Sister of Charity," contained in the work issued this season by the publishers of the present volume, viz.: "The Escaped Nun; or, Disclosures of Convent Life," &c. Of the authenticity of those two narratives we can give the public the strongest assurance.

After the city of Rome had been taken by siege by the French army, in 1849, the priests claimed possession of a female orphan-asylum, which had something of the nature of a nunnery. The republican government had given liberty to all recluses, and opened all secret institutions. (When will Americans do the same?)

Subsequently, when the papists attempted to reinstate the old system, the females remonstrated, barred the doors, and armed themselves with knives and spits from the kitchen, but the French soldiers succeeded in reducing them by force. During the contest the cry of the women was, "We will not be the wives of the priests!"

In one of the convents in that city, opened by the republicans, were found evidences of some of the worst crimes mentioned by Maria Monk; and in another were multitudes of bones, including those of children.

A strong effort will probably be made again, by the parties exposed by this book, to avoid the condemnation which it throws upon convents—the strongholds of superstition, corruption, and foreign influence, in the United States. The Romish publications, although greatly reduced in number within a few years, will probably pour out much of their unexhausted virulence, as it is their vocation to misrepresent, deny, and vilify. They will be ready to pronounce a general anathema on all who dare to reprint, or even to read or believe, such strong accusations against the "holy retreats" of those whom they pretend are "devoted to lives of piety." But we will challenge them to do it again, by placing some of their iron bishops and even popes in the forefront.

In the year 1489, in the reign of Henry VII, Pope Innocent VIII published a bull for the Reformation of Monasteries, entitled, in Latin, "De Reformatione Monasceriorum," in which he says that, "members of monasteries and other religious places, both Clemian, Cistercian, and Praemonstratensian, and various other orders in the Kingdom of England"—"lead a lascivious and truly dissolute life." And that the papist reader may receive this declaration with due reverence, we copy the preceding words in Latin, as written by an infallible pope, the man whose worshippers address him as "Vicegerent of God on earth." Of course his words must convince them, if ours do not: "Vitam lascivam ducunt, et nimium dissolutam." "Swine Priory," in 1303, had a Prioress named Josiana, whose conduct made the name of her house quite appropriate. In France, in the Council of Troyes, A. D. 999, the Archbishop said, "In convents of monks, canons, and nuns, we have lay abbots residing with their wives, sons, daughters, soldiers and dogs;" and he charges the whole clergy with being in a deprived and sinful state. But the particulars now before us, of such shameful things in Germany, Italy, &c., for ages, would fill a larger volume than this.

Now, let the defenders of nunneries repeat, if they dare, their hackneyed denunciations of those who deny their sanctity. Here stand some of their own bishops and popes before us; and the anathemas must fall first upon mitres and tiaras! Americans will know how much confidence to place in the pretended purity of institutions, whose iniquity and shame have been thus proclaimed, age after age, in a far more extensive manner than by this book. But we can at any time shut their mouths by the mere mention of "Den's Theology," which they must not provoke us to refer to.

CHAPTER I

EARLY RECOLLECTIONS

Early Life—Religious Education neglected—First Schools—Entrance into the School of the Congregational Nunnery—Brief Account of the Nunneries in Montreal—The Congregational Nunnery—The Black Nunnery—The Grey Nunnery—Public Respect for these Institutions—Instruction Received—The Catechism—The Bible.

My parents were both from Scotland, but had been resident in Lower Canada some time before their marriage, which took place in Montreal; and in that city I spent most of my life. I was born at St. John's, where they lived for a short time. My father was an officer under the British Government, and my mother has enjoyed a pension on that account ever since his death.[1]

According to my earliest recollections, he was attentive to his family; and a particular passage from the Bible, which often occurred to my mind in after life, I may very probably have been taught by him, as after his death I do not recollect to have received any religious instruction at home; and was not even brought up to read the scriptures: my mother, although nominally a Protestant, not being accustomed to pay attention to her children in this respect. She was rather inclined to think well of the Catholics, and often attended their churches. To my want of religious instruction at home, and the ignorance of my Creator, and my duty, which was its natural effect. I think I can trace my introduction to Convents, and the scenes which I am to describe in this narrative.

When about six or seven years of age, I went to school to a Mr. Workman, a Protestant, who taught in Sacrament street, and remained several months. There I learned to read and write, and arithmetic as far as division. All the progress I ever made in those branches was gained in that school, as I have never improved in any of them since.

A number of girls of my acquaintance went to school to the nuns of the Congregational Nunnery, or Sisters of Charity, as they are sometimes called. The schools taught by them are perhaps more numerous than some of my readers may imagine. Nuns are sent out from that Convent to many of the towns and villages of Canada to teach small schools; and some of them are established as instructresses in different parts of the United States. When I was

---

[1] See the affidavit of William Miller, in the Appendix.

1

about ten years old, my mother asked me one day if I should not like to learn to read and write French; and I then began to think seriously of attending the school in the Congregational Nunnery. I had already some acquaintance with that language, sufficient to speak it a little, as I heard it every day, and my mother knew something of it.

I have a distinct recollection of my first entrance into the Nunnery; and the day was an important one in my life, as on it commenced my acquaintance with a Convent. I was conducted by some of my young friends along Notre Dame street till we reached the gate. Entering that, we walked some distance along the side of a building towards the chapel, until we reached a door, stopped, and rung a bell. This was soon opened, and entering, we proceeded through a long covered passage till we took a short turn to the left, soon after which we reached the door of the school-room. On my entrance, the Superior met me, and told me first of all that I must always dip my fingers into the holy water at her door, cross myself, and say a short prayer; and this she told me was always required of Protestant as well as Catholic children.

There were about fifty girls in the school, and the nuns professed to teach something of reading, writing, arithmetic, and geography. The methods, however, were very imperfect, and little attention was devoted to them, the time being in a great degree engrossed with lessons in needle-work, which was performed with much skill. The nuns had no very regular parts assigned them in the management of the schools. They were rather rough and unpolished in their manners, often exclaiming, "c'est un menti" (that's a lie), and "mon Dieu" (my God), on the most trivial occasions. Their writing was quite poor, and it was not uncommon for them to put a capital letter in the middle of a word. The only book on geography which we studied, was a catechism of geography, from which we learnt by heart a few questions and answers. We were sometimes referred to a map, but it was only to point out Montreal or Quebec, or some other prominent name, while we had no instruction beyond.

It may be necessary for the information of some of my readers, to mention that there are three distinct Convents in Montreal, all of different kinds; that is, founded on different plans, and governed by different rules. Their names are as follows:—

1st. The Congregational Nunnery.

2d. The Black Nunnery, or Convent of Sister Bourgeoise.

3d The Grey Nunnery.

The first of these professes to be devoted entirely to the education of girls. It would require however only a proper

2

examination to prove that, with the exception of needle-work, hardly anything is taught excepting prayers and the catechism; the instruction in reading, writing, &c., in fact, amounting to very little, and often to nothing. This Convent is adjacent to that next to be spoken of, being separated from it only by a wall. The second professes to be a charitable institution for the care of the sick, and the supply of bread and medicines for the poor; and something is done in these departments of charity, although but an insignificant amount, compared with the size of the buildings, and the number of the inmates.

The Grey Nunnery, which is situated in a distant part of the city, is also a large edifice, containing departments for the care of insane persons and foundlings. With this, however, I have less personal acquaintance than with either of the others. I have often seen two of the Grey nuns, and know that their rules, as well as those of the Congregational Nunnery, do not confine them always within their walls, like those of the Black Nunnery. These two Convents have their common names (Black and Grey) from the colours of the dresses worn by their inmates.

In all these three Convents, there are certain apartments into which strangers can gain admittance, but others from which they are always excluded. In all, large quantities of various ornaments are made by the nuns, which are exposed for sale in the Ornament Rooms, and afford large pecuniary receipts every year, which contribute much to their incomes. In these rooms visitors often purchase such things as please them from some of the old[2] and confidential nuns who have the charge of them.

From all that appears to the public eye, the nuns of these Convents are devoted to the charitable objects appropriate to each, the labour of making different articles, known to be manufactured by them, and the religious observances, which occupy a large portion of their time. They are regarded with much respect by the people at large; and now and then when a novice takes the veil, she is supposed to retire from the temptations and troubles of this world into a state of holy seclusion, where, by prayer, self-mortification, and good deeds, she prepares herself for heaven. Sometimes the Superior of a Convent obtains the character of working miracles; and when such a one dies, it is published through the country, and crowds throng the Convent, who think indulgences are to be derived from bits of her clothes or other things she has possessed; and many have sent articles to be touched to her bed or chair, in which a degree of virtue is thought to remain. I used to

---

[2] The term "old nun," does not always indicate superior age.

participate in such ideas and feelings, and began by degrees to look upon a nun as the happiest of women, and a Convent as the most peaceful, holy, and delightful place of abode. It is true, some pains were taken to impress such views upon me. Some of the priests of the Seminary often visited the Congregation Nunnery, and both catechised and talked with us on religion. The Superior of the Black Nunnery adjoining, also, occasionally came into the School, enlarged on the advantages we enjoyed in having such teachers, and dropped something now and then relating to her own Convent, calculated to make us entertain the highest ideas of it, and to make us sometimes think of the possibility of getting into it.

Among the instructions given us by the priests, some of the most pointed were those directed against the Protestant Bible. They often enlarged upon the evil tendency of that book, and told us that but for it many a soul now condemned to hell, and suffering eternal punishment, might have been in happiness. They could not say any thing in its favour: for that would be speaking against religion and against God. They warned us against it, and represented it as a thing very dangerous to our souls. In confirmation of this, they would repeat some of the answers taught us at catechism, a few of which I will here give. We had little catechisms ("Le Petit Catechism") put into our hands to study; but the priests soon began to teach us a new set of answers, which were not to be found in our books, and from some of which I received new ideas, and got, as I thought, important light on religious subjects, which confirmed me more and more in my belief in the Roman Catholic doctrines. These questions and answers I can still recall with tolerable accuracy, and some of them I will add here. I never have read them, as we were taught them only by word of mouth.

Question. "Pourquoi le bon Dieu n'a pas fait tous les commandemens?"

Réponse. "Parce que l'homme n'est pas si fort qu'il peut garder tous ses commandemens."

Q. "Why did not God make all the commandments?"

A. "Because man is not strong enough to keep them."

And another. Q. "Pourquoi l'homme ne lit pas l'Evangile?"

R. "Parce que l'esprit de l'homme est trop borné et trop faîble pour comprendre qu'est ce que Dieu a écrit."

Q. "Why are men not to read the New Testament?"

A. "Because the mind of man is too limited and weak to understand what God has written."

These questions and answers are not to be found in the common catechisms in use in Montreal and other places where I have been, but all the children in the Congregational Nunnery were taught them, and many more not found in these books.

4

CHAPTER II

CONGREGATIONAL NUNNERY

Story told by a fellow Pupil against a Priest—Other Stories—Pretty Mary—Confess to Father Richards—My subsequent Confessions—Left the Congregational Nunnery.

There was a girl thirteen years old whom I knew in the School, who resided in the neighborhood of my mother, and with whom I had been familiar. She told me one day at school of the conduct of a priest with her at confession, at which I was astonished. It was of so criminal and shameful a nature, I could hardly believe it, and yet I had so much confidence that she spoke the truth, that I could not discredit it.

She was partly persuaded by the priest to believe that he could not sin, because he was a priest, and that anything he did to her would sanctify her; and yet she seemed doubtful how she should act. A priest, she had been told by him, is a holy man, and appointed to a holy office, and therefore what would be wicked in other men, could not be so in him. She told me that she had informed her mother of it, who expressed no anger nor disapprobation, but only enjoined it upon her not to speak of it; and remarked to her, that as priests were not like other men, but holy, and sent to instruct and save us, whatever they did was right.

I afterward confessed to the priest that I had heard the story, and had a penance to perform for indulging a sinful curiosity in making inquiries; and the girl had another for communicating it. I afterward learned that other children had been treated in the same manner, and also of similar proceedings in other places.

Indeed, it was not long before such language was used to me, and I well remember how my views of right and wrong were shaken by it. Another girl at the School, from a place above Montreal, called the Lac, told me the following story of what had occurred recently in that vicinity. A young squaw, called la Belle Marie,(pretty Mary,) had been seen going to confession at the house of the priest, who lived a little out of the village. La Belle Marie was afterwards missed, and her murdered body was found in the river. A knife was also found covered with blood, bearing the priest's name. Great indignation was excited among the Indians, and the priest immediately absconded, and was never heard from again. A note was found on his table addressed to him, telling him to fly if he was guilty.

It was supposed that the priest was fearful that his conduct might be betrayed by this young female; and he undertook to clear himself by killing her.

These stories struck me with surprise at first, but I gradually began to feel differently, even supposing them true, and to look upon the priests as men incapable of sin; besides, when I first went to confession, which I did to Father Richards, in the old French church (since taken down), I heard nothing improper; and it was not until I had been several times, that the priests became more and more bold, and were at length indecent in their questions and even in their conduct when I confessed to them in the Sacristie. This subject I believe is not understood nor suspected among Protestants; and it is not my intention to speak of it very particularly, because it is impossible to do so without saying things both shameful and demoralizing.

I will only say here, that when quite a child, I had from the mouths of the priests at confession what I cannot repeat, with treatment corresponding; and several females in Canada have recently assured me, that they have repeatedly, and indeed regularly, been required to answer the same and other like questions, many of which present to the mind deeds which the most iniquitous and corrupt heart could hardly invent.

There was a frequent change of teachers in the School of the Nunnery; and no regular system was pursued in our instruction. There were many nuns who came and went while I was there, being frequently called in and out without any perceptible reason. They supply school teachers to many of the country towns, usually two for each of the towns with which I was acquainted, besides sending Sisters of Charity to different parts of the United States. Among those whom I saw most, was Saint Patrick, an old woman for a nun (that is, about forty), very ignorant, and gross in her manners, with quite a beard on her face, and very cross and disagreeable. She was sometimes our teacher in sewing, and was appointed to keep order among us. We were allowed to enter only a few of the rooms in the Congregational Nunnery, although it was not considered one of the secluded Convents.

In the Black Nunnery, which is very near the Congregational, is an hospital for sick people from the city; and sometimes some of our boarders, such as are indisposed, were sent there to be cured. I was once taken ill myself and sent there, where I remained a few days.

There were beds enough for a considerable number more. A

physician attended it daily; and there are a number of the veiled nuns of that Convent who spend most of their time there.

These would also sometimes read lectures and repeat prayers to us.

After I had been in the Congregational Nunnery about two years, I left it,[3] and attended several different schools for a short time; but I soon became dissatisfied, having many and severe trials to endure at home, which my feelings will not allow me to describe; and as my Catholic acquaintances had often spoken to me in favour of their faith, I was inclined to believe it true, although, as I before said, I knew little of any religion. While out of the nunnery, I saw nothing of religion. If I had, I believe I should never have thought of becoming a nun.

CHAPTER III

BLACK NUNNERY

Preparations to become a Novice in the Black
Nunnery—Entrance—Occupations of the Novices—The Apartments to which
they had Access—First Interview with Jane Ray—Reverence for the
Superior—Her Reliques—The Holy Good Shepherd or nameless
Nun—Confession of Novices.

At length I determined to become a Black nun, and called upon one of the oldest priests in the Seminary, to whom I made known my intention.

The old priest to whom I applied was Father Rocque. He is still alive. He was at that time the oldest priest in the Seminary, and carried the Bon Dieu, (Good God,) as the sacramental wafer is called. When going to administer it in any country place, he used to ride with a man before him, who rang a bell as a signal. When the Canadians heard it, whose habitations he passed, they would come and prostrate themselves to the earth, worshipping it as God. He

---

[3] See the 2d affidavit.

7

was a man of great age, and wore large curls, so that he somewhat resembled his predecessor, Father Roue. He was at that time at the head of the Seminary. This institution is a large edifice, situated near the Congregational and Black Nunneries, being on the east side of Notre Dame street. It is the general rendezvous and centre of all the priests in the District of Montreal, and, I have been told, supplies all the country with priests as far down as Three Rivers, which place, I believe, is under the charge of the Seminary of Quebec. About one hundred and fifty priests are connected with that of Montreal, as every small place has one priest, and a number of larger ones have two.

Father Rocque promised to converse with the Superior of the Convent, and proposed my calling again, at the end of two weeks, at which time I visited the Seminary again, and was introduced by him to the Superior of the Black Nunnery. She told me she must make some inquiries, before she could give me a decided answer; and proposed to me to take up my abode a few days at the house of a French family in St. Lawrence suburbs, a distant part of the city. Here I remained about a fortnight; during which time I formed some acquaintance with the family, particularly with the mistress of the house, who was a devoted Papist, and had a high respect for the Superior, with whom she stood on good terms.

At length, on Saturday morning about ten o'clock, I called and was admitted into the Black Nunnery, as a novice, much to my satisfaction, for I had a high idea of a life in a Convent, secluded, as I supposed the inmates to be, from the world and all its evil influences, and assured of everlasting happiness in heaven. The Superior received me, and conducted me into a large room, where the novices, (who are called in French Postulantes,) were assembled, and engaged in their customary occupation of sewing.

Here were about forty of them, and they were collected in groups in different parts of the room, chiefly near the windows; but in each group was found one of the veiled nuns of the Convent, whose abode was in the interior apartments, to which no novice was to be admitted. As we entered, the Superior informed the assembly that a new novice had come, and she desired any present who might have known me in the world to signify it.

Two Miss Fougnées, and a Miss Howard, from Vermont, who had been my fellow-pupils in the Congregational Nunnery, immediately recognised me. I was then placed in one of the groups, at a distance from them, and furnished by a nun called Sainte Clotilde, with materials to make a kind of purse, such as the priests use to carry the consecrated wafer in, when they go to administer the sacrament to the sick. I well remember my feelings at that time,

8

sitting among a number of strangers, and expecting with painful anxiety the arrival of the dinner hour. Then, as I knew, ceremonies were to be performed, for which I was but ill prepared, as I had not yet heard the rules by which I was to be governed, and knew nothing of the forms to be repeated in the daily exercises, except the creed in Latin, and that imperfectly. This was during the time of recreation, as it is called. The only recreation there allowed, however, is that of the mind, and of this there is but little. We were kept at work, and permitted to speak with each other only on such subjects as related to the Convent, and all in the hearing of the old nuns who sat by us. We proceeded to dinner in couples, and ate in silence while a lecture was read.

The novices had access to only eight of the apartments of the Convent; and whatever else we wished to know, we could only conjecture. The sleeping room was in the second story, at the end of the western wing. The beds were placed in rows, without curtains or anything else to obstruct the view; and in one corner was a small room partitioned off, in which was the bed of the night-watch, that is, the old nun that was appointed to oversee us for the night. In each side of the partition were two holes, through which she could look out upon us whenever she pleased. Her bed was a little raised above the level of the others. There was a lamp hung in the middle of our chamber which showed every thing to her distinctly; and as she had no light in her little room, we never could perceive whether she was awake or asleep. As we knew that the slightest deviation from the rules would expose us to her observation, as well as to that of our companions, in whom it was a virtue to betray one another's faults, as well as to confess our own, I felt myself under a continual exposure to suffer what I disliked, and had my mind occupied in thinking of what I was to do next, and what I must avoid.

I soon learned the rules and ceremonies we had to regard, which were many; and we had to be very particular in their observance. We were employed in different kinds of work while I was a novice. The most beautiful specimen of the nuns' manufacture which I saw was a rich carpet made of fine worsted, which had been begun before my acquaintance with the Convent, and was finished while I was there. This was sent as a present to the King of England, as an expression of gratitude for the money annually received from the government. It was about forty yards in length, and very handsome. We were ignorant of the amount of money thus received. The Convent of Grey Nuns has also received funds from the government, though on some account or other, had not for several years.

I was sitting by a window at one time, with a girl named Jane

9

M'Coy, when one of the old nuns cams up and spoke to us in a tone of liveliness and kindness which seemed strange, in a place where everything seemed so cold and reserved. Some remark which she made was evidently intended to cheer and encourage me, and made me think that she felt some interest in me. I do not recollect what she said, but I remember it gave me pleasure. I also remember that her manner struck me singularly. She was rather old for a nun, that is, probably thirty; her figure large, her face wrinkled, and her dress careless. She seemed also to be under less restraint than the others, and this, I afterward found, was the case. She sometimes even set the rules at defiance. She would speak aloud when silence was required, and sometimes walk about when she ought to have kept her place: she would even say and do things on purpose to make us laugh; and although often blamed for her conduct, had her offences frequently passed over, when others would have been punished with penances.

I learnt that this woman had always been singular. She never would consent to take a saint's name on receiving the veil, and had always been known by her own, which was Jane Ray. Her irregularities were found to be numerous, and penances were of so little use in governing her, that she was pitied by some, who thought her partially insane. She was, therefore, commonly spoken of as mad Jane Ray; and when she committed a fault, it was often apologized for by the Superior or other nuns, on the ground that she did not know what she did.

The occupations of a novice in the Black Nunnery are not such as some of my readers may suppose. They are not employed in studying the higher branches of education; they are not offered any advantages for storing their mind, or polishing their manners; they are not taught even reading, writing, or arithmetic; much less any of the more advanced branches of knowledge. My time was chiefly employed, at first, in work and prayers. It is true, during the last year I studied a great deal, and was required to work but very little; but it was the study of prayers in French and Latin, which I had merely to commit to memory, to prepare for the easy repetition of them on my reception, and after I should be admitted as a nun.

Among the wonderful events which had happened in the Convent, that of the sudden conversion of a gay young lady of the city into a nun, appeared to me one of the most remarkable. The story which I first heard, while a novice, made a deep impression upon my mind. It was nearly as follows:

The daughter of a wealthy citizen of Montreal was passing the church of Bon Secours, one evening, on her way to a ball, when she was suddenly thrown down upon the steps or near the door, and received a severe shock. She was taken up, and removed first, I think, into the church, but soon into the Black Nunnery, which she soon determined to join as a nun; instead, however, of being required to pass through a long novitiate (which usually occupies about two years and a-half, and is abridged only where the character is peculiarly exemplary and devout), she was permitted to take the veil without delay; being declared by God to a priest to be in a state of sanctity. The meaning of this expression is, that she was a real saint, and already in a great measure raised above the world and its influences, and incapable of sinning, possessing the power of intercession, and being a proper object to be addressed in prayer. This remarkable individual, I was further informed, was still in the Convent, though I never was allowed to see her; she did not mingle with the other nuns, either at work, worship, or meals; for she had no need of food, and not only her soul, but her body, was in heaven a great part of her time. What added, if possible, to the reverence and mysterious awe with which I thought of her, was the fact I learned, that she had no name. The titles used in speaking of her were, the holy saint, reverend mother, or saint bon pasteur (the holy good shepherd).

It is wonderful that we could have carried our reverence for the Superior as far as we did, although it was the direct tendency of many instructions and regulations, indeed of the whole system, to permit, even to foster a superstitious regard for her.

One of us was occasionally called into her room, to cut her nails or dress her hair; and we would often collect the clippings, and distribute them to each other, or preserve them with the utmost care. I once picked up all the stray hairs I could find, after combing her head, bound them together, and kept them for some time, until she told me I was not worthy to possess things so sacred. Jane McCoy and I were once sent to alter a dress for the Superior. I gathered up all the bits of thread, made a little bag, and put them into it for safe preservation. This I wore a long time around my neck, so long, indeed, that I wore out a number of strings, which, I remember, I replace with new ones. I believed it to possess the power of removing pain, and often prayed to it to cure the tooth-ache, &c. Jane Ray sometimes professed to outgo us all in devotion to the Superior, and would pick up the feathers after making her bed. These she would distributed among us, saying, "When the Superior dies, reliques will begin to grow scarce, and you had better supply yourselves in season." Then she would treat the whole matter in some way to turn it into ridicule. Equally contradictory would she appear, when occasionally she would obtain leave from the Superior to tell her dreams. With a serious face, which sometimes imposed

11

upon all of us, and made us half believe she was in a perfect state of sanctity, she would narrate in French some unaccountable vision which she said she had enjoyed. Then turning round, would say, "There are some who do not understand me; you all ought to be informed." And then she would say something totally different in English, which put us to the greatest agony for fear of laughing. Sometimes she would say that she expected to be Superior herself, one of these days, and other things which I have not room to repeat.

While I was in the Congregational Nunnery, I had gone to the parish church whenever I was to confess; for although the nuns had a private confession-room in the building, the boarders were taken in parties through the streets on different days by some of the nuns, to confess in the church; but in the Black Nunnery, as we had a chapel and priests attending in the confessionals, we never left the building.

Our confessions there as novices, were always performed in one way, so that it may be sufficient to describe a single case. Those of us who were to confess at a particular time, took our places on our knees near the confessional-box, and after having repeated a number of prayers, &c., prescribed in our books, came up one at a time and kneeled beside a fine wooden lattice-work, which entirely separated the confessor from us, yet permitted us to place our faces almost to his ear, and nearly concealed his countenance from view, even when so near. I recollect how the priests used to recline their heads on one side, and often covered their faces with their handkerchiefs, while they heard me confess my sins, and put questions to me, which were often of the most improper and even revolting nature, naming crimes both unthought of and inhuman. Still, strange as it may seem, I was persuaded to believe that all this was their duty, or at least that it was done without sin.

Veiled nuns would often appear in the chapel at confession; though, as I understood, they generally confessed in private. Of the plan of their confession-rooms I had no information; but I supposed the ceremony to be conducted much on the same plan as in the chapel and in the church, viz. with a lattice interposed between the confessor and the confessing.

Punishments were sometimes resorted to, while I was a novice, though but seldom. The first time I ever saw a gag, was one day when a young novice had done something to offend the Superior. This girl I always had compassion for; because she was very young, and an orphan. The Superior sent for a gag, and expressed her regret at being compelled, by the bad conduct of the child, to proceed to such a punishment; after which she put it into her mouth, so far as to keep it open, and then let it remain some

12

time before she took it out. There was a leathern strap fastened to each end, and buckled to the back part of the head.

CHAPTER IV

Displeased with the Convent—Left it—Residence at St. Denis— Reliques—Marriage—Return to the Black Nunnery—Objections made by some Novices—Ideas of the Bible.

After I had been in the nunneries four or five years, from the time I commenced school at the Congregational Convent, one day I was treated by one of the nuns in a manner which displeased me, and because I expressed some resentment, was required to beg her pardon. Not being satisfied with this, although I complied with the command, nor with the coolness with which the Superior treated me, I determined to quit the Convent at once, which I did without asking leave. There would have been no obstacle to my departure, I presume, novice as I then was, if I had asked permission; but I was too much displeased to wait for that, and went home without speaking to any one on the subject.

I soon after visited the town of St. Denis, where I saw two young ladies with whom I had formerly been acquainted in Montreal, and one of them a former schoolmate at Mr. Workman's school. After some conversation with me, and learning that I had known a lady who kept school in the place, they advised me to apply to her to be employed as her assistant teacher; for she was then instructing the government school in that place. I visited her, and found her willing, and I engaged at once as her assistant.

The government society paid her 20_l_: a-year: she was obliged to teach ten children gratuitously; might receive fifteen pence a month (about a quarter of a dollar), for each of ten scholars more; and then she was at liberty, according to the regulations, to demand as much as she pleased for the other pupils. The course of instruction, as required by the society, embraced only reading, writing, and what was called ciphering, though I think improperly. The only books used were a spelling-book, l'Instruction de la Jeunesse, the Catholic New Testament, and l'Histoire de Canada. When these had been read through, in regular succession, the children were dismissed as having completed their education. No

13

difficulty is found in making the common French Canadians content with such an amount of instruction as this; on the contrary, it is often very hard indeed to prevail upon them to send their children at all, for they say it takes too much of the love of God from them to sent them to school. The teacher strictly complied with the requisitions of the society in whose employment she was, and the Roman Catholic catechism was regularly taught in the school, as much from choice as from submission to authority, as she was a strict Catholic. I had brought with me the little bag I have before mentioned, in which I had so long kept the clippings of the thread left after making a dress for the Superior. Such was my regard for it, that I continued to wear it constantly round my neck, and to feel the same reverence for its supposed virtues as before. I occasionally had the toothache during my stay at St. Denis, and then always relied on the influence of my little bag. On such occasions I would say—

"By the virtue of this bag, may I be delivered from the toothache;" and

I supposed that when it ceased, it was owing to that cause.

While engaged in this manner, I became acquainted with a man who soon proposed marriage; and young and ignorant of the world as I was, I heard his offers with favour. On consulting with my friend, she expressed an interest for me, advised me against taking such a step, and especially as I knew little about the man, except that a report was circulated unfavorable to his character. Unfortunately, I was not wise enough to listen to her advice, and hastily married. In a few weeks, I had occasion to repent of the step I had taken, as the report proved true—a report which I thought justified, and indeed required, our separation. After I had been in St. Denis about three months, finding myself thus situated, and not knowing what else to do, I determined to return to the Convent, and pursue my former intention of becoming a Black nun, could I gain admittance. Knowing the many inquiries that the Superior would make relative to me, during my absence before leaving St. Denis, I agreed with the lady with whom I had been associated as a teacher (when she went to Montreal, which she did very frequently), to say to the Lady Superior that I had been under her protection during my absence, which would satisfy her, and stop further inquiry; as I was sensible, that, should they know I had been married, I should not gain admittance.

I soon returned to Montreal, and on reaching the city, I visited the Seminary, and in another interview with the Superior of it, communicated my wish, and desired him to procure my re-admission as a novice. Little delay occurred.

After leaving me for a short time, he returned, and told me

14

that the Superior of the Convent had consented, and I was soon introduced into her presence. She blamed me for my conduct in leaving the nunnery, but told me that I ought to be ever grateful to my guardian angel for taking care of me, and bringing me in safety back to that retreat. I requested that I might be secured against the reproaches and ridicule of all the novices and nuns, which I thought some might be disposed to cast upon me unless prohibited by the Superior; and this she promised me. The money usually required for the admission of novices had not been expected from me. I had been admitted the first time without any such requisition; but now I chose to pay it for my re-admission. I knew that she was able to dispense with such a demand as well in this as the former case, and she knew that I was not in possession of any thing like the sum required.

But I was bent on paying to the Nunnery, and accustomed to receive the doctrine often repeated to me before that time, that when the advantage of the church was consulted, the steps taken were justifiable, let them be what they would, I therefore resolved to obtain money on false pretences, confident that if all were known, I should be far from displeasing the Superior. I went to the brigade major, and asked him to give me the money payable to my mother from her pension, which amounted to about thirty dollars, and without questioning my authority to receive it in her name, he gave it me.

From several of her friends I obtained small sums under the name of loans, so that altogether I had soon raised a number of pounds, with which I hastened to the nunnery, and deposited a part in the hands of the Superior. She received the money with evident satisfaction, though she must have known that I could not have obtained it honestly; and I was at once re-admitted as a novice.

Much to my gratification, not a word fell from the lips of any of my old associates in relation to my unceremonious departure, nor my voluntary return. The Superior's orders, I had not a doubt, had been explicitly laid down, and they certainly were carefully obeyed, for I never heard an allusion made to that subject during my subsequent stay in the Convent, except that, when alone, the Superior would herself sometimes say a little about it.

There were numbers of young ladies who entered awhile as novices, and became weary or disgusted with some things they observed, and remained but a short time. One of my cousins, who lived at Lachine, named Reed, spent about a fortnight in the Convent with me. She, however, conceived such an antipathy against the priests, that she used expressions which offended the Superior.

The first day she attended mass, while at dinner with us in full community, she said before us all: "What a rascal that priest was, to preach against his best friend!"

All stared at such an unusual exclamation, and some one inquired what she meant.

"I say," she continued, "he has been preaching against him who gives him his bread. Do you suppose that if there were no devil, there would be any priests?"

This bold young novice was immediately dismissed: and in the afternoon we had a long sermon from the Superior on the subject.

It happened that I one day got a leaf of an English Bible, which had been brought into the Convent, wrapped round some sewing silk, purchased at a store in the city. For some reason or other, I determined to commit to memory a chapter it contained, which I soon did. It is the only chapter I ever learnt in the Bible, and I can now repeat it. It is the second of St. Matthew's gospel, "Now when Jesus was born in Bethlehem of Judea," &c.

It happened that I was observed reading the paper, and when the nature of it was discovered, I was condemned to do penance for my offence.

Great dislike to the Bible was shown by those who conversed with me about it, and several have remarked to me, at different times, that if it were not for that book, Catholics would never be led to renounce their own faith.

I heard passages read from the Evangile, relating to the death of Christ; the conversion of Paul; a few chapters from St. Matthew, and perhaps a few others. The priest would also sometimes take a verse or two, and preach from it. I read St. Peter's Life, but only in the book called the "Lives of the Saints." He, I understand, has the keys of heaven and hell, and has founded our church. As for St. Paul, I remember, as I was taught to understand it, that he was once a great persecutor of the Roman Catholics, until he became convicted, and confessed to one of the father confessors, I don't know which. For who can expect to be forgiven who does not become a Catholic, and confess?

CHAPTER V

Received Confirmation—Painful Feelings—Specimen of Instruction received on the Subject.

The day on which I received confirmation was a distressing one to me. I believed the doctrine of the Roman Catholics, and according to them I was guilty of three mortal sins; concealing something at confession, sacrilege, in putting the body of Christ in the sacrament under my feet, and receiving it while not in a state of grace; and now, I had been led into all those sins in consequence of my marriage, which I never had acknowledged, as it would cut me off from being admitted as a nun.

On the day, therefore, when I went to the church to be confirmed, with a number of others, I suffered extremely from the reproaches of my conscience. I knew, at least I believed, as I had been told, that a person who had been anointed with the holy oil of confirmation on the forehead, and dying in the state in which I was, would go down to hell, and in the place where the oil had been rubbed, the names of my sins would blaze out on my forehead; these would be a sign by which the devils would know me; and they would torment me the worse for them. I was thinking of all this, while I sat in the pew, waiting to receive the oil. I felt, however, some consolation, as I often did afterward when my sins came to mind; and this consolation I derived from another doctrine of the same church: viz. that a bishop could absolve me from all these sins any minute before my death; and I intended to confess them all to a bishop before leaving the world. At length, the moment for administering the "sacrament" arrived, and a bell was rung. Those who had come to be confirmed had brought tickets from their confessors, and these were thrown into a hat, carried around by a priest who in turn handed each to the bishop, by which he learnt the name of each of us, and applied a little of the oil to our foreheads. This was immediately rubbed off by a priest with a bit of cloth, quite roughly.

I went home with some qualms of conscience, and often thought with dread of the following tale, which I have heard told to illustrate the sinfulness of conduct like mine.

A priest was once travelling, when, just as he was passing by a house, his horse fell on his knees, and would not rise. His rider dismounted, and went in to learn the cause of so extraordinary an occurrence. He found there a woman near death, to whom a priest

17

was trying to administer the sacrament, but without success; for every time she attempted to swallow it, it was thrown back out of her mouth into the chalice. He perceived it was owing to unconfessed sin, and took away the holy wafer from her: on which his horse rose from his knees, and he pursued his journey.

I often remembered also that I had been told, that we shall have as many devils biting us, if we go to hell, as we have unconfessed sins on our consciences.

I was required to devote myself for about a year, to the study of the prayers and the practice of the ceremonies necessary on the reception of a nun. This I found a very tedious duty; but as I was released in a great degree from the daily labors usually demanded of novices, I felt little disposition to complain.

CHAPTER VI

Taking the Veil—Interview afterward with the Superior—Surprise and horror at her Disclosure—Resolution to Submit.

I was introduced into the Superior's room on the evening preceding the day on which I was to take the veil, to have an interview with the Bishop. The Superior was present, and the interview lasted about half an hour. The Bishop on this as on other occasions appeared to me habitually rough in his manners. His address was by no means prepossessing.

Before I took the veil, I was ornamented for the ceremony, and was clothed in a rich dress belonging to the Convent, which was used on such occasions; and placed not far from the altar in the chapel, in the view of a number of spectators who had assembled, perhaps about forty. Taking the veil is an affair which occurs so frequently in Montreal, that it has long ceased to be regarded as a novelty; and, although notice had been given in the French parish church as usual, only a small audience had assembled, as I have mentioned.

Being well prepared with a long training, and frequent rehearsals, for what I was to perform, I stood waiting in my large flowing dress for the appearance of the Bishop. He soon presented himself, entering by the door behind the altar; I then threw myself at his feet, and asked him to confer upon me the veil. He expressed his consent, and threw it over my head, saying, "Receive the veil, O thou spouse of Jesus Christ;" and then turning to the Superior, I threw myself prostrate at her feet, according to my instructions, repeating what I had before done at rehearsals, and made a movement as if to kiss her feet. This she prevented, or appeared to prevent, catching me by a sudden motion of her hand, and granted my request. I then kneeled before the Holy Sacrament, that is, a very large round wafer held by the Bishop between his fore-finger and thumb, and made my vows.

This wafer I had been taught to regard with the utmost veneration, as the real body of Jesus Christ, the presence of which made the vows uttered before it binding in the most solemn manner.

After taking the vows, I proceeded to a small apartment behind the altar, accompanied by four nuns, where was a coffin prepared with my nun name engraven upon it:

"SAINT EUSTACE."

My companions lifted it by four handles attached to it, while I threw off my dress, and put on that of a nun of Soeur Bourgeoise; and then we all returned to the chapel. I proceeded first, and was followed by the four nuns; the Bishop naming a number of worldly pleasures in rapid succession, in reply to which I as rapidly repeated—"Je renonce, je renonce, je renonce"—[I renounce, I renounce, I renounce.]

The coffin was then placed in front of the altar, and I advanced to lay myself in it. This coffin was to be deposited, after the ceremony, in an outhouse, to be preserved until my death, when it was to receive my corpse. There were reflections which I naturally made at the time, but I stepped in, extended myself, and lay still. A pillow had been placed at the head of the coffin, to support my head in a comfortable position. A large, thick black cloth was then spread over me, and the chanting of Latin hymns immediately commenced. My thoughts were not the most pleasing during the time I lay in that situation. The pall, or Drap Mortel, as the cloth is called, had a strong smell of incense, which was always disagreeable to me, and then proved almost suffocating. I recollected also a story I had heard of a novice, who, in taking the veil, lay down in her coffin like me, and was covered in the same manner, but on the removal of the covering was found dead.

When I was uncovered, I rose, stepped out of my coffin, and kneeled. The Bishop then addressed these words to the Superior, "Take care and keep pure and spotless this young virgin, whom Christ has consecrated to himself this day." After which the music commenced, and here the whole was finished. I then proceeded from the chapel, and returned to the Superior's room, followed by the other nuns, who walked two by two, in their customary manner, with their hands folded on their breasts, and their eyes cast down upon the floor. The nun who was to be my companion in future, then walked at the end of the procession. On reaching the Superior's door, they all left me, and I entered alone, and found her with the Bishop and two priests.

The Superior now informed me, that having taken the black veil, it only remained that I should swear the three oaths customary on becoming a nun; and that some explanations would be necessary from her. I was now, she told me, to have access to every part of the edifice, even to the cellar, where two of the sisters were imprisoned for causes which she did not mention. I must be informed, that one of my great duties was, to obey the priests in all things; and this I soon learnt, to my utter astonishment and horror, was to live in the practice of criminal intercourse with them. I expressed some of the feelings which this announcement excited in me, which came upon me like a flash of lightning, but the only effect was to set her arguing with me, in favor of the crime, representing it as a virtue acceptable to God, and honorable to me. The priests, she said, were not situated like other men, being forbidden to marry; while they lived secluded, laborious, and self-denying lives for our salvation. They might, indeed, be considered our saviours, as without their services we could not obtain the pardon of sin, and must go to hell. Now, it was our solemn duty, on withdrawing from the world, to consecrate our lives to religion, to practice every species of self-denial. We could not become too humble, nor mortify our feelings too far; this was to be done by opposing them, and acting contrary to them; and what she proposed was, therefore, pleasing in the sight of God. I now felt how foolish I had been to place myself in the power of such persons as were around me.

From what she said I could draw no other conclusion, but that I was required to act like the most abandoned of beings, and that all my future associates were habitually guilty of the most heinous and detestable crimes. When I repeated my expressions of surprise and horror, she told me that such feelings were very common at first, and that many other nuns had expressed themselves as I did, who had long since changed their minds. She even said, that on her entrance into the nunnery, she had felt like me.

Doubts, she declared, were among our greatest enemies. They would lead us to question every point of duty, and induce us to waver at every step. They arose only from remaining imperfection, and were always evidence of sin. Our only way was to dismiss them immediately, repent, and confess them. They were deadly sins, and would condemn us to hell, if we should die without confessing them. Priests, she insisted, could not sin. It was a thing impossible. Everything that they did, and wished, was of course right. She hoped I would see the reasonableness and duty of the oaths I was to take, and be faithful to them.

She gave me another piece of information which excited other feelings in me, scarcely less dreadful. Infants were sometimes born in the convent; but they were always baptized and immediately strangled! This secured their everlasting happiness; for the baptism purified them from all sinfulness, and being sent out of the world before they had time to do anything wrong, they were at once admitted into heaven. How happy, she exclaimed, are those who secure immortal happiness to such little beings! Their little souls would thank those who kill their bodies, if they had it in their power!

Into what a place, and among what society, had I been admitted! How differently did a Convent now appear from what I had supposed it to be! The holy women I had always fancied the nuns to be, the venerable Lady Superior, what were they? And the priests of the seminary adjoining, some of whom indeed I had had reason to think were base and profligate men, what were they all? I now learnt they were often admitted into the nunnery, and allowed to indulge in the greatest crimes, which they and others called virtues.

After having listened for some time to the Superior alone, a number of the nuns were admitted, and took a free part in the conversation. They concurred in everything which she had told me, and repeated, without any signs of shame or compunction, things which criminated themselves. I must acknowledge the truth, and declare that all this had an effect upon my mind. I questioned whether I might not be in the wrong, and felt as if their reasoning might have some just foundation. I had been several years under the tuition of Catholics, and was ignorant of the Scriptures, and unaccustomed to the society, example, and conversation of Protestants; had not heard any appeal to the Bible as authority, but had been taught, both by precept and example, to receive as truth everything said by the priests. I had not heard their authority questioned, nor anything said of any other standard of faith but their declarations. I had long been familiar with the corrupt and licentious expressions which some of them use at confessions, and believed that other women were also. I had no standard of duty to refer to, and no judgment of my own which I knew how to use, or thought of using.

All around me insisted that my doubts proved only my own ignorance and sinfulness; that they knew by experience they would soon give place to true knowledge, and an advance in religion; and I felt something like indecision.

Still, there was so much that disgusted me in the discovery I had now made, of the debased characters around me, that I would most gladly have escaped from the nunnery, and never returned. But that was a thing not to be thought of. I was in their power, and this I deeply felt, while I thought there was not one among the whole number of nuns to whom I could look for kindness. There was one, however, who began to speak to me at length in a tone that gained something of my confidence,—the nun whom I have mentioned before as distinguished by her oddity, Jane Ray, who made us so much amusement when I was a novice. Although, as I have remarked, there was nothing in her face, form, or manners, to give me any pleasure, she addressed me with apparent friendliness; and while she seemed to concur in some things spoken by them, took an opportunity to whisper a few words in my ear, unheard by them, intimating that I had better comply with everything the Superior desired, if I would save my life. I was somewhat alarmed before, but I now became much more so, and determined to make no further resistance. The Superior then made me repeat the three oaths; and when I had sworn them, I was shown into one of the community rooms, and remained some time with the nuns, who were released from their usual employments, and enjoying a recreation day, on account of the admission of a new sister. My feelings during the remainder of that day, I shall not attempt to describe; but pass on to mention the ceremonies which took place at dinner. This description may give an idea of the manner in which we always took our meals, although there were some points in which the breakfast and supper were different.

At 11 o'clock the bell rung for dinner, and the nuns all took their places in a double row, in the same order as that in which they left the chapel in the morning, except that my companion and myself were stationed at the end of the line. Standing thus for a moment, with our hands placed one on the other over the breast, and hidden in our large cuffs, with our heads bent forward, and eyes fixed on the floor; an old nun who stood at the door, clapped her hands as a signal for us to proceed, and the procession moved on, while we all commenced the repetition of litanies. We walked on in this order, repeating all the way, until we reached the door of the dining-room, where we were divided into two lines; those on the right passing down one side of the long table, and those on the left the other, till all were in, and each stopped in her place. The plates were all ranged, each with a knife, fork, and spoon, rolled up in a napkin, and tied round with a linen band marked with the owner's name. My own plate, knife, fork, &c., were prepared like the rest, and on the band around them I found my new name written:—"SAINT EUSTACE."

There we stood till all had concluded the litany; when the old nun who had taken her place at the head of the table next the door, said the prayer before meat, beginning "Benedicite," and we sat down. I do not remember of what our dinner consisted, but we usually had soup and some plain dish of meat, the remains of which were occasionally served up at supper as a fricassee. One of the nuns who had been appointed to read that day, rose and began to lecture from a book put into her hands by the Superior, while the rest of us ate in perfect silence. The nun who reads during dinner stays afterward to dine. As fast as we finished our meals, each rolled up her knife, fork, and spoon in her napkin, and bound them together with the band, and set with hands folded. The old nun then said a short prayer, rose, stepped a little aside, clapped her hands, and we marched towards the door, bowing as we passed before a little chapel or glass box, containing a wax image of the infant Jesus.

Nothing important occurred until late in the afternoon, when, as I was sitting in the community-room, Father Dufrèsne called me out, saying he wished to speak with me. I feared what was his intention; but I dared not disobey. In a private apartment, he treated me in a brutal manner; and from two other priests I afterward received similar usage that evening. Father Dufrèsne afterward appeared again; and I was compelled to remain in company with him until morning.

I am assured that the conduct of the priests in our Convent has never been exposed, and is not imagined by the people of the United States. This induces me to say what I do, notwithstanding the strong reasons I have to let it remain unknown. Still, I cannot force myself to speak on such subjects except in the most brief manner.

CHAPTER VII

Daily Ceremonies—Jane Ray among the Nuns.

On Thursday morning, the bell rung at half-past six to awaken us. The old nun who was acting as night-watch immediately spoke aloud:

"Voici le Seigneur qui vient." (Behold the Lord cometh.) The nuns all responded:

"Allons-y devant lui." (Let us go and meet him.)

We then rose immediately, and dressed as expeditiously as possible, stepping into the passage-way at the foot of our beds as soon as we were ready, and taking places each beside her opposite companion. Thus we were soon drawn up in a double row the whole length of the room, with our hands folded across our breasts, and concealed in the broad cuffs of our sleeves. Not a word was uttered. When the signal was given, we all proceeded to the community-room, which is spacious, and took our places in rows facing the entranced, near which the Superior was seated in a vergiere, or large chair.

We first repeated, "Au nom du Père, du Fils, et du Saint Esprit—Ainsi soit il." (In the name of the Father, the Son, and the Holy Ghost—Amen.)

We then kneeled and kissed the floor; then, still on our knees, we said a very long prayer, beginning: Divin Jesus, Sauveur de mon âme, (Divine Jesus, Saviour of my soul). Then came the Lord's prayer, three Hail Marys, four creeds, and five confessions (confesse à Dieu).

Next we repeated the ten commandments. Then we repeated the Acts of Faith, and a prayer to the Virgin in Latin, (which, like every thing else in Latin, I never understood a word of.) Next we said the litanies of the holy name of Jesus, in Latin, which was afterward to be repeated several times in the course of the day. Then came the prayer for the beginning of the day; then bending down, we commenced the Orison Mental (or Mental Orison), which lasted about an hour and a half.

This exercise was considered peculiarly solemn. We were told in the nunnery that a certain saint was saved by the use of it, as he never omitted it. It consists of several parts: First, the Superior read to us a chapter from a book, which occupied five minutes. Then profound silence prevailed for fifteen minutes, during which we were meditating upon it. Then she read another chapter of equal

24

length, on a different subject and we meditated upon that another quarter of an hour; and after a third reading and meditation, we finished the exercise with a prayer, called an act of contrition, in which we asked forgiveness for the sins committed during the Orison.

During this hour and a half I became very weary, having before been kneeling for some time, and having then to sit in another position more uncomfortable, with my feet under me, my hands clasped, and my body bent humbly forward, with my head bowed down.

When the Orison was over, we all rose to the upright kneeling posture, and repeated several prayers, and the litanies of the providences, "providence de Dieu," &c.; then followed a number of Latin prayers, which we repeated on the way to mass, for in the nunnery we had mass daily.

When mass was over we proceeded in our usual order to the eating-room to breakfast, practising the same forms which I have described at dinner. Having made our meal in silence, we repeated the litanies of the "holy name of Jesus" as we proceeded to the community-room; and such as had not finished them on their arrival, threw themselves upon their knees, and remained there until they had gone through with them, and then kissing the floor, rose again.

At nine o'clock commenced the lecture, which was read by a nun appointed to perform that duty that day; all the rest of us in the room being engaged in work.

The nuns were at this time distributed in different community-rooms, at different kinds of work, and in each were listening to a lecture. This exercise continued until ten o'clock, when the recreation-bell rang. We still continued our work, but the nuns began to converse with each other, on subjects permitted by the rules in the hearing of the old nuns, one of whom was seated in each of the groups.

At half-past ten the silence bell rang, and then conversation instantly ceased, and the recitation of some Latin prayers commenced, which continued half an hour.

At eleven o'clock the dinner-bell rang, and then we proceeded to the dining-room, and went through the forms and ceremonies of the preceding day. We proceeded two by two. The old nun who had the command of us, clapped her hands as the first couple reached the door, when we stopped. The first two dipped their fingers into the font, touched the holy water to the breast, forehead, and each side, thus forming a cross, said, "In the name of the Father, Son, and Holy Ghost, Amen," and then walked on to the dining-room, repeating the litanies. The rest followed their example. On reaching the door the couples divided, and the two rows of nuns marching up, stopped and faced the table against their plates. There we stood, repeating the close of the litany aloud. The old nun then pronounced

"BENEDICITE,"

and we sat down. One of our number began to read a lecture, which continued during the whole meal: she stays to eat after the rest have retired. When we had dined, each of us folded up her napkin, and again folded her hands. The old nun then repeated a short prayer in French, and stepping aside from the head of the table, let us pass out as we came in. Each of us bowed in passing the little chapel near the door, which is a glass case, containing a waxen figure of the infant Jesus. When we reached the community-room we took our places in rows, and kneeled upon the floor, while a nun read aloud, "Douleurs de notre Sainte Marie" (the sorrows of our holy Mary.) At the end of each verse we responded "Ave Maria." We then repeated again the litanies of the Providences, and the

"BENIS," &c.

Then we kissed the floor, and rising, took our work, with leave to converse on permitted subjects; that is what is called recreation till one o'clock. We then began to repeat litanies, one at a time in succession, still engaged at sewing, for an hour.

At two o'clock commenced the afternoon lectures, which lasted till near three. At that hour one of the nuns stood up in the middle of the room, and asked each of us a question out of the catechism; and such as were unable to answer correctly, were obliged to kneel down, until that exercise was concluded, upon as many dry peas as there were verses in the chapter out of which they were questioned. This seems like a penance of no great importance; but I have sometimes kneeled on peas until I suffered great inconvenience, and even pain. It soon makes one feel as if needles were running through the skin: whoever thinks it a trifle, had better try it.

At four o'clock recreation commenced, when we were allowed, as usual, to speak to each other, while at work.

At half-past four we began to repeat prayers in Latin, while we worked, and concluded about five o'clock, when we commenced repeating the "prayers for the examination of conscience," the "prayer after confession," the "prayer before sacrament," and the "prayer after sacrament." Thus we continued our work until dark, when we laid it aside, and began to go over the same prayers which we had repeated in the morning, with the exception of the orison mental; instead of that long exercise, we examined our consciences, to determine whether we had performed the resolution we had made in the morning; and such as had kept it, repeated an "acte de joie," or expression of gratitude; while such as had not, said an "acte de contrition."

When the prayers were concluded, any nun who had been disobedient in the day, knelt and asked pardon of the Superior and her companions "for the scandal she had caused them;" and then requested the Superior to give her a penance to perform. When all the penances, had been imposed, we all proceeded to the eating-room to supper, repeating litanies on the way.

At supper the ceremonies were the same as at dinner, except that there was no lecture read. We ate in silence, and went out bowing to the chapelle, and repeating litanies. Returning to the community-room which we had left, we had more prayers to repeat, which are called La couronne, (crown,) which consists of the following parts:

1st, *Four Paters*, 2d, *Four Ave Marias*, 3d, *Four Gloria Patris*, 4th, *Benis*, &c.

At the close of these we kissed the floor; after which we had recreation till half-past eight o'clock, being allowed to converse on permitted subjects, but closely watched, and not allowed to sit in corners.

At half-past eight a bell was rung, and a chapter was read to us, in a book of meditations, to employ our minds upon during our waking hours at night.

Standing near the door, we dipped our fingers in the holy water, crossed and blessed ourselves, and proceeded up to the sleeping-room, in the usual order, two by two. When we had got into bed, we repeated a prayer beginning with

"Mon Dieu, je vous donne mon coeur,"
"God, I give you my heart;"

and then an old nun, bringing some holy water, sprinkled it on our beds to drive away the devil, while we took some and crossed ourselves again.

At nine o'clock the bell rung, and all who were awake repeated a prayer, called the offrande; those who were asleep were considered as excused.

After my admission among the nuns, I had more opportunity than before, to observe the conduct of mad Jane Ray. She behaved quite differently from the rest, and with a degree of levity irreconcilable with the rules. She was, as I have described her, a large woman, with nothing beautiful or attractive in her face, form, or manners; careless in her dress, and of a restless disposition, which prevented her from steadily applying herself to any thing for any length of time, and kept her roving about, and almost perpetually talking to somebody or other. It would be very difficult to give an accurate description of this singular woman; dressed in the plain garments of the nuns, bound by the same vows, and accustomed to the same life, resembling them in nothing else, and frequently interrupting all their employments. She was apparently almost always studying or pursuing some odd fancy; now rising from sewing, to walk up and down, or straying in from another apartment, looking about, addressing some of us, and passing out again, or saying something to make us laugh, in periods of the most profound silence. But what showed that she was no novelty, was the little attention paid to her, and the levity with which she was treated by the old nuns; even the Superior every day passed over irregularities in this singular person, which she would have punished with penances, or at least have met with reprimands, in any other. From what I saw of her, I soon perceived that she betrayed two distinct traits of character; a kind disposition towards such as she chose to prefer, and a pleasure in teasing those she disliked, or such as had offended her.

CHAPTER VIII

Description of Apartments in the Black Nunnery, in order.—1st Floor—2d Floor—The Founder—Superior's Management with the Friends of Novices—Religious Lies—Criminality of Concealing Sins at Confession.

I will now give from memory, a general description of the interior of the Convent of Black nuns, except the few apartments which I never saw. I may be inaccurate in some things, as the apartments and passages of that spacious building are numerous and various; but I am willing to risk my credit for truth and sincerity on the general correspondence between my description and things as they are. And this would, perhaps be as good a case as any by which to test the truth of my statements, were it possible to obtain access to the interior. It is well known, that none but veiled nuns, the bishop, and priests, are ever admitted; and, of course, that I cannot have seen what I profess to describe, if I have not been a Black nun.[4] The priests who read this book, will acknowledge to themselves the truth of my description; but will, of course deny it to the world, and probably exert themselves to destroy or discredit, I offer to every reader the following description, knowing that time may possibly throw open those secret recesses, and allow the entrance of those who can satisfy themselves, with their own eyes, of its truth. Some of my declarations may be thought deficient in evidence; and this they must of necessity be in the present state of things. But here is a kind of evidence on which I rely, as I see how unquestionable and satisfactory it must prove, whenever it shall be obtained.

If the interior of the Black Nunnery, whenever it shall be examined, is materially different from the following description, then I can claim no confidence of my readers. If it resembles it, they will, I presume, place confidence in some of those declarations, on which I may never be corroborated by true and living witnesses.

I am sensible that great changes may be made in the furniture of apartments; that new walls may be constructed, or old ones removed; and I have been credibly informed, that masons have been employed in the nunnery since I left it. I well know, however, that entire changes cannot be made; and that enough must remain as it was to substantiate my description, whenever the truth shall be known.

The First Story.

Beginning at the extremity of the right wing of the Convent, towards Notre Dame-street, on the first story, there is—

1st. The nuns' private chapel, adjoining which is a passage to a small projection of the building, extending from the upper story to the ground, with very small windows. Into the passage we were sometimes required to bring wood from the yard and pile it up for use.

2d. A large community-room, with plain benches fixed against the wall to sit, and lower ones in front to place our feet upon. There is a fountain in the passage near the chimney at the farther end, for washing the hands and face, with a green curtain sliding on a rod before it. This passage leads to the old nuns' sleeping-room on the right, and the Superior's sleeping-room, just beyond it, as well as to a staircase which conducts to the nuns' sleeping-room, or dortoir, above. At the end of the passage is a door opening into—

3d. The dining-room; this is larger than the community-room,

---

[4] I ought to have made an exception here, which I may enlarge upon in future Certain other persons are sometimes admitted.

and has three long tables for eating, and a chapelle, or collection of little pictures, a crucifix, and a small image of the infant Saviour in a glass case. This apartment has four doors, by the first of which we are supposed to have entered, while one opens to a pantry, and the third and fourth to the two next apartments.

4th. A large community-room, with tables for sewing, and a staircase on the opposite left-hand corner.

5th. A community-room for prayer, used by both nuns and novices. In the farther right-hand corner is a small room partitioned off, called the room for the examination of conscience, which I had visited while a novice by permission of the Superior, and where nuns and novices occasionally resorted to reflect on their character, usually in preparation for the sacrament, or when they had transgressed some of the rules. This little room was hardly large enough to contain half a dozen persons at a time.

6th. Next beyond is a large community-room for Sundays. A door leads to the yard, and thence to a gate in the wall on the cross street.

7th. Adjoining this is a sitting-room, fronting on the cross street, with two windows, and a store-room on the side opposite them. There is but little furniture, and that very plain.

8th. From this room a door leads into what I may call the wax-room, as it contains many figures in wax, not intended for sale. There we sometimes used to pray, or meditate on the Saviour's passion. This room projects from the main building; leaving it, you enter a long passage, with cupboards on the right, in which are stored crockery-ware, knives and forks, and other articles of table furniture, to replace those worn out or broken—all of the plainest description; also, shovels, tongs, &c. This passage leads to—

9th. A corner room, with a few benches, &c., and a door leading to a gate on the street. Here some of the medicines were kept, and persons were often admitted on business, or to obtain medicines with tickets from the priests; and waited till the Superior or an old nun could be sent for. Beyond this room we were never allowed to go; and I cannot speak from personal knowledge of what came next.

The Second Story.

Beginning, as before, at the western extremity of the same wing, but on the second story, the farthest apartment in that direction which I ever entered was—

1st. The nuns' sleeping-room, or dormitory, which I have already described. Here is an access to the projection mentioned in speaking of the first story. The stairs by which we came up to bed are at the farther end of the room; and near them a crucifix and font

30

of holy water. A door at the end of the room opens into a passage, with two small rooms, and closets between them, containing bedclothes. Next you enter—

2d. A small community-room, beyond which is a passage with a narrow staircase, seldom used, which leads into the fourth community-room, in the first story. Following the passage just mentioned, you enter by a door—

3d. A little sitting-room, furnished in the following manner: with chairs, a sofa, on the north side, covered with a red-figured cover and fringe, a table in the middle, commonly bearing one or two books, an inkstand, pens, &c. At one corner is a little projection into the room, caused by a staircase leading from above to the floor below, without any communication with the second story. This room has a door opening upon a staircase leading down to the yard, on the opposite side of which is a gate opening into the cross street. By this way the physician is admitted, except when he comes later than usual. When he comes in, he usually sits a little while, until a nun goes into the adjoining nuns' sick-room, to see if all is ready, and returns to admit him. After prescribing for the patients he goes no farther, but returns by the way he enters; and these two are the only rooms into which he is ever admitted, except the public hospital.

4th. The nuns' sick-room adjoins the little sitting-room on the east, and has, I think, four windows towards the north, with beds ranged in two rows from end to end, and a few more between them, near the opposite extremity. The door from the sitting-room swings to the left, and behind it is a table, while a glass case, to the right, contains a wax figure of the infant Saviour, with several sheep. Near the northeastern corner of this room are two doors, one of which opens into a long and narrow passage leading to the head of the great staircase that conducts to the cross street. By this passage the physician sometimes finds his way to the sick-room, when he comes later than usual. He rings the bell at the gate, which I was told had a concealed pull, known only to him and the priests, proceeds up-stairs and through the passage, rapping three times at the door of the sick-room, which is opened by a nun in attendance, after she has given one rap in reply. When he has visited his patients, and prescribed for them, he returns by the same way.

5th. Next beyond this sick-room, is a large unoccupied apartment, half divided by two partial partitions, which leave an open space in the middle. Here some of the old nuns commonly sit in the day-time.

6th. A door from this apartment opens into another not appropriated to any particular use, but containing a table, where

31

medicines are sometimes prepared by an old nun, who is usually found there. Passing through this room, you enter a passage with doors on its four sides: that on the left, which is kept fastened on the inside, leads to the staircase and gate; that in front, to private sick-rooms soon to be described.

7th. That on the right leads to another, appropriated to nuns suffering with the most loathsome disease. There were usually a number of straw mattresses, in that room, as I well knew, having helped to carry them in after the yard-man had filled them. A door beyond enters into a store-room, which extends also beyond this apartment. On the right, another door opens into another passage; crossing which, you enter by a door—

8th. A room with a bed and screen in one corner, on which nuns were laid to be examined before their introduction into the sick-room last mentioned. Another door, opposite the former, opens into a passage, in which is a staircase leading down.

9th. Beyond this is a spare-room, sometimes used to store apples, boxes of different things, &c.

10th. Returning now to the passage which opens on one side upon the stairs to the gate, we enter the only remaining door, which leads into an apartment usually occupied by some of the old nuns, and frequently by the Superior.

11th, and 12th. Beyond this are two more sick-rooms, in one of which those nuns stay who are waiting their accouchment, and in the other, those who have passed it.

13th. The next is a small sitting-room, where a priest waits to baptize the infants previous to their murder. A passage leads from this room, on the left, by the doors of two succeeding apartments, neither of which have I ever entered.

14th. The first of them is the "holy retreat," or room occupied by the priests, while suffering the penalty of their licentiousness.

15th. The other is a sitting-room, to which they have access. Beyond these the passage leads to two rooms, containing closets for the storage of various articles, and two others where persons are received who come on business.

The public hospitals succeed, and extend a considerable distance, I believe, to the extremity of the building. By a public entrance in that part, priests often come into the nunnery; and I have often seen some of them thereabouts, who must have entered by that way. Indeed, priests often get into the "holy retreat" without exposing themselves to the view of persons in other parts of the Convent, and have been first known to be there, by the yard-man being sent to the Seminary for their clothes.

The Congregational Nunnery was founded by a nun called

Sister Bourgeoise. She taught a school in Montreal, and left property for the foundation of a Convent. Her body is buried, and her heart is kept, under the nunnery, in an iron chest, which has been shown to me, with the assurance that it continues in perfect preservation, although she has been dead more than one hundred and fifty years. In the chapel is the following inscription: "Soeur Bourgeoise, Fondatrice du Couvent"—Sister Bourgeoise, Founder of the Convent.

Nothing was more common than for the Superior to step hastily into our community-rooms, while numbers of us were assembled there, and hastily communicate her wishes in words like these:—

"Here are the parents of such a novice: come with me, and bear me out in this story." She would then mention the outlines of a tissue of falsehoods, she had just invented, that we might be prepared to fabricate circumstances, and throw in whatever else might favor the deception. This was justified, and indeed most highly commended, by the system of faith in which we were instructed.

It was a common remark made at the initiation of a new nun into the Black nun department, that is, to receive the black veil, that the introduction of another novice into the Convent as a veiled nun, caused the introduction of a veiled nun into heaven as a saint, which was on account of the singular disappearance of some of the older nuns at the entrance of new ones!

To witness the scenes which often occurred between us and strangers, would have struck a person very powerfully, if he had known how truth was set at naught. The Superior, with a serious and dignified air, and a pleasant voice and aspect, would commence a recital of things most favorable to the character of the absent novice, and representing her as equally fond of her situation, and beloved by the other inmates. The tale told by the Superior, whatever it was, however unheard before, might have been any of her statements, was then attested by us, who, in every way we could think of, endeavored to confirm her declarations, beyond the reach of doubt.

Sometimes the Superior would intrust the management of such a case to some of the nuns, whether to habituate us to the practice in which she was so highly accomplished, or to relieve herself of what would have been a serious burden to most other persons, or to ascertain whether she could depend upon us, or all together, I cannot tell. Often, however, have I seen her throw open a door, and say, in a hurried manner, "Who can tell the best story?"

One point, on which we received frequent and particular,

instructions was, the nature of falsehoods. On this subject I have heard many a speech, I had almost said many a sermon; and I was led to believe that it was one of great importance, one on which it was a duty to be well informed, as well as to act. "What!" exclaimed a priest one day—"what, a nun of your age, and not know the difference between a wicked and a religious lie!"

He then went on, as had been done many times previously in my hearing, to show the essential difference between the two different kinds of falsehoods. A lie told merely for the injury of another, for our own interest alone, or for no object at all, he painted as a sin worthy of penance. But a lie told for the good of the church or Convent, was meritorious, and of course the telling of it a duty. And of this class of lies there were many varieties and shades. This doctrine has been inculcated on me and my companions in the nunnery, more times than I can enumerate: and to say that it was generally received, would be to tell a part of the truth. We often saw the practice of it, and were frequently made to take part in it. Whenever anything which the Superior thought important, could be most conveniently accomplished by falsehood, she resorted to it without scruple.

There was a class of cases in which she more frequently relied on deception than any other.

The friends of the novices frequently applied at the Convent to see them, or at least to inquire after their welfare. It was common for them to be politely refused an interview, on some account or other, generally a mere pretext; and then the Superior usually sought to make as favorable an impression as possible on the visitors. Sometimes she would make up a story on the spot, and tell the strangers; requiring some of us to confirm it, in the most convincing way we could.

At other times she would prefer to make over to us the task of deceiving, and we were commended in proportion to our ingenuity and success.

Some nun usually showed her submission, by immediately stepping forward. She would then add, perhaps, that the parents of such a novice, whom she named, were in waiting, and it was necessary that they should be told such, and such, and such things. To perform so difficult a task well, was considered a difficult duty, and it was one of the most certain ways to gain the favour of the Superior. Whoever volunteered to make a story on the spot, was sent immediately to tell it, and the other nuns present were hurried off with her under strict injunctions to uphold her in every thing she might state. The Superior, as there was every reason to believe, on all such occasions, when she did not herself appear, hastened to the

34

apartment adjoining that in which the nuns were going, there to listen through the thin partition, to hear whether all performed their parts aright. It was not uncommon for her to go rather further, when she wanted time to give such explanations as she could have desired. She would then enter abruptly, ask, "Who can tell a good story this morning?" and hurry us off without a moment's delay, to do our best at a venture, without waiting for instructions. It would be curious, could a stranger from "the wicked world" outside the Convent witness such a scene. One of the nuns, who felt in a favourable humour to undertake the proposed task, would step promptly forward, and signify her readiness in the usual way: by a knowing wink of one eye, and slight toss of the head.

"Well go and do the best you can," the superior would say; "and all the rest of you must mind and swear to it." The latter part of the order, at least, was always performed; for in every such case, all the nuns present appeared as unanimous witnesses of everything that was uttered by the spokesman of the day.

We were constantly hearing it repeated, that we must never again look upon ourselves as our own; but must remember, that we were solemnly and irrevocably devoted to God. Whatever was required of us, we were called upon to yield under the most solemn considerations. I cannot speak on every particular with equal freedom: but I wish my readers clearly to understand the condition in which we were placed, and the means used to reduce us to what we had to submit to. Not only were we required to perform the several tasks imposed upon us at work, prayers, and penances, under the idea that we were performing solemn duties to our Maker, but every thing else which was required of us, we were constantly told, was something indispensable in his sight. The priests, we admitted were the servants of God, specially appointed by his authority, to teach us our duty, to absolve us from sin, and to lead us to heaven. Without their assistance, we had allowed we could never enjoy the favour of God; unless they administered the sacraments to us, we could not enjoy everlasting happiness. Having consented to acknowledge all this, we had no other objection to urge against admitting any other demand that might be made for or by them. If we thought an act ever so criminal, the Superior would tell us that the priests acted under the direct sanction of God, and could not sin. Of course, then, it could not be wrong to comply with any of their requests, because they could not demand any thing but what was right. On the contrary, to refuse to do any thing they asked, would necessarily be sinful. Such doctrines admitted, and such practices performed, it will not seem wonderful when I mention that we often felt something of their preposterous character.

Sometimes we took a pleasure in ridiculing some of the favourite themes of our teachers; and I recollect one subject particularly, which at one period afforded us repeated merriment. It may seem irreverent in me to give the account, but I do it to show how things of a solemn nature were sometimes treated in the Convent, by women bearing the title of saints. A Canadian Novice, who spoke very broken English, one day remarked that she was performing some duty "for the God." This peculiar expression had something ridiculous to the ears of some of us; and it was soon repeated again and again, in application to various ceremonies which we had to perform. Mad Jane Ray seized upon it with avidity, and with her aid it soon took the place of a by-word in conversation, so that we were constantly reminding each other, that we were doing this and that thing, how trifling and unmeaning soever, "for the God." Nor did we stop here: when the superior called upon us to bear witness to one of her religious lies, or to fabricate the most spurious one the time would admit; to save her the trouble, we were sure to be reminded, on our way to the strangers' room, that we were doing it "for the God." And so it was when other things were mentioned—every thing which belonged to our condition, was spoken of in similar terms.

I have hardly detained the reader long enough on the subject, to give him a just impression of the stress laid on confession. It is one of the great points to which our attention was constantly directed. We were directed to keep a strict and constant watch over our thoughts; to have continually before our minds the rules of the Convent, to compare the one with the other, remember every devotion, and tell all, even the smallest, at confession, either to the Superior or to the priest. My mind was thus kept in a continual state of activity, which proved very wearisome; and it required the constant exertion of our teachers, to keep us up to the practice they inculcated.

Another tale recurs to me, of those which were frequently told us to make us feel the importance of unreserved confession. A nun of our Convent, who had hidden some sin from her confessor, died suddenly, and without any one to confess her. Her sisters assembled to pray for the peace of her soul, when she appeared, and informed them, that it would be of no use, but rather troublesome to her, as her pardon was impossible.[5] The doctrine is, that prayers made for

---

[5] Since the first edition, I have found this tale related in a Romish book, as one of very ancient date. It was told to us as having taken place in our Convent.

souls guilty of unconfessed sin, do but sink them deeper in hell; and this is the reason I have heard given for not praying for Protestants.

The authority of the priests in everything, and the enormity of every act which opposes it, were also impressed upon our minds, in various ways, by our teachers. A "Father" told us the following story one day at catechism.

A man once died who had failed to pay some money which the priest had asked of him; he was condemned to be burnt in purgatory until he should pay it but had permission to come back to this world, and take a human body to work in. He made his appearance therefore again on earth, and hired himself to a rich man as a labourer. He worked all day with the fire burning in him, unseen by other people; but while he was in bed that night, a girl in an adjoining room, perceiving the smell of brimstone, looked through a crack in the wall, and saw him covered with flames. She informed his master, who questioned him the next morning, and found that his hired man was secretly suffering the pains of purgatory, for neglecting to pay a certain sum of money to the priest. He, therefore furnished him the amount due; it was paid, and the servant went off immediately to heaven. The priest cannot forgive any debt due unto him, because it is the Lord's estate.

While at confession, I was urged to hide nothing from the priest, and have been told by them, that they already knew what was in my heart, but would not tell, because it was necessary for me to confess it. I really believed that the priests were acquainted with my thoughts; and often stood in great awe of them. They often told me they had power to strike me dead at any moment.

CHAPTER IX

Nuns with similar names—Squaw Nuns—First visit to the Cellar—Description of it—Shocking discovery there—Superior's Instructions—Private Signal of the Priests—Books used in the Nunnery—Opinions expressed of the Bible—Specimens of what I know of the Scriptures.

I found that I had several namesakes among the nuns, for there were two others who already bore my new name, Saint

37

Eustace. This was not a solitary case, for there were five Saint Marys, and three Saint Monros, besides two novices of that name. Of my namesakes I have little to say, for they resembled most of the nuns; being so much cut off from intercourse with me and the other sisters, that I never saw anything in them, nor learnt any thing about them, worth mentioning.

Several of my new companions were squaws, who had taken the veil at different times. They were from some of the Indian settlements in the country, but were not distinguishable by any striking habits of character from other nuns, and were generally not very different in their appearance when in their usual dress, and engaged in their customary occupations. It was evident, that they were treated with much kindness and lenity by the Superior and the old nuns; and this I discovered was done in order to render them as well contented and happy in their situation as possible. I should have attributed the motives for this partiality to their wishing that they might not influence others to keep away, had I not known they were, like ourselves, unable to exert such an influence. And therefore, I could not satisfy my own mind why this difference was made. Many of the Indians were remarkably devoted to the priests, believing every thing they were taught; and as it is represented to be not only a high honor, but a real advantage to a family, to have one of its members become a nun, Indian parents will often pay large sums of money for the admission of their daughters into a convent. The father of one of the squaws, I was told, paid to the Superior nearly her weight in silver on her reception, although he was obliged to sell nearly all his property to raise the money. This he did voluntarily, because he thought himself overpaid by having the advantage of her prayers, self-sacrifices, &c. for himself and the remainder of his family. The squaws sometimes served to amuse us; for when we were partially dispirited or gloomy, the Superior would occasionally send them to dress themselves in their Indian garments, which usually excited us to merriment.

Among the squaw nuns whom I particularly remember, was one of the Sainte Hypolites, not the one who figured in a dreadful scene, described in another part of this narrative, but a woman of a far more mild and humane character.

Three or four days after my reception, the Superior sent me into the cellar for coal; and after she had given me directions, I proceeded down a staircase, with a lamp in my hand. I soon found myself upon the bare earth, in a spacious place, so dark, that I could not at once distinguish its form, or size, but I observed that it had very solid stone walls, and was arched overhead, at no great elevation. Following my directions, I proceeded onward from the foot of the stairs, where appeared to be one end of the cellar. After walking about fifteen paces, I passed three small doors, on the right, fastened with large iron bolts on the outside, pushed into posts of stone-work, and each having a small opening above, covered with a fine grating, secured by a smaller bolt. On my left, were three similar doors, resembling these, and placed opposite them.

Beyond these, the space became broader; the doors evidently closed small compartments, projecting from the outer wall of the cellar. I soon stepped upon a wooden floor, on which were heaps of wool, coarse linen, and other articles, apparently deposited there for occasional use. I soon crossed the floor, and found the bare earth again under my feet.

A little farther on, I found the cellar again contracted in size, by a row of closets, or smaller compartments projecting on each side. These were closed by doors of a different description from the first, having a simple fastening, and no opening through them. Just beyond, on the left side, I passed a staircase leading up, and then three doors, much resembling those first described, standing opposite three more, on the other side of the cellar. Having passed these, I found the cellar enlarged as before, and here the earth appeared as if mixed with some whitish substance, which attracted my attention.

As I proceeded, I found the whiteness increase, until the surface looked almost like snow, and in a short time I observed before me, a hole dug so deep into the earth that I could perceive no bottom. I stopped to observe it.—It was circular, perhaps twelve or fifteen feet across; in the middle of the cellar, and unprotected by any kind of curb, so that one might easily have walked into it, in the dark.

The white substance which I had observed, was spread all over the surface around it; and lay in such quantities on all sides, that it seemed as if a great deal of it must have been thrown into the hole. It immediately occurred to me that the white substance was lime, and that this must be the place where the infants were buried, after being murdered, as the Superior had informed me. I knew that lime is often used by Roman Catholics in burying-places; and in this way I accounted for its being scattered about the spot in such quantities.

This was a shocking thought to me; but I can hardly tell how it affected me, as I had already been prepared to expect dreadful things in the Convent, and had undergone trials which prevented me from feeling as I should formerly have done in similar circumstances.

I passed the spot, therefore, with distressing thoughts, it is

39

true, about the little corpses, which might be in that secret burying-place, but with recollections also of the declarations which I had heard, about the favor done their souls by sending them straight to heaven, and the necessary virtue accompanying all the actions of the priests.

Whether I noticed them or not, at the time, there is a window or two on each, nearly against the hole, in at which are sometimes thrown articles brought to them from without, for the use of the Convent. Through the windows on my right, which opens into the yard, towards the cross street, lime is received from carts; and I then saw a large heap of it near the place.

Passing the hole, I came to a spot where was another projection on each side, with three cells like those I first described.—Beyond them, in another broad part of the cellar, were heaps of vegetables, and other things, on the right; and on the left I found the charcoal I was in search of. This was placed in a heap against the wall, as I might then have observed, near a small high window, like the rest, at which it is thrown in. Beyond this spot, at a short distance, the cellar terminated.

The top quite to that point, is arched overhead, though at different heights, for the earth on the bottom is uneven, and in some places several feet higher than in others.

Not liking to be alone in so spacious and gloomy a part of the Convent, especially after the discovery I had made, I hastened to fill my basket with coal, and to return.

Here then I was, in a place which I had considered as the nearest imitation of heaven to be found on earth, among a society where deeds were constantly perpetrated, which I had believed to be most criminal, and I had now found the place in which harmless infants were unfeelingly thrown out of sight, after being murdered.

And yet, such is the power of instruction and example, although not satisfied, as many around me seemed to be, that all was righteous and proper, I sometimes was half inclined to believe it, for the priests could do no sin, and this was done by priests.

Among the first instructions I received from the Superior, were such as prepared me to admit priests into the nunnery from the street at irregular hours. It is no secret, that priests enter and go out; but if they were to be watched by any person in St. Paul's street all day long, no irregularity might be suspected; and they might be supposed to visit the Convent for the performance of religious ceremonies merely.

But if a person was near the gate at midnight, he might sometimes form a different opinion; for when a stray priest is shut out of the Seminary, or is otherwise put to the need of seeking a

40

lodging, he is always sure of being admitted to the black nunnery. Nobody but a priest or the physician can ring the bell at the sick-room door; much less can any others gain admittance. The pull of the bell is entirely concealed, somewhere on the outside of the gate, I have been told.

He makes himself known as a priest by a peculiar kind of hissing sound, made by the tongue against the teeth, while they are kept closed, and the lips open. The nun within, who delays to open the door, until informed what kind of an applicant is there, immediately recognizes the signal, and replies with two inarticulate sounds, such as are often used instead of yes, with the mouth closed.

The Superior seemed to consider this part of my instructions quite important, and taught me the signals. I had often occasion to use them; I have been repeatedly called to the door, in the night, while watching in a sick room, and on reaching it, heard the short hissing sound I have mentioned; then, according to my standing orders, unfastened the door, admitted the priest, who was at liberty to go where he pleased. I will name Mr. Bierze, from St. Denis.

The books used in the nunnery, at least such as I recollect of them, were the following. Most of these are lecture books, or such as are used by the daily readers, while we were at work, and meals. These were all furnished by the Superior, out of her library, to which we never had access. She was informed when we had done with one book, and then exchanged it for such another as she pleased to select.

Le Miroir du Chrétien (Christian Mirror), History of Rome, History of the Church, Life of Soeur Bourgeoise, (the founder of the Convent), in two volumes, L'Ange Conducteur (the Guardian Angel), L'Ange Chrétien (the Christian Angel), Les Vies des Saints (Lives of Saints), in several volumes, Dialogues, a volume consisting of conversations between a Protestant Doctor, called Dr. D. and a Catholic gentleman, on the articles of faith, in which, after much ingenious reasoning, the former was confuted. One large book, the name of which I have forgotten, occupied us nine or ten months at our lectures, night and morning. L'Instruction de la Jeunesse (the Instruction of Youth), containing much about Convents, and the education of persons in the world, with a great deal on confessions, &c. Examen de la Conscience, (Examination of Conscience), is a book frequently used.

I may here remark, that I never saw a Bible in the Convent from the day I entered as a novice, until that on which I effected my escape. The Catholic New Testament, commonly called the Evangile, was read to us about three or four times a year. The

41

Superior directed the reader what passage to select; but we never had it in our hands to read when we pleased. I often heard the Protestant Bible spoken of in bitter terms, as a most dangerous book, and one which never ought to be in the hands of common people.

CHAPTER X

Manufacture of Bread and Wax Candles carried on in the Convent—Superstitions—Scapularies—Virgin Mary's pincushion— Her House—The Bishop's power over fire—My Instructions to Novices—Jane Ray—Vacillation of feelings.

Large quantities of bread are made in the Black Nunnery every week, for besides what is necessary to feed the nuns, many of the poor are supplied. When a priest wishes to give a loaf of bread to a poor person, he gives him an order, which is presented at the Convent. The making of bread is therefore one of the most laborious employments in the Institution.

The manufacture of wax candles was another important branch of business in the nunnery. It was carried on in a small room, on the first floor, thence called the Ciergerie, or wax-room; cierge being the French word for a wax candle. I was sometimes sent to read the daily lecture and catechism to the nuns employed there, but found it a very unpleasant task, as the smell rising from the melted wax gave me a sickness at the stomach. The employment was considered rather unhealthy, and those were assigned to it who had the strongest constitutions. The nuns who were more commonly employed in that room, were Sainte Marie, Sainte Catharine, Sainte Charlotte, Sainte Francis, Sainte Hyacinthe, Sainte Hypolite, and others. But with these, as with other persons in the Convent, I was never allowed to speak, except under circumstances before mentioned. I was sent to read, and was not allowed even to answer the most trivial question, if one were asked me. Should a nun say, "what o'clock is it?" I never should have dared to reply, but was required to report her to the Superior.

Much stress was laid on the sainte scapulaire, or, holy scapulary. This is a small band of cloth or silk, formed and wrought in a peculiar manner, to be tied around the neck by two strings, fastened to the ends. I have made many of them, having been sometimes set to make them in the Convent. On one side is worked a kind of double cross, (thus, XX) and on the other I. II. S., the meaning of which I do not exactly know. Such a band is called a scapulary, and many miracles are attributed to its power. Children on first receiving the communion are often presented with scapularies, which they are taught to regard with great reverence. We were told of the wonders effected by their means, in the addresses made to us, by priests at catechism or lectures. I will repeat one or two of the stories which occur to me.

A Roman Catholic servant woman, who had concealed some of her sins at confession, acted so hypocritical a part as to make her mistress believe her a décote, or a strict observer of her duty. She even imposed upon her confessor, to such a degree, that he gave her a scapulary. After he had given it, however, one of the saints in heaven informed him in a vision, that the holy scapulary must not remain on the neck of so great a sinner; and that it must be restored to the church. She lay down that night with the scapulary round her throat, but in the morning was found dead, with her head cut off, and the scapulary was discovered in the church. The belief was, that the devil could not endure to have so holy a thing on one of his servants, and had pulled so hard to get it off, as to draw the silken thread with which it was tied, through her neck; after which, by some divine power it was restored to the church.

Another story was as follows. A poor Roman Catholic was once taken prisoner by the heretics. He had a sainte scapulaire on his neck, when God seeing him in the midst of his foes, took it from his neck by a miracle, and held it up in the air above the throng of heretics; more than one hundred of whom were converted, by seeing it thus supernaturally suspended.

I had been informed by the Superior, on my first admission as a nun, that there was a subterraneous passage, leading from the cellar of our Convent into that of the Congregational Nunnery; but, though I had so often visited the cellar, I had never seen it. One day, after I had been received three or four months, I was sent to walk through it upon my knees with another nun, as a penance. This, and other penances, were sometimes put upon us by the priests, without any reason assigned. The common way, indeed, was to tell us of the sin for which a penance was imposed, but we were left many times to conjecture. Now and then the priests would inform us at a subsequent confession, when he happened to recollect something about it, as I thought, and not because he reflected, or cared much about the subject.

43

The nun who was with me led me through the cellar, passing to the right of the secret burying place, and showed me the door of the subterraneous passage, which was at the extremity towards the Congregational Nunnery. The reasons why I had not noticed it before, I presume, were that it was made to shut close and even with the wall, and all that part of the cellar was whitewashed. The door, which is of wood, and square, opens with a latch into a passage, about four feet and a half high. We immediately got upon our knees, commenced saying the prayers required, and began to move slowly along the dark and narrow passage. It may be fifty or sixty feet in length; when we reached the end, we opened a door, and found ourselves in the cellar of the Congregational Nunnery, at some distance from the outer wall; for the covered way is carried in towards the middle of the cellar by two low partitions covered at the top. By the side of the door, was placed a list of names of the Black nuns, with a slide, that might be drawn over any of them. We covered our names in this manner, as evidence of having performed the duty assigned us; and then returned backwards on our knees, by the way we had come. This penance I repeatedly performed afterwards; and by this way, as I have occasion elsewhere to mention, nuns from the Congregational Nunnery, sometimes entered our Convent for worse purposes.

We were frequently assured, that miracles are still performed; and pains were taken to impress us deeply on this subject. The Superior often spoke to us of the Virgin Mary's pincushion, the remains of which it is pretended are preserved in the Convent, though it has crumbled quite to dust. We regarded this relic with such veneration, that we were afraid even to look at it, and we often heard the following story related, when the subject was introduced.

A priest in Jerusalem once had a vision, in which he was informed that the house in which the Virgin had lived, should be removed from its foundations, and transported to a distance. He did not think the communication was from God, and therefore disregarded it; but the house was soon after missed, which convinced him that the vision was true, and he told where the house might be found. A picture of the house is preserved in the Nunnery, and was sometimes shown us. There are also wax figures of Joseph sawing wood, and Jesus as a child, picking up the chips. We were taught to sing a little song relating to this, the chorus of which I remember.

"Saint Joseph charpentier,
Petit Jesus ramassait les copeaux
Pour fair bouillir la marmite."

44

St. Joseph was a carpenter, little Jesus collected chips to make the pot boil.

I began to speak of miracles, and I recollect a story of one, about a family in Italy saved from shipwreck by a priest, who were in consequence converted and had two sons honoured with the priest's office.

I had heard before I entered the Convent, about a great fire which destroyed a number of houses in the Quebec suburbs, and which some said the Bishop extinguished with holy water. I once heard a Catholic and a Protestant disputing on this subject, and when I went to the Congregational Nunnery, I sometimes heard the children, alluding to the same story, say at an alarm of fire, "Is it a Catholic fire? Then why does not the Bishop run?"

Among the topics on which the bishop addressed the nuns in the Convent this was one. He told us the story one day, and said he could have sooner interfered and stopped the flames, but that at last, finding they were about to destroy too many Catholic houses, he threw holy water on the fire, and extinguished it. I believed this, and also thought that he was able to put out any fire, but that he never did it, except when inspired.

The holy water which the Bishop had consecrated, was considered much more efficacious, than any blessed by a common priest; and this it was which was used in the Convent in sprinkling our beds. It had virtue in it, to keep off any evil spirits.

Now that I was a nun, I was occasionally sent to read lectures to the novices, as other nuns had been while I was a novice. There were but few of us, who were thought capable of reading English well enough, and therefore, I was more frequently sent than I might otherwise have been. The Superior often said to me, as I was going among the novices:

"Try to convert them—save their souls—you know you will have a higher place in heaven for every one you convert."

For whatever reason, Mad Jane Ray seemed to take great delight in crossing and provoking the Superior and old nuns; and often she would cause an interruption when it was most inconvenient and displeasing to them. The preservation of silence was insisted upon most rigidly, and penances of such a nature were imposed for breaking it, that it was a constant source of uneasiness with me, to know that I might infringe the rules in so many ways, and that inattention might at any moment subject me to something very unpleasant. During the periods of meditation, therefore, and those of lecture, work, and repose, I kept a strict guard upon myself, to escape penances, as well as to avoid sin; and the silence of the

45

other nuns, convinced me that they were equally watchful, and from the same motives.

My feelings, however, varied at different times, and so did those of many, if not all my companions, excepting the older ones, who took their turns in watching us. We sometimes felt disposed for gaiety, and threw off all ideas that talking was sinful, even when forbidden by the rules of the Convent. And even when I felt that I might perhaps be doing wrong, I reflected that confession, and certainly penance, would soon wipe off the guilt.

I may remark here, that I ere long found out several things, important to be known, to a person living under such rules. One of these was, that it was much better to confess to a priest, a sin committed against the rules, because he would not require one of the penances I most disliked, viz.: those which exposed of me to the observation of the nuns, or which demanded self-debasement before them, like begging their pardon, kissing the floor, or the Superior's feet, &c., and, besides, he as a confessor was said to be bound to secrecy, and could not inform the Superior against me. My conscience being as effectually unburthened by my confession to the priest, as I had been taught to believe, I therefore preferred not to tell my sins to any one else; and this course I found was preferred by others for the same good reasons.

To Jane Ray, however, it sometimes appeared to be a matter of perfect indifference, who knew her violations of rule, or to what penances she exposed herself.

Often and often, while perfect silence prevailed among the nuns, at meditation, or while nothing was to be heard except the voice of the reader appointed for the day, no matter whose life or writings were presented for our contemplations, Jane would break forth with some remark or question, that would attract general attention, and often cause a long and total interruption. Sometimes she would make some harmless remark or inquiry aloud, as if through mere inadvertency, and then her well-known voice, so strongly associated with every thing singular and ridiculous, would arrest the attention of us all, and generally incline us to smile, and even force us to laugh. The Superior would then usually utter some hasty remonstrance, and many a time have I heard her pronounce some penance upon her; but Jane had ever some apology ready, or some reply calculated to irritate still farther, or to prove to every one, that no punishment would be effectual on her. Sometimes this singular woman would appear to be actuated by opposite feelings and motives; for although she usually delighted in drawing others into difficulty, and has thrown many a severe penance even upon her greatest favourites; on other occasions she appeared totally regardless of consequences herself, and preferred to take all the blame, anxious only to shield others.

I have repeatedly known her to break silence in the community, as if she had no object, or none beyond that of causing disturbance, or exciting a smile, and as soon as it was noticed, exclaim: "Say it's me, say it's me!"

Sometimes she would even expose herself to punishments in place of another who was guilty; and thus I found it difficult fully to understand her. In some cases she seemed decidedly out of her wits, as the Superior and priests commonly preferred to represent her; but generally I saw in her what prevented me from accounting her insane.

Among her most common tricks were such as these: She gave me the name of the "Devout English Reader," because I was often appointed to make the lecture to the English girls; and sometimes, after taking a seat near me, under pretence of deafness, would whisper it in my hearing, because she knew my want of self-command when excited to laughter. Thus she often exposed me to penances for a breach of decorum, and set me to biting my lips, to avoid laughing outright in the midst of a solemn lecture. "Oh! you devout English Reader!" would sometimes come upon me suddenly from her lips, with something in it so ludicrous that I had to exert myself to the utmost to avoid observation.

This came so often at one time, that I grew uneasy, and told her I must confess it, to unburden my conscience; I had not done so before, because she would complain of me, for giving way to temptation.

Sometimes she would pass behind us as we stood at dinner ready to sit down, and softly moving back our chairs, leave us to fall down upon the floor. This she repeatedly has done; and While we were laughing together, she would spring forward, kneel to the Superior, and beg her pardon and a penance.

CHAPTER XI

Alarming Order from the Superior—Proceed to execute it—Scene in an upper Room—Sentence of Death, and Murder—My own distress—Reports made to friends of St. Francis.

But I must now come to one deed, in which I had some part, and which I look back upon with greater horror and pain, than any occurrences in the Convent, in which I was not the principal sufferer. It is not necessary for me to attempt to excuse myself in this or any other case. Those who have any disposition to judge fairly, will exercise their own judgment in making allowances for me, under the fear and force, the commands and examples, around me. I, therefore, shall confine myself, as usual, to the simple narrative of facts. The time was about five months after I took the veil; the weather was cool, perhaps in September or October. One day, the Superior sent for me and several other nuns, to receive her commands at a particular room. We found the Bishop and some priests with her; and speaking in an unusual tone of fierceness and authority, she said, "Go to the room for the Examination of Conscience, and drag Saint Francis up-stairs." Nothing more was necessary than this unusual command, with the tone and manner which, accompanied it, to excite in me most gloomy anticipation. It did not strike me as strange, that St. Francis should be in the room to which the Superior directed us. It was an apartment to which we were often sent to prepare for the communion, and to which we voluntarily went, whenever we felt the compunctions which our ignorance of duty, and the misinstructions we received, inclined us to seek relief from self-reproach. Indeed, I had seen her there a little before. What terrified me was, first, the Superior's angry manner, second, the expression she used, being a French term, whose [illegible] we had learnt in the Convent, and whose meaning is rather softened when translated into drag; third, the place to which we were directed to take the interesting young nun, and the persons assembled there as I supposed to condemn her. My fears were such, concerning the fate that awaited her, and my horror at the idea that she was in some way to be sacrificed, that I would have given any thing to be allowed to stay where I was. But I feared the consequence of disobeying the Superior, and proceeded with the rest towards the room for the examination of conscience.

The room to which we were to proceed from that, was in the second story, and the place of many a scene of a shameful nature. It is sufficient for me to say, after what I have said in other parts of this book, that things had there occurred which made me regard the place with the greatest disgust Saint Francis had appeared melancholy for some time. I well knew that she had cause, for she had been repeatedly subject to trials which I need not name—our common lot. When we reached the room where we had been bidden to seek her, I entered the door, my companions standing behind me, as the place was so small as hardly to hold five persons at a time.

The young nun was standing alone near the middle of the room; she was probably about twenty, with light hair, blue eyes, and a very fair complexion. I spoke to her in a compassionate voice, but at the same time with such a decided manner, that she comprehended my full meaning—

"Saint Francis, we are sent for you."

Several others spoke kindly to her, but two addressed her very harshly. The poor creature turned round with a look of meekness, and without expressing any unwillingness or fear, without even speaking a word, resigned herself to our hands. The tears came into my eyes. I had not a moment's doubt that she considered her fate as sealed, and was already beyond the fear of death. She was conducted, or rather hurried to the staircase, which was near by, and then seized by her limbs and clothes, and in fact almost dragged up-stairs, in the sense the Superior had intended. I laid my own hands upon her—I took hold of her too,—more gentle indeed than some of the rest; yet I encouraged and assisted them in carrying her. I could not avoid it. My refusal would not have saved her, nor prevented her being carried up; it would only have exposed me to some severe punishment, as I believed some of my companions, would have seized the first opportunity to complain of me.

All the way up the staircase, Saint Francis spoke not a word, nor made the slightest resistance. When we entered with her the room to which she was ordered, my heart sank within me. The Bishop, the Lady Superior, and five priests, viz. Bonin, Richards, Savage, and two others, I now ascertained, were assembled for her trial, on some charge of great importance.

When we had brought our prisoner before them, Father Richards began to question her, and she made ready but calm replies. I cannot pretend to give a connected account of what ensued: my feelings were wrought up to such a pitch, that I knew not what I did, nor what to do. I was under a terrible apprehension that, if I betrayed my feelings which almost overcame me, I should fall under the displeasure of the cold-blooded persecutors of my poor innocent sister; and this fear on the one hand, with the distress I felt for her on the other, rendered me almost frantic. As soon as I entered the room, I had stepped into a corner, on the left of the entrance, where I might partially support myself, by leaning against the wall, between the door and window. This support was all that prevented me from falling to the floor, for the confusion of my thoughts was so great, that only a few of the words I heard spoken on either side made any lasting impression upon me. I felt as if struck with some insupportable blow; and death would not have been more frightful to me. I am inclined to the belief, that Father

Richards wished to shield the poor prisoner from the severity of her fate, by drawing from her expressions that might bear a favorable construction. He asked her, among other things, if she was not sorry for what she had been overheard to say, (for she had been betrayed by one of the nuns,) and if she would not prefer confinement in the cells, to the punishment which was threatened her. But the Bishop soon interrupted him, and it was easy to perceive, that he considered her fate as sealed, and was determined she should not escape. In reply to some of the questions put to her, she was silent; to others I heard her voice reply that she did not repent of words she had uttered, though they had been reported by some of the nuns who had heard them; that she still wished to escape from the Convent; and that she had firmly resolved to resist every attempt to compel her to the commission of crimes which she detested. She added, that she would rather die than cause the murder of harmless babes.

"That is enough, finish her!" said the Bishop.

Two nuns instantly fell upon the young woman, and in obedience to directions, given by the Superior, prepared to execute her sentence.

She still maintained all the calmness and submission of a lamb. Some of those who took part in this transaction, I believe, were as unwilling as myself; but of others I can safely say, that I believe they delighted in it. Their conduct certainly exhibited a most blood-thirsty spirit. But, above all others present, and above all human fiends I ever saw, I think Sainte Hypolite was the most diabolical. She engaged in the horrid task with all alacrity, and assumed from choice the most revolting parts to be performed. She seized a gag, forced it into the mouth of the poor nun, and when it was fixed between her extended jaws, so as to keep them open at their greatest possible distance, took hold of the straps fastened at each end of the stick, crossed them behind the helpless head of the victim, and drew them tight through the loop prepared, as a fastening.

The bed which had always stood in one part of the room, still remained there; though the screen, which had usually been placed before it, and was made of thick muslin, with only a crevice through which a person behind might look out, had been folded up on its hinges in the form of a W, and placed in a corner. On the bed the prisoner was laid with her face upward, and then bound with cords, so that she could not move. In an instant another bed was thrown upon her. One of the priests, named Bonin, sprung like a fury first upon it, and stamped upon it, with all his force. He was speedily followed by the nuns, until there were as many upon the bed as

50

could find room, and all did what they could, not only to smother, but to bruise her. Some stood up and jumped upon the poor girl with their feet, some with their knees, and others in different ways seemed to seek how they might best beat the breath out of her body, and mangle it, without coming in direct contact with it, or seeing the effects of their violence. During this time, my feelings were almost too strong to be endured. I felt stupefied, and was scarcely conscious of what I did. Still, fear for myself remained in a sufficient degree to induce me to some exertion, and I attempted to talk to those who stood next, partly that I might have an excuse for turning away from the dreadful scene.

After the lapse of fifteen or twenty minutes, and when it was presumed that the sufferer had been smothered, and crushed to death, Father Bonin and the nuns ceased to trample upon her, and stepped from the bed. All was motionless and silent beneath it.

They then began to laugh at such inhuman thoughts as occurred to some of them, rallying each other in the most unfeeling manner, and ridiculing me for the feelings which I in vain endeavoured to conceal. They alluded to the resignation of our murdered companion, and one of them tauntingly said, "She would have made a good Catholic martyr." After spending some moments in such conversation, one of them asked if the corpse should be removed. The Superior said it had better remain a little while. After waiting a short time longer, the feather-bed was taken off, the cords unloosed, and the body taken by the nuns and dragged down stairs. I was informed that it was taken into the cellar, and thrown unceremoniously into the hole which I have already described, covered with a great quantity of lime, and afterwards sprinkled with a liquid, of the properties and name of which I am ignorant. This liquid I have seen poured into the hole from large bottles, after the necks were broken off, and have heard that it is used in France to prevent the effluvia rising from cemeteries.

I did not soon recover from the shock caused by this scene; indeed it still recurs to me, with most gloomy impressions. The next day there was a melancholy aspect over everything, and recreation time passed in the dullest manner; scarcely anything was said above a whisper.

I never heard much said afterward about Saint Francis.

I spoke with one of the nuns, a few words, one day, but we were all cautioned not to expose ourselves very far, and could not place much reliance in each other. The murdered nun had been brought to her shocking end through the treachery of one of our number, in whom she confided.

I never knew with certainty who had reported her remarks to

the Superior, but suspicion fastened on one, and I never could regard her but with detestation.

I was more inclined to blame her than some of those employed in the execution; for there could have been no necessity for the betrayal of her feelings. We all knew how to avoid exposing each other.

I was often sent by the Superior to overhear what was said by novices and nuns: when they seemed to shun her, she would say, "Go and listen, they are speaking English;" and though I obeyed her, I never informed her against them. If I wished to clear my conscience, I would go to a priest, and confess, knowing that he dared not communicate what I said to any person, and that he would not impose as heavy penances as the Superior.

We were always at liberty to choose another confessor when we had any sin to confess, which we were unwilling to tell one to whom we should otherwise have gone.

Not long after the murder just related, a young woman came to the nunnery, and asked for permission to see Saint Francis. It was my former friend, with whom I had been an assistant teacher, Miss Louise Bousquet, of St. Denis. From this, I supposed the murdered nun might have come from that town, or its vicinity. The only answer returned to the inquiry was, that Saint Francis was dead.

Some time afterward, some of St. Francis' friends called to inquire after her, and they were told that she had died a glorious death; and further told, that she made some heavenly expressions, which were repeated in order to satisfy her friends.

CHAPTER XII

Description of the Room of the Three States, and the pictures in it— Jane Ray ridiculing Priests—Their criminal Treatment of us at Confession—Jane Ray's Tricks with the Nuns' Aprons, Handkerchiefs, and Nightgowns—Apples.

The pictures in the room of the Three States were large, and painted by some artist who understood how to make horrible ones. They appeared to be stuck to the walls. The light is admitted from small and high windows, which are curtained, and is rather faint, so as to make every thing look gloomy. The story told us was, that they were painted by an artist to whom God had given power to represent things exactly they are in heaven, hell, and purgatory.

In heaven, the picture of which hangs on one side of the apartment, multitudes of nuns and priests are put in the highest places, with the Virgin Mary at the head, St. Peter and other saints far above the great numbers of good Catholics of other classes, who were crowded in below.

In purgatory are multitudes of people; and in one part, called "The place of lambs," are infants who died unbaptized. "The place of darkness," is that part of purgatory in which adults are collected; and there they are surrounded with flames, waiting to be delivered by the prayers of the living.

In hell, the picture of which, and that of purgatory, were on the wall opposite that of heaven, the human faces were the most horrible that can be imagined. Persons of different descriptions were represented, with the most distorted features, ghastly complexions, and every variety of dreadful expression; some with wild beasts gnawing at their heads, others furiously biting the iron bars which kept them in, with looks which could not fail to make a spectator shudder.

I could hardly persuade myself that the figures were not living, and the impression they made on my feelings was powerful. I was often shown the place where nuns go who break their vows, as a warning. It is the hottest place in hell, and worse, in every point of view, even than that to which Protestants are assigned; because they are not so much to be blamed, as we were sometimes assured, as their ministers and the Bible, by which they are perverted.

Whenever I was shut in that room, as I was several times, I prayed for "les âmes des fidèles trépassés:" the souls of those faithful ones who have long been in purgatory, and have no relations living to pray for them.

My feelings were often of the most painful description, while I remained alone with those frightful pictures.

Jane Ray was once put in, and uttered the most dreadful shrieks. Some of the old nuns proposed to the Superior to have her gagged: "No" she replied; "go and let out that devil, she makes me sin more than all the rest."

Jane could not endure the place; and she afterward gave names to many of the worst figures in the pictures. On catechism-days she would take a seat behind a cupboard-door, where the priest could not see her, while she faced the nuns, and would make us laugh. "You are not so attentive to your lesson as you used to be," he would begin to say, while we were endeavouring to suppress our laughter.

Jane would then hold up the first letter of some priest's name, whom she had before compared with one of the faces in "hell," and look so that we could hardly preserve our gravity. I remember she named the wretch who was biting at the bars of hell, with a serpent gnawing his head, with chains and padlocks on, Father Dufresne; and she would say—"Does not he look like him, when he comes in to Catechism with his long solemn face, and begins his speeches with, 'My children, my hope is, you have lived very devout lives?'"

The first time I went to confession after taking the veil, I found abundant evidence that the priests did not treat even that ceremony, which is called a solemn sacrament, with respect enough to lay aside the detestable and shameless character they so often showed on other occasions. The confessor sometimes sat in the room of examination of conscience, and sometimes in the Superior's room, and always alone, except the nun who was confessing. He had a common chair placed in the middle of the floor, and instead of being placed behind a grate, or lattice, as in the chapel, had nothing before or around him. There were no spectators to observe him, and of course any such thing would have been unnecessary.

A number of nuns usually confessed on the same day, but only one could be admitted into the room at the time. They took their places just without the door, on their knees, and went through the preparation prescribed by the rules of confession; repeating certain prayers, which always occupy a considerable time. When one was ready, she rose from her knees, entered, and closed the door behind her; and no other one even dared touch the latch until she came out.

I shall not tell what was transacted at such times, under the pretence of confessing, and receiving absolution from sin: far more guilt was often incurred than pardoned; and crimes of a deep die were committed, while trifling irregularities, in childish ceremonies, were treated as serious offences. I cannot persuade myself to speak plainly on such a subject, as I must offend the virtuous ear. I can only say, that suspicion cannot do any injustice to the priests, because their sins cannot be exaggerated.

Some idea may be formed of the manner in which even such women as many of my sister nuns were regarded the confessors, when I state, that there was often a contest among us, to avoid entering the apartment as long as we could, endeavouring to make each other go first, as that was what most of us dreaded.

During the long and tedious days, which filled up the time between the occurrences I have mentioned, nothing, or little took place to keep up our spirits. We were fatigued in body with labour, or with sitting, debilitated by the long continuance of our religious exercises, and depressed in feelings by our miserable and hopeless condition. Nothing but the humors of mad Jane Ray, could rouse us for a moment from our languor and melancholy.

To mention all her devices, would require more room than is here allowed, and a memory of almost all her words and actions for years. I had early become a favourite with her, and had opportunity to learn more of her character than most of the other nuns. As this may be best learnt from hearing what she did, I will here recount a few of her tricks, just as they happen to present themselves to my memory, without regard to the order of time.

She one day, in an unaccountable humour, sprinkled the floor plentifully with holy water, which brought upon her a severe lecture from the Superior, as might have been expected. The Superior said it was a heinous offence; she had wasted holy water enough to save many souls from purgatory; and what would they not give for it! She then ordered Jane to sit in the middle of the floor, and when the priest came, he was informed of her offence. Instead, however, of imposing one of those penances to which she had often been subjected, but with so little effect, he said to her, "Go to your place, Jane; we forgive you for this time."

I was once set to iron aprons with Jane; aprons and pocket-handkerchiefs are the only articles of dress which are ever ironed in the Convent. As soon as we were alone, she remarked, "Well, we are free from the rules, while we are at this work;" and although she knew she had no reason for saying so, she began to sing, and I soon joined her, and thus we spent the time, while we were at work, to the neglect of the prayers we ought to have said.

We had no idea that we were in danger of being overheard, but it happened that the Superior was overhead all the time, with several nuns, who were preparing for confession: she came down and said, "How is this?" Jane Ray coolly replied, that we had employed our time in singing hymns, and referred to me. I was afraid to confirm so direct a falsehood, in order to deceive the Superior, though I had often told more injurious ones of her fabrication, or at her orders, and said very little in reply to Jane's request.

The Superior plainly saw the trick that was attempted, and ordered us both to the room for the examination of conscience, where we remained till night, without a mouthful to eat. The time was not, however, unoccupied; I received such a lecture from Jane, as I have very seldom heard, and she was so angry with me that we did not speak to each other for two weeks.

At length she found something to complain of against me, had me subjected to a penance, which led to our begging each other's pardon, and we became perfectly satisfied, reconciled, and as good friends as ever.

One of the most disgusting penances we ever had to submit to, was that of drinking the water in which the Superior had washed her feet. Nobody could ever laugh at this penance except Jane Ray. She would pretend to comfort us, by saying, she was sure it was better than mere plain, clear water.

Some of the tricks which I remember, were played by Jane with nuns' clothes. It was a rule that the oldest aprons in use should go to the youngest received, and the old nuns were to wear all the new ones. On four different occasions, Jane stole into the sleeping-room at night, and unobserved by the watch, changed a great part of the aprons, placing them by the beds of nuns to whom they did not belong. The consequence was, that in the morning they dressed themselves in such haste, as never to discover the mistakes they made, until they were all ranged at prayers; and then the ridiculous appearance which many of them cut, disturbed the long devotions. I laugh so easily, that on such occasions, I usually incurred a full share of penances, I generally, however, got a new apron, when Jane played this trick; for it was part of her object, to give the best aprons to her favourites, and put off the ragged ones on some of the old nuns whom she most hated.

Jane once lost her pocket-handkerchief. The penance for such an offence is, to go without any for five weeks. For this she had no relish, and requested me to pick one from some of the nuns on the way up-stairs. I succeeded in getting two: this Jane said was one too many; and she thought it dangerous for either of us to keep it, lest a search should be made. Very soon the two nuns were complaining that they had lost their handkerchiefs, and wondering what could have become of them, as they were sure that they had been careful. Jane seized an opportunity, and slipped one into a straw bed, where it remained until the bed was emptied to be filled with new straw.

As the winter was coming on, one year, she complained to me that we were not as well supplied with warm night-clothes as two of the nuns she named, whom she said she "abominated." She soon after found means to get possession of their fine warm flannel nightgowns, one of which she gave to me, while the other she put on at bed time. She presumed the owners would have a secret search for them; and in the morning hid them in the stove, after the fire had gone out, which was kindled a little before the hour of rising, and then suffered to burn down.

This she did every morning, taking them out at night, through the winter. The poor nuns who owned the garments were afraid to complain of their loss, lest they should have some penance laid on them, and nothing was ever said about them. When the weather began to grow warm in the spring Jane returned the nightgowns to the beds of the nuns, from whom she had borrowed them, and they were probably as much surprised to find them again, as they had before been at losing them.

Jane once found an opportunity to fill her apron with a quantity of fine apples, called fameuses, which came in her way, and, hastening up to the sleeping-room, hid them under my bed. Then, coming down, she informed me, and we agreed to apply for leave to make our elevens, as it is called. The meaning of this is, to repeat a certain round of prayers, for nine days in succession, to some saint we choose to address for assistance, in becoming more charitable, affectionate or something else. We easily obtained permission, and hastened up-stairs to begin our nine days' feast on the apples; when, much to our surprise, they had all been taken away, and there was no way to avoid the disagreeable fate we had brought upon ourselves. Jane therefore began to search the beds of the other nuns; but not finding any trace of the apples, she became doubly vexed and stuck pins in those which belonged to her enemies.

When bedtime came, they were much scratched in getting in bed, which made them break silence, and that subjected them to penances.

CHAPTER XIII

Jane Ray's Tricks continued—The Broomstick Ghost—Sleep-walking—Salted Cider—Changing Beds—Objects of some of her Tricks—Feigned Humility—Alarm—Treatment of a new Nun—A nun made by stratagem.

One night, Jane, who had been sweeping the sleeping-room, for a penance, dressed up the broom-stick, when she had completed her work, with a white cloth on the end, so tied as to resemble an old woman dressed in white, with long arms sticking out. This she stuck through a broken pane of glass, and placed it so that it appeared to be looking in at the window, by the font of holy water. There it remained until the nuns came up to bed. The first who

57

stopped at the font, to dip her finger in, caught a glimpse of the singular object, and started with terror. The next was equally terrified, as she approached, and the next and the next.

We all believed in ghosts; and it was not wonderful that such an object should cause alarm, especially as it was but a short time after the death of one of the nuns. Thus they went on, each getting a fright in turn, yet all afraid to speak. At length, one more alarmed, or with less presence of mind than the rest, exclaimed, "Oh, mon Dieu! Je ne me coucherais pas!" When the night-watch called out, "Who's that?" she confessed she had broken silence, but pointed at the cause; and then, all the nuns assembling at a distance from the window, Jane offered to advance boldly, and ascertain the nature of the apparition, which they thought a most resolute intention. We all stood looking on, when she stepped to the window, drew in the broomstick, and showed us the ridiculous puppet, which had alarmed so many superstitious fears.

Some of her greatest feats she performed as a sleep walker. Whether she ever walked in her sleep or not, I am unable with certainty, to say. She however often imposed upon the Superior and old nuns, by making them think so, when I knew she did not; and yet, I cannot positively say that she always did. I have remarked, that one of the old nuns was always placed in our sleeping-room at night, to watch us. Sometimes she would be inattentive, and sometimes fall into a doze. Jane Ray often seized such times to rise from her bed, and walk about, occasionally seizing one of the nuns in bed, in order to frighten her. This she generally affected; and many times we have all been awakened, by screams of terror. In our alarm, some of us frequently broke silence, and gave occasion to the Superior to lay us under penances. Many tunes, however, we escaped with a mere reprimand, while Jane usually received expressions of compassion:—"Poor creature! she would not do so if she were in perfect possession of her reason." And Jane displayed her customary artfulness, in keeping up the false impression. As soon as she perceived that the old nun was likely to observe her, she would throw her arms about, or appear unconscious of what she was doing, falling upon a bed, or standing stock-still, until exertions had been made to rouse her from her supposed lethargy.

We were once allowed to drink cider at dinner, which was quite an extraordinary favour. Jane, however, on account of her negligence of all work, was denied the privilege, which she much resented. The next day when dinner arrived, we began to taste our new drink, but it was so salt we could not swallow it. Those of us who at first discovered it, were, as usual, afraid to speak; but we set down our cups, and looked round, till the others made the same discovery, which they all soon did, and most of them in the same manner. Some, however, at length, taken by surprise, uttered some ludicrous exclamation, on tasting the salted cider, and then an old nun, looking cross, would cry out:—

"Ah! tu casses la silence!" (Ah! you've broken silence.)

And thus we soon got a-laughing, beyond our power of suppressing it. At recreation, that day, the first question asked by many of us, was, "How did you like your cider?"

Jane Ray never had a fixed place to sleep in. When the weather began to grow warm in the spring, she usually pushed some bed out of its place, near a window, and put her own beside it; and when the winter approached, she would choose a spot near the stove, and occupy it with her bed, in spite of all remonstrance. We were all convinced that it was generally best to yield to her.

She was often set to work, in different ways; but, whenever she was dissatisfied with doing any thing, would devise some trick that would make the Superior, or old nuns, drive her off; and whenever any suspicion was expressed, of her being in her right mind, she would say, that she did not know what she was doing; that all the difficulty arose from her repeating prayers too much, which wearied and distracted her mind.

I was once directed to assist Jane Ray, in shifting the beds of the nuns. When we came to those of some of the sisters, whom she most disliked, she said, now we will pay them for some of the penances we have suffered on their account; and taking some thistles, she mixed them with the straw. At night, the first of them who got into bed, felt the thistles, and cried out. The night-watch exclaimed, as usual, "You are breaking silence there." And then another screamed, as she was scratched by the thistles and another. The old nun then called on all who had broken silence to rise, and ordered them to sleep under their beds, as a penance, which they silently complied with. Jane and I afterward confessed, when it was all over, and took some trifling penance which the priest imposed.

Those nuns who fell most under the displeasure of mad Jane Ray, as I have intimated before, were those who had the reputation of being most ready to inform of the trifling faults of others and especially those who acted without any regard to honour, by disclosing what they had pretended to listen to in confidence. Several of the worst tempered "saints" she held in abhorrence; and I have heard her say, that such and such, she abominated. Many a trick did she play upon these, some of which were painful to them in their consequences, and a good number of them have never been traced to this day. Of all the nuns, however, none other was regarded by her with so much detestation as Saint Hypolite; for she was always believed to have betrayed Saint Francis, and to have caused her murder. She was looked upon by us as the voluntary cause of her death, and of the crime which those of us committed, who, unwillingly, took part in her execution. We, on the contrary, being under the worst of fears for ourselves, in case of refusing to obey our masters and mistress, thought ourselves chargeable with less guilt, as unwilling assistants in a scene, which it was impossible for us to prevent or delay. Jane has often spoken to me of the suspected informer, and always in terms of the greatest bitterness.

The Superior sometimes expressed commiseration for mad Jane Ray, but I never could tell whether she really believed her insane or not. I was always inclined to think that she was willing to put up with some of her tricks, because they served to divert our minds from the painful and depressing circumstances in which we were placed. I knew the Superior's powers and habits of deception also, and that she would deceive us as willingly as any one else.

Sometimes she proposed to send Jane to St. Anne's, a place near Quebec, celebrated for the pilgrimages made to it by persons differently afflicted. It is supposed that some peculiar virtue exists there, which will restore health to the sick; and I have heard stories told in corroboration of the common belief. Many lame and blind persons, with others, visit St. Anne's every year, some of whom may be seen travelling on foot, and begging their food. The Superior would sometimes say that it was a pity that a woman like Jane Ray, capable of being so useful, should be unable to do her duties in consequence of a malady which she thought might be cured by a visit to St Anne's.

Yet to St. Anne's Jane never was sent, and her wild and various tricks continued as before. The rules of silence, which the others were so scrupulous in observing, she set at naught every hour; and as for other rules, she regarded them with as little respect when they stood in her way. She would now and then step out and stop the clock by which our exercises were regulated, and sometimes, in this manner, lengthened out our recreations till near twelve. At last the old nuns began to watch against such a trick, and would occasionally go out to see if the clock was going.

She once made a request that she might not eat with the other nuns, which was granted, as it seemed to proceed from a spirit of genuine humility, which made her regard herself as unworthy of our society.

It being most convenient, she was sent to the Superior's table to make her meals after her; and it did not at first occur to the Superior, that Jane, in this manner, profited by the change, by getting much better food than the rest of us. Thus there seemed to be always something deeper than anybody at first suspected, at the bottom of everything she did.

She was once directed to sweep a community-room, under the sleeping-chamber. This office had before been assigned to the other nuns, as a penance; but the Superior, considering that Jane Ray did little or nothing, determined thus to furnish her with some employment.

She declared to us that she would not sweep it long, as we might soon be assured. It happened that the stove by which that community-room was warmed in the winter, had its pipe carried through the floor of our sleeping-chamber, and thence across it, in a direction opposite that in which the pipe of our stove was carried. It being then warm weather, the first-mentioned pipe had been taken down, and the hole left unstopped. After we had all retired to our beds, and while engaged in our silent prayers, we were suddenly alarmed by a bright blaze of fire, which burst from the hole in the floor, and threw sparks all around us. We thought the building was burning, and uttered cries of terror regardless of the penances, the fear of which generally kept us silent.

The utmost confusion prevailed; for although we had solemnly vowed never to flee from the Convent even if it was on fire, we were extremely alarmed, and could not repress our feelings. We soon learnt the cause, for the flames ceased in a moment or two, and it was found that mad Jane Ray, after sweeping a little in the room beneath, had stuck a quantity of wet powder on the end of her broom, thrust it up through the hole in the ceiling into our apartment, and with a lighted paper set it on fire.

The date of this alarm I must refer to a time soon after that of the election riots, for I recollect that she found means to get possession of some of the powder which was prepared at that time, for an emergency to which some thought the Convent was exposed.

She once asked for pen and paper, and when the Superior told her that if she wrote to her friends she must see it, she replied, that it was for no such purpose; she wanted to write her confession, and thus make it once for all. She wrote it, handed it to the priest, and he gave it to the Superior, who read it to us. It was full of offences which she had never committed, evidently written to throw ridicule on confessions, and one of the most ludicrous productions I ever saw.

Our bedsteads were made with narrow boards laid across them, on which the beds were laid. One day, while we were in the bedchamber together, she proposed that we should misplace these boards. This was done, so that at night nearly a dozen nuns fell down upon the floor on getting into bed. A good deal of confusion

61

naturally ensued, but the authors were not discovered. I was so conscience-stricken, however, that a week afterward, while we examined our consciences together, I told her I must confess the sin the next day. She replied, "Do as you like, but you will be sorry for it."

The next day, when we came before the Superior, I was just going to kneel and confess, when Jane, almost without giving me time to shut the door, threw herself at the Superior's feet, and confessed the trick, and a penance was immediately laid on me for the sin I had concealed.

There was an old nun, who was a famous talker, whom used to call La Mère, (Mother). One night, Jane Ray got up, and secretly changed the caps of several of the nuns, and hers among the rest. In the morning there was great confusion, and such a scene as seldom occurred. She was severely blamed by La Mère, having been informed against by some of the nuns; and at last became so much enraged, that she attacked the old woman, and even took her by the throat. La Mère called on all present to come to her assistance, and several nuns interfered. Jane seized the opportunity afforded in the confusion to beat some of her worst enemies quite severely, and afterwards said, that she had intended to kill some of the rascally informers.

For a time Jane made us laugh so much at prayers, that the Superior forbade her going down with us to morning prayers, and she took the opportunity to sleep in the morning. When this was found out, she was forbidden to get into her bed again after leaving it, and then she would creep under it and take a nap on the floor. This she told us of one day, but threatened us if we ever betrayed her. At length, she was missed at breakfast, as she would sometimes oversleep herself, and the Superior began to be more strict, and always inquired, in the morning whether Jane Ray was in her place. When the question was general, none of us answered; but when it was addressed to some nun near her by name, as, "Saint Eustace, is Jane Ray in her place?" then we had to reply.

Of all the scenes that occurred during my stay in the Convent, there was none which excited the delight of Jane more than one which took place in the chapel one day at mass, though I never had any particular reason to suppose that she had brought it about.

Some person, unknown to me to this day, had put some substance or other, of a most nauseous smell, into the hat of a little boy, who attended at the altar, and he, without observing the trick, put it upon his head. In the midst of the ceremonies he approached some of the nuns, who were almost suffocated with the odour; and as he occasionally moved from place to place some of them began to beckon to him to stand further off, and to hold their noses, with looks of disgust. The boy was quite unconscious of the cause of the difficulty, and paid them no attention; but the confusion soon became so great, through the distress of some, and the laughing of others, that the Superior noticed the circumstance, and beckoned to the boy to withdraw. All attempts, however, to engage us in any work, prayer, or meditation, were found ineffectual. Whenever the circumstances in the chapel came to mind, we would laugh out. We had got into such a state, that we could not easily restrain ourselves. The Superior, yielding to necessity, allowed us recreation for the whole day.

The Superior used sometimes to send Jane to instruct the novices in their English prayers. She would proceed to her task with all seriousness; but sometimes chose the most ridiculous, as well as irreverent passages, from songs, and other things, which she had before somewhere learnt, which would set us, who understood her, laughing. One of her rhymes, I recollect, began with:

> "The Lord of love, look from above,
> Upon this turkey hen."

Jane for a time slept opposite me, and often in the night would rise, unobserved, and slip into my bed, to talk with me, which she did in a low whisper, and return again with equal caution.

She would tell me of the tricks she had played, and such as she meditated, and sometimes make me laugh so loud, that I had much to do in the morning with begging pardons, and doing penances.

One winter's day, she was sent to light a fire; but after she had done so, remarked privately to some of us: "My fingers were too cold—you'll see if I do it again." The next day, there was a great stir in the house, because it was said that mad Jane Ray had been seized with a fit while making a fire, and she was taken up apparently insensible, and conveyed to her bed. She complained to me, who visited her in the course of the day, that she was likely to starve, as food was denied her; and I was persuaded to pin a stocking under my dress, and secretly put food into it from the table. This I afterward carried to her and relieved her wants.

One of the things which I blamed Jane most for, was a disposition to quarrel with any nun who seemed to be winning the favour of the Superior. She would never rest until she had brought such a one into some difficulty.

We were allowed but little soap; and Jane, when she found her supply nearly gone, would take the first piece she could find. One day there was a general search made for a large piece that was missed; when, soon after I had been searched, Jane Ray passed me and slipped it into my pocket; she was soon after searched herself and then secretly came for it again.

While I recall these particulars of our nunnery, and refer so often to the conduct and language of one of the nuns, I cannot speak of some things which I believed or suspected, on account of my want of sufficient knowledge. But it is a pity you have not Jane Ray for a witness; she knows many things of which I am ignorant. She must be in possession of facts that should be known. Her long residence in the Convent, her habits of roaming about it, and of observing every thing, must have made her acquainted with things which would be heard with interest. I always felt as if she knew everything. She would often go and listen, or look through the cracks into the Superior's room, while any of the priests were closeted with her, and sometimes would come and tell me what she witnessed. I felt myself bound to confess in such cases, and always did so.

She knew, however, that I only told it to the priest or to the Superior, and without mentioning the name of my informant, which I was at liberty to withhold, so that she was not found out. I often said to her, "Don't tell me, Jane, for I must confess it." She would reply:

"It is better for you to confess it than for me." I thus became, even against my will, informed of scenes, supposed by the actors of them to be secret.

Jane Ray once persuaded me to accompany her into the Superior's room, to hide with her under the sofa, and await the appearance of a visitor whom she expected, that we might overhear what passed between them. We had been long concealed, when the Superior came in alone and sat for some time, when fearing she might detect us in the stillness which prevailed, we began to repent of our temerity. At length however, she suddenly withdrew, and thus afforded us a welcome opportunity to escape.

I was passing one day through a part of the cellar, where I had not often occasion to go, when the toe of my shoe hit something. I tripped and fell down. I rose again, and holding my lamp to see what had caused my fall, I found an iron ring, fastened to a small square trapdoor. This I had the curiosity to raise, and saw four or five steps leading down, but there was not light enough to see more, and I feared to be noticed by somebody and reported to the Superior; so closing the door again, I left the spot. At first, I could not imagine the use for such a passage; but it afterward occurred to me, that this might open to the subterranean passage to the Seminary, for I never before could account for the appearance of many of the priests, who often appeared and disappeared among us, particularly at night, when I knew the gates were closed. They could, as I now saw, come up to the door of the Superior's room at any hour, then up the stairs into our sleeping-room, or where they chose. And often they were in our beds before us.

I afterward ascertained that my conjectures were correct, and that a secret communication was kept up, in this manner, between the two institutions, at the end towards Notre Dame-street, at a considerable depth under ground. I often afterward, met priests in the cellar, when sent there for coal and other articles, as they had to pass up and down the common cellar stairs on their way.

My wearisome daily prayers and labours, my pain of body, and depression of mind which were so much increased by penances I had suffered, and those which I constantly feared, and the feelings of shame, remorse, and horror, which sometimes arose, brought me into a state which I cannot describe.

In the first place, my frame was enfeebled by the uneasy postures I was required to keep for so long a time during prayers. This alone I thought was sufficient to undermine my health and destroy my life. An hour and a half every morning I had to sit on the floor of the community-room, with my feet under me, my body bent forward, and my head hanging on one side—in a posture expressive of great humility, it is true, but very fatiguing to keep for such an unreasonable length of time. Often I found it impossible to avoid falling asleep in this posture, which I could do without detection, by bending a little lower than usually. The signal to rise, or the noise made by the rising of the other nuns, then woke me, and I got up with the rest unobserved.

Before we took the posture just described, we had to kneel for a long time without bending the body, keeping quite erect, with the exception of the knees only, with the hands together before the breast. This I found the most distressing attitude for me, and never assumed it without feeling a sharp pain in my chest, which I often thought would soon lead me to my grave—that is, to the great common receptacle for the dead, under the chapel. And this upright kneeling posture we were obliged to resume as soon as we rose from the half-sitting posture first mentioned; so that I usually felt myself exhausted and near to fainting before the conclusion of morning services.

I found the meditations extremely tedious, and often did I sink into sleep while we were all seated in silence on the floor. When required to tell my meditations, as it was thought to be of no great importance what we said, I sometimes found I had nothing to tell but a dream, and told that, which passed off very well.

65

Jane Ray appeared to be troubled still more than myself with wandering thoughts; and when blamed for them, would reply, "I begin very well; but directly I begin to think of some old friend of mine, and my thoughts go a-wandering from one country to another."

Sometimes I confessed my falling asleep; and often the priests have talked to me about the sin of sleeping in time of meditation. At last, one of them proposed to me to prick myself with a pin, which I have often done, and so roused myself for a time.

My close confinement in the Convent, and the want of opportunities to breathe the open air, might have proved more injurious to me than they did, had I not employed a part of my time in more active labours than those of sewing, &c., to which I was chiefly confined. I took part occasionally in some of the heavy work, as washing, &c.

The events which I am now to relate, occurred about five months after my admission into the Convent as a nun; but I cannot fix the time with precision, as I know not of any thing which took place in the world about the same period. The circumstance I clearly remember; but, as I have elsewhere remarked, we were not accustomed to keep any account of time.

Information was given to us one day, that another novice was to be admitted among us; and we were required to remember and mention her often in our prayers, that she might have faithfulness in the service of her holy spouse. No information was given us concerning her beyond this fact: not a word about her age, name, or nation. On all similar occasions the same course was pursued, and all that the nuns ever learnt concerning one another was what they might discover by being together, and which usually amounted to little or nothing.

When the day of her admission arrived, though I did not witness the ceremony in the chapel, it was a gratification to us all on one account, because we were all released from labour, and enjoyed a great recreation-day.

Our new sister, when she was introduced to the "holy" society of us "saints," proved to be young, of about the middle size, and very good-looking for a Canadian; for I soon ascertained that she was one of my own countrywomen. The Canadian females are generally not handsome. I never learnt her name, nor any thing of her history. She had chosen Saint Martin for her nun name. She was admitted in the morning, and appeared melancholy all day. This I observed was always the case; and the remarks made by others, led me to believe that they, and all they had seen, had felt sad and miserable for a longer or shorter time. Even the Superior, as it may be recollected, confessed to me that she had experienced the same feelings when she was received. When bedtime arrived, she proceeded to the chamber with the rest of us, and was assigned a bed on the side of the room opposite my own, and a little beyond. The nuns were all soon in bed, the usual silence ensued, and I was making my customary mental prayer and composing myself to sleep, when I heard the most piercing and heart-rending shrieks proceed from our new comrade. Every nun seemed to rise as if by one impulse, for no one could hear such sounds, especially in such total silence, without being greatly excited. A general noise succeeded, for many voices spoke together, uttering cries of surprise, compassion, or fear. It was in vain for the night-watch to expect silence: for once we forgot rules and penances, and gave vent to our feelings, and she could do nothing but call for the Superior. Strange as it may seem, mad Jane Ray, who found an opportunity to make herself heard for an instant, uttered an exclamation in English, which so far from expressing any sympathy for the sufferer, seemed to betray feelings hardened to the last degree against conscience and shame. This caused a laugh among some of those who understood her, and had become hardened to their own trials, and of course in a great measure to those of others.

I heard a man's voice mingled with the cries and shrieks of the nun. Father Quiblier, of the Seminary, I had felt confident, was in the Superior's room at the time when we retired; and several of the nuns afterward assured me that it was he. The Superior soon made her appearance, and in a harsh manner commanded silence. I heard her threaten gagging her, and then say, "You are no better than anybody else, and if you do not obey, you shall be sent to the cells."

One young girl was taken into the Convent during my abode there, under peculiar circumstances. I was acquainted with the whole affair, as I was employed to act a part in it.

Among the novices, was a young lady of about seventeen, the daughter of an old rich Canadian. She had been remarkable for nothing that I know of except the liveliness of her disposition. The Superior once expressed to us a wish to have her take the veil, though the girl herself had never had any such intention, that I knew of. Why the Superior wished to receive her, I could only conjecture. One reason might have been, that she expected to receive a considerable sum from her father. She was, however, strongly desirous of having the girl in our community, and one day said: "Let us take her in by a trick, and tell the old man she felt too humble to take the veil in public."

Our plans then being laid, the unsuspecting girl was induced by us, in sport, as we told her, and made her believe, to put on such a splendid robe as I had worn on my admission, and to pass through some of the ceremonies of taking the veil. After this, she was seriously informed, that she was considered as having entered the Convent in earnest, and must henceforth bury herself to the world, as she would never be allowed to leave it. We put on her a nun's dress, though she wept, and refused, and expressed the greatest repugnance. The Superior threatened, and promised, and flattered, by turns, until the poor girl had to submit; but her appearance long showed that she was a nun only by compulsion.

In obedience to the directions of the Superior, we exerted ourselves to make her contented, especially when she was first received, when we got round her, and told her we had felt so for a time, but having since become acquainted with the happiness of a nun's life, were perfectly content and would never be willing to leave the Convent. An exception seemed to be made in her favor, in one respect: for I believe no criminal attempt was made upon her, until she had been some time an inmate of the nunnery.

Soon after her reception, or rather her forcible entry into the Convent, her father called to make inquiry about his daughter. The Superior first spoke with him herself, and then called us to repeat her plausible story, which I did with accuracy. If I had wished to say any thing else, I never should have dared.

We told the foolish old man, that his daughter, whom we all loved, had long desired to become a Nun, but had been too humble to wish to appear before spectators, and had, at her own desire, been favored with a private admission into the community.

The benefit conferred upon himself and his family, by this act of self-consecration I reminded him, must be truly great and valuable; as every family which furnishes a priest, or a nun, is justly looked upon as receiving the peculiar favor of heaven on that account. The old Canadian firmly believed every word I was forced to tell him, took the event as a great blessing, and expressed the greatest readiness to pay more than the customary fee to the Convent. After the interview, he withdrew, promising soon to return and pay a handsome sum to the convent, which he performed with all despatch, and the greatest cheerfulness. The poor girl never heard that her father had taken the trouble to call to see her, much less did she know any thing of the imposition passed upon him. She remained in the Convent when I left it.

The youngest girl who ever took the veil of our sisterhood, was only fourteen years of age, and considered very pious. She lived but a short time. I was told that she was ill-treated by the priests, and believe her death was in consequence.

CHAPTER XV

Influencing Novices—Difficulty of convincing persons from the United States—Tale of the Bishop in the City—The Bishop in the Convent—The Prisoners in the Cells—Practice in Singing—Narratives, Jane Ray's Hymns, The Superior's best Trick.

It was considered a great duty to exert ourselves to influence novices in favor of the Roman Catholic religion; and different nuns, were, at different times, charged to do what they could, by conversation, to make favourable impressions on the minds of some, who were particularly indicated to us by the Superior. I often heard it remarked, that those who were influenced with the greatest difficulty, were young ladies from the United States; and on some of those, great exertions were made.

Cases in which citizens of the States were said to have been converted to the Roman Catholic faith, were sometimes spoken of, and always as if they were considered highly important.

The Bishop, as we were told, was on the public square, on the day of an execution, when, as he said, a stranger looked at him in some peculiar manner, which made him confidently believe God intended to have him converted by his means. When he went home, he wrote a letter for him, and the next day found him again in the same place, and gave him the letter, which led to his becoming a Roman Catholic. This man, it was added, proved to be a citizen of the States.

The Bishop, as I have remarked, was not very dignified on all occasions, and sometimes acted in such a manner as would not have appeared well in public.

One day I saw him preparing for mass; and because he had difficulty in getting on his robe, showed evident signs of anger. One of the nuns remarked: "The Bishop is going to perform a passionate mass." Some of the others exclaimed: "Are you not ashamed to speak so of my lord!" And she was rewarded with a penance.

But it might be hoped that the Bishop would be free from the crimes of which I have declared so many priests to have been guilty. I am far from entertaining such charitable opinions of him; and I had good reasons, after a time.

I was often required to sleep on a sofa, in the room of the present Superior, as I may have already mentioned.

One night, not long after I was first introduced there, for that purpose, and within the first twelve months of my wearing the veil, having retired as usual, at about half-past nine, not long after we had got into bed, the alarm-bell from without, which hangs over the Superior's bed, was rung. She told me to see who was there; and going down, I heard the signal given, which I have before mentioned, a peculiar kind of hissing sound made through the teeth. I answered with a low, "Hum-hum;" and then opened the door. It was Bishop Lartigue, the present Bishop of Montreal. He said to me, "Are you a Novice or a Received?" meaning a Received nun. I answered a "Received."

He then requested me to conduct him to the Superior's room, which I did. He went to the bed, drew the curtains behind him, and I lay down again upon the sofa, until morning, when the Superior called me, at an early hour, about daylight, and directed me to show him the door, to which I conducted him, and he took his departure.

I continued to visit the cellar frequently, to carry up coal for the fires, without anything more than a general impression that there were two nuns, somewhere imprisoned in it. One day while there on my usual errand, I saw a nun standing on the right of the cellar, in front of one of the cell doors I had before observed; she was apparently engaged with something within. This attracted my attention. The door appeared to close in a small recess, and was fastened with a stout iron bolt on the outside, the end of which was secured by being let into a hole in the stone-work which formed the posts. The door, which was of wood, was sank a few inches beyond the stone-work, rose and formed an arch overhead. Above the bolt was a window supplied with a fine grating, which swung open, a small bolt having been removed from it, on the outside. The nun I had observed seemed to be whispering with some person within, through the little window: but I hastened to get my coal, and left the cellar, presuming that was the prison. When I visited the place again, being alone, I ventured to the spot, determined to learn the truth, presuming that the imprisoned nuns, of whom the Superior had told me on my admission, were confined there. I spoke at the window where I had seen the nun standing, and heard a voice reply in a whisper. The aperture was so small, and the place so dark, that I could see nobody; but I learnt that a poor wretch was confined there a prisoner. I feared that I might be discovered, and after a few words, which I thought could do no harm, I withdrew.

My curiosity was now alive, to learn every thing I could about so mysterious a subject. I made a few inquiries of Saint Xavier, who only informed me that they were punished for refusing to obey the Superior, Bishop, and Priests. I afterward found that the other nuns were acquainted with the fact I had just discovered. All I could learn, however, was, that the prisoner in the cell whom I had spoken with, and another in the cell just beyond, had been confined there

70

several years without having been taken out; but their names, connexions, offences, and everything else relating to them, I could never learn, and am still as ignorant of as ever. Some conjectured that they had refused to comply with some of the rules of the Convent or requisitions of the Superior; others, that they were heiresses whose property was desired for the convent, and who would not consent to sign deeds of it. Some of the nuns informed me, that the severest of their sufferings arose from fear of supernatural beings.

I often spoke with one of them in passing near their cells, when on errands in the cellar, but never ventured to stop long, or to press my inquiries very far. Besides, I found her reserved, and little disposed to converse freely, a thing I could not wonder at when I considered her situation, and the characters of persons around her. She spoke like a woman in feeble health, and of broken spirits. I occasionally saw other nuns speaking to them, particularly at mealtimes, when they were regularly furnished with food, which was such as we ourselves ate.

Their cells were occasionally cleaned and then the doors were opened. I never looked into them, but was informed that the ground was their only floor. I presumed that they were furnished with straw to lie upon, as I always saw a quantity of old straw scattered about that part of the cellar, after the cells had been cleansed. I once inquired of one of them, whether they could converse together, and she replied that they could, through a small opening between their cells, which I could not see.

I once inquired of the one I spoke with in passing, whether she wanted anything, and she replied, "Tell Jane Ray I want to see her a moment if she can slip away." When I went up I took an opportunity to deliver my message to Jane, who concerted with me a signal to be used in future, in case a similar request should be made through me. This was a sly wink at her with one eye, accompanied with a slight toss of my head. She then sought an opportunity to visit the cellar, and was soon able to hold an interview with the poor prisoners, without being noticed by any one but myself. I afterward learnt that mad Jane Ray was not so mad, but she could feel for those miserable beings, and carry through measures for their comfort. She would often visit them with sympathizing words, and, when necessary, conceal part of her food while at table, and secretly convey it into their dungeons. Sometimes we would combine for such an object; and I have repeatedly aided her in thus obtaining a larger supply of food than they had been able to obtain from others.

I frequently thought of the two nuns confined in the cells, and occasionally heard something said about them, but very little. Whenever I visited the cellar and thought it safe, I went up to the first of them and spoke a word or two, and usually got some brief reply, without ascertaining that any particular change took place with either of them. The one with whom I ever conversed, spoke English perfectly well, and French I thought as well. I supposed she must have been well educated, for I could not tell which was her native language. I remember that she frequently used these words when I wished to say more to her, and which alone showed that she was constantly afraid of punishment: "Oh, there's somebody coming—do go away!" I have been told that the other prisoner also spoke English.

It was impossible for me to form any certain opinion about the size or appearance of those two miserable creatures, for their cells were perfectly dark, and I never caught the slightest glimpse even of their faces. It is probable they were women not above the middle size, and my reason for this presumption is the following: I was sometimes appointed to lay out the clean clothes for all the nuns in the Convent on Saturday evening, and was always directed to lay by two suits for the prisoners. Particular orders were given to select the largest sized garments for several tall nuns; but nothing of the kind was ever said in relation to the clothes for those in the cells.

I had not been long a veiled nun, before I requested of the Superior permission to confess to the "Saint Bon Pasteur," (Holy Good Shepherd,) that is, the mysterious and nameless nun whom I had heard of while a novice. I knew of several others who had confessed to her at different times, and of some who had sent their clothes to be touched by her when they were sick; and I felt a desire to unburden my heart of certain things, which I was loath to acknowledge to the Superior, or any of the priests.

The Superior made me wait a little, until she could ascertain whether the "Saint Bon Pasteur" was ready to admit me; and after a time returned, and told me to enter the old nuns' room. That apartment has twelve beds, arranged like the berths of a ship by threes; and as each is broad enough to receive two persons, twenty-four may be lodged there, which was about the number of old nuns in the Convent during the most of my stay in it. Near an opposite corner of the apartment was a large glass case, with no appearance of a door, or other opening, in any part of it: and in that case stood the venerable nun, in the dress of the community, with her thick veil spread over her face, so as to conceal it entirely. She was standing, for the place did not allow room for sitting, and moved a little, which was the only sign of life, as she did not speak. I fell upon my knees before her, and began to confess some of my imperfections, which lay heavy upon my mind, imploring her aid and intercession, that I might be delivered from them. She appeared to listen to me with patience, but still never returned a word in reply. I became much affected as I went on, and at length began to weep bitterly; and when I withdrew, was in tears. It seemed to me that my heart was remarkably relieved after this exercise, and all the requests I had made, I found, as I believed, strictly fulfilled. I often, afterward, visited the old nuns' room for the same purpose, and with similar results, so that my belief in the sanctity of the nameless nun, and my regard for her intercession were unbounded.

What is remarkable, though I repeatedly was sent into that A room to dust it, or to put it in order, I remarked that the glass case was vacant, and no signs were to be found either of the nun or of the way by which she had left it; so that a solemn conclusion rested upon my mind, that she had gone on one of her frequent visits to heaven.

A priest would sometimes come in the daytime to teach us to sing, and this was done with some parade or stir, as if it were considered, or meant to be considered as a thing of importance.

The instructions, however, were entirely repetitions of the words and tunes, nothing being taught even of the first principles of the science. It appeared to me, that although hymns alone were sung, the exercise was chiefly designed for our amusement, to raise our spirits a little, which were apt to become depressed. Mad Jane Ray certainly usually treated the whole thing as a matter of sport, and often excited those of us who understood English to a great degree of mirth. She had a very fine voice, which was so powerful as generally to be heard above the rest. Sometimes she would be silent when the other nuns began; I and the Superior would often call out, "Jane Ray, you don't sing." She always had some trifling excuse ready, and commonly appeared unwilling to join the rest. After being urged or commanded by the Superior, she would then strike up some English song, or profane parody, which was rendered ten times more ridiculous by the ignorance of the Lady Superior and the majority of the nuns. I cannot help laughing now when I remember how she used to stand with perfect composure and sing,

"I wish I was married and nothing to rue,
With plenty of money and nothing to do."

"Jane Ray, you don't sing right," the Superior would exclaim. "Oh," she would reply, with perfect coolness, "that is the English for,

'Seigneur Dieu de clemence,
Reçois ce grand pécheur;'"

73

and, as sung by her, a person ignorant of the language would naturally be imposed upon. It was extremely difficult for me to conceal my laughter. I have always had greater exertion to make in repressing it than most other persons; and mad Jane Ray often took advantage of this.

Saturday evening usually brought with it much unpleasant work for some of us. We received the Sacrament every Sunday; and in preparation for it, on Saturday evening we asked pardon of the Superior and of each other "for the scandal we had caused since we last received the Sacrament," and then asked the Superior's permission to receive it on the following day. She inquired of each nun who necessarily asked her permission, whether she, naming her as Saint somebody, had concealed any sin that should hinder her from receiving it; and if the answer was in the negative, she granted her permission.

On Saturdays we were catechised by a priest, being assembled in a community-room. He sat on the right of the door in a chair. He often told us stories, and frequently enlarged on the duty enticing novices into the nunnery. "Do you not feel" he would say, "now that you are safely out of the world, sure of heaven? But remember how many poor people are yet in the world. Every novice you influence to the black veil, will add to your honour in heaven. Tell them how happy you are."

The Superior played one trick while I was in the Convent, which always passed for one of the most admirable she ever carried into execution. We were pretty good judges in a case of this kind, for, as may be presumed, we were rendered familiar with the arts of deception under so accomplished a teacher.

There was an ornament on hand in the nunnery, of an extraordinary kind, which was prized at ten pounds; but it had been made and exposed to view so long, that it became damaged and quite unsaleable. We were one day visited by an old priest from the country, who was evidently somewhat intoxicated; and as he withdrew to go to his lodgings, in the Seminary, where the country priests often stay, the Superior conceived a plan for disposing of the old ornament. "Come," said she, "we will send it to the old priest, and swear he has bought it!"

We all approved of the ingenious device, for it evidently might be classed among the pious frauds we had so often had recommended to us both by precept and example; and the ornament was sent to him the next morning, as his property when paid for. He soon came to the Convent, and expressed the greatest surprise that he had been charged with purchasing such a thing, for which he had no need and no desire.

The Superior heard this declaration with patience, but politely insisted that it was a fair bargain; and we then surrounded the old priest, with the strongest assertions that such was the fact, and that nobody would ever have thought of his purchasing it unless he had expressly engaged to take it. The poor old man was entirely put down. He was certain of the truth: but what could he do: resist or disprove a direct falsehood pronounced by the Superior of a Convent, and sworn to by all her holy nuns? He finally expressed his conviction that we were right: he was compelled to pay his money.

CHAPTER XVI

Frequency of the Priests' Visits to the Nunnery—Their Freedom and Crimes—Difficulty of learning their Names—Their Holy Retreat—Objections in our minds—Means used to counteract Conscience—Ingenious Arguments.

Some of the priests from the Seminary were in the nunnery every day and night, and often several at a time. I have seen nearly all of them at different times, though there are about one hundred and fifty in the district of Montreal. There was a difference in their conduct; though I believe every one of them was guilty of licentiousness; while not one did I ever see who maintained a character any way becoming the profession of a priest. Some were gross and degraded in a degree which few of my readers can ever have imagined; and I should be unwilling to offend the eye, and corrupt the heart of any one, by an account of their words and actions. Few imaginations can conceive deeds so abominable as they practised, and often required of some of the poor women, under the fear of severe punishments, and even of death. I do not hesitate to say with the strongest confidence, that although some of the nuns became lost to every sentiment of virtue and honour, especially one from the Congregational Nunnery whom I have before mentioned, Saint Patrick, the greater part of them loathed the practices to which they were compelled to submit by the Superior and priests, who kept them under so dreadful a bondage.

Some of the priests whom I saw I never knew by name, and the names of others I did not learn for a time, and at last only by accident.

They were always called "Mon père," my father; but sometimes, when they had purchased something in the ornament-room, they would give their real names, with directions where it should be sent. Many names, thus learnt, and in other ways, were whispered about from nun to nun, and became pretty generally known. Several of the priests, some of us had seen before we entered the Convent.

Many things of which I speak, from the nature of the case, must necessarily rest chiefly upon my own word, until further evidence can be obtained: but there are some facts for which I can appeal to the knowledge of others. It is commonly known in Montreal that some of the priests occasionally withdraw from their customary employments, and are not to be seen for some time, it being understood that they have retired for religious study, meditation and devotion, for the improvement of their hearts. Sometimes they are thus withdrawn from the world for weeks: but there is no fixed period.

This was a fact I knew before I took the veil; for it is a frequent subject of remark, that such or such a Father is on a "holy retreat." This is a term which conveys the idea of a religious seclusion from the world for sacred purposes. On the re-appearance of the priest after such a period, in the church or the streets, it is natural to feel a peculiar impression of his devout character—an impression very different from that conveyed to the mind of one who knows matters as they really are. Suspicions have been indulged by some in Canada on this subject, and facts are known by at least a few. I am able to speak from personal knowledge: for I have been a nun of Soeur Bourgeoise.

The priests are liable, by their dissolute habits, to occasional attacks of disease, which render it necessary, or at least prudent, to submit to medical treatment.

In the Black Nunnery they find private accommodations, for they are free to enter one of the private hospitals whenever they please; which is a room set apart on purpose for the accommodation of the priests, and is called a retreat-room. But an excuse is necessary to blind the public, and this they find is the pretence that they make of being in a "Holy Retreat." Many such cases I have known; and I can mention the names of priests who have been confined in this Holy Retreat. They are very carefully attended by the Superior and old nuns, and their diet mostly consists of vegetable soups, &c., with but little meat, and that fresh. I have seen an instrument of surgery laying upon the table in that holy room, which is used only for particular purposes.

Father Tabeau, a Roman priest, was on one of his holy

retreats about the time when I left the nunnery. There are sometimes a number confined there at the same time. The victims of these priests frequently share the same fate.

I have often reflected how grievously I had been deceived in my opinion of a nun's condition! All the holiness of their lives, I now saw, was merely pretended. The appearance of sanctity and heavenly mindedness which they had shown among us novices, I found was only a disguise to conceal such practices as would not be tolerated in any decent society in the world; and as for peace and joy like that of heaven, which I had expected to find among them, I learnt too well that they did not exist there.

The only way in which such thoughts were counteracted, was by the constant instructions given us by the Superior and priests, to regard every doubt as a mortal sin. Other faults we might have, as we were told over and over again, which, though worthy of penances, were far less sinful than these. For a nun to doubt that she was doing her duty in fulfilling her vows and oaths, was a heinous offence, and we were exhorted always to suppress our doubts, to confess them without reserve, and cheerfully to submit to severe penances on account of them, as the only means of mortifying our evil dispositions, and resisting the temptations of the devil. Thus we learnt in a good degree to resist our minds and consciences, when we felt the first rising of a question about the duty of doing any thing required of us.

To enforce this upon us, they employed various means. Some of the most striking stories told us at catechism by the priests, were designed for this end. One of these, I will repeat. One day, as a priest assured us who was hearing us say the catechism on Saturday afternoon, as one Monsieur ——, a well-known citizen of Montreal, was walking near the cathedral, he saw Satan giving orders to numerous evil spirits who had assembled around him. Being afraid of being seen, and yet wishing to observe what was done, he hid himself where he could observe all that passed. Satan despatched his devils to different parts of the city, with directions to do their best for him; and they returned in a short time, bringing in reports of their success in leading persons of different classes to the commission of various sins, which they thought would be agreeable to their master. Satan, however, expressed his dissatisfaction, and ordered them out again; but just then a spirit from the Black Nunnery came, who had not been seen before, and stated that he had been trying for seven years to persuade one of the nuns to doubt, and had just succeeded. Satan received the intelligence with the highest pleasure; and turning to the spirits around him, said:

"You have not half done your work—he has done much more than all of you."

In spite, however, of our instructions and warnings, our fears and penances, such doubts would intrude; and I have often indulged them for a time, and at length, yielding to the belief that I was wrong in giving place to them, would confess them, and undergo with cheerfulness such new penances as I was loaded with. Others too would occasionally entertain and privately express such doubts; though we all had been most solemnly warned by the cruel murder of Saint Francis. Occasionally some of the nuns would go further, and resist the restraints or punishments imposed upon them; and it was not uncommon to hear screams, sometimes of a most piercing and terrific kind, from nuns suffering under discipline.

Some of my readers may feel disposed to exclaim against me, for believing things, which will strike them as so monstrous and abominable. To such, I would say, without pretending to justify myself—You know little of the position in which I was placed: in the first place, ignorant of any other religions doctrines; and in the second, met at every moment by some ingenious argument, and the example of a large community, who received all the instructions of the priests as of undoubted truth, and practised upon them. Of the variety and speciousness of the arguments used, you cannot have any correct idea. They were often so ready with replies, examples, anecdotes and authorities, to enforce their doctrines, that it seemed to me they could never have learnt it all from books, but must have been taught by wicked spirits. Indeed, when I reflect upon their conversations, I am astonished at their art and address, and find it difficult to account for their subtlety and success in influencing my mind, and persuading me to anything they pleased. It seems to me, that hardly anybody would be safe in their hands. If you were to go to confession twice, I believe you would feel very differently from what you do now. They have such a way of avoiding one thing, and speaking of another, of affirming this, and doubting or disputing that, of quoting authorities, and speaking of wonders and miracles recently performed, in confirmation of what they teach, as familiarly known to persons whom they call by name, and whom they pretend to offer as witnesses, though they never give you an opportunity to speak with them—these, and many other means, they use in such away, that they always blinded my mind, and I should think, would blind the minds of others.

CHAPTER XVII

Treatment of young Infants in the Convent—Talking in Sleep—Amusements—Ceremonies at the public interment of deceased Nuns—Sudden disappearance of the Old Superior—Introduction of the new one—Superstition—Alarm of a Nun—Difficulty of Communication with other Nuns.

It will be recollected, that I was informed immediately after receiving the veil, that infants were occasionally murdered in the Convent. I was one day in the nuns' private sick room, when I had an opportunity, unsought for, of witnessing deeds of such a nature. It was, perhaps, a month after the death of Saint Francis. Two little twin babes, the children of Sainte Catharine, were brought to a priest, who was in the room, for baptism. I was present while the ceremony was performed, with the Superior and several of the old nuns, whose names I never knew, they being called Ma tante, Aunt.

The priests took turns in attending to confession and catechism in the Convent, usually three months at a time, though sometimes longer periods. The priest then on duty was Father Larkin. He is a good-looking European, and has a brother who is a professor in the college. He baptized, and then put oil upon the heads of the infants, as is the custom after baptism. They were then taken, one after another, by one of the old nuns, in the presence of us all. She pressed her hand upon the mouth and nose of the first, so tight that it could not breathe, and in a few minutes, when the hand was removed, it was dead. She then took the other, and treated it in the same way. No sound was heard, and both the children were corpses. The greatest indifference was shown by all present during this operation; for all, as I well knew, were long accustomed to such scenes. The little bodies were then taken into the cellar, thrown into the pit I have mentioned, and covered with a quantity of lime.

I afterward saw another new-born infant treated in the same manner, in the same place; but the actors in the scene I choose not to name, nor the circumstances, as everything connected with it is of a peculiarly trying and painful nature to my own feelings.

These were the only instances of infanticide I witnessed; and it seemed to be merely owing to accident that I was then present. So far as I know, there were no pains taken to preserve secrecy on this subject; that is, I saw no attempt made to keep any of the inmates of the Convent in ignorance of the murder of children. On the contrary, others were told, as well as myself, on their first admission as veiled nuns, that all infants born in the place were baptized and killed, without loss of time; and I had been called to witness the murder of the three just mentioned, only because I happened to be in the room at the time.

That others were killed in the same manner during my stay in the nunnery, I am well assured.

How many there were I cannot tell, and having taken no account of those I heard of, I cannot speak with precision; I believe, however, that I learnt through nuns, that at least eighteen or twenty infants were smothered, and secretly buried in the cellar, while I was a nun.

One of the effects of the weariness of our bodies and minds, was our proneness to talk in our sleep. It was both ludicrous and painful to hear the nuns repeat their prayers in the course of the night, as they frequently did in their dreams. Required to keep our minds continually on the stretch, both in watching our conduct, in remembering the rules and our prayers, under the fear of the consequences of any neglect, when we closed our eyes in sleep, we often went over again the scenes of the day; and it was no uncommon thing for me to hear a nun repeat one or two of our long exercises in the dead of night. Sometimes, by the time she had finished, another, in a different part of the room, would happen to take a similar turn, and commence a similar recitation; and I have known cases in which several such unconscious exercises were performed, all within an hour or two.

We had now and then a recreation day, when we were relieved from our customary labor, and from all prayers except those for morning and evening. The greater part of our time was then occupied with different games, particularly backgammon and drafts, and in such conversation as did not relate to our past lives, and the outside of the Convent. Sometimes, however, our sports would be interrupted on such days by the entrance of one of the priests, who would come in and propose that his fete, the birth-day of his patron saint, should be kept by "the saints." We saints!

Several nuns died at different times while I was in the Convent; how many I cannot say, but there was a considerable number: I might rather say, many in proportion to the number in the nunnery. The proportion of deaths I am sure was very large. There were always some in the nuns' sick-rooms, and several interments took place in the chapel. When a Black nun is dead, the corpse is dressed as if living, and placed in the chapel in a sitting posture, within the railing round the altar, with a book in the hand, as if reading. Persons are then freely admitted from the street, and some of them kneel and pray before it. No particular notoriety is given, I believe, to this exhibition out of the Convent; but such a case usually excites some attention.

The living nuns are required to say prayers for the delivery of their deceased sister from purgatory, being informed, as in all other such cases, that if she is not there, and has no need of our intercession, our prayers are in no danger of being thrown away, as they will be set down to the account of some of our departed friends, or at least to that of the souls which have no acquaintances to pray for them.

It was customary for us occasionally to kneel before a dead nun thus seated in the chapel, and I have often performed that task. It was always painful, for the ghastly countenance being seen whenever I raised my eyes, and the feeling that the position and dress were entirely opposed to every idea of propriety in such a case, always made me melancholy.

The Superior sometimes left the Convent, and was absent for an hour, or several hours, at a time, but we never knew of it until she had returned, and were not informed where she had been. I one day had reason to presume that she had recently paid a visit to the priests' farm, though I had no direct evidence that such was the fact. The priests' farm is a fine tract of land belonging to the Seminary, a little distance from the city, near the Lachine road, with a large old-fashioned edifice upon it. I happened to be in the Superior's room on the day alluded to, when she made some remark on the plainness and poverty of her furniture. I replied, that she was not proud, and could not be dissatisfied on that account; she answered—

"No; but if I was, how much superior is the furniture at the priests' farm! the poorest room there is furnished better than the best of mine."

I was one day mending the fire in the Superior's room, when a priest was conversing with her on the scarcity of money; and I heard him say, that very little money was received by the priests for prayers, but that the principal part came with penances and absolutions.

One of the most remarkable and unaccountable things that happened in the Convent, was the disappearance of the old Superior. She had performed her customary part during the day, and had acted and appeared just as usual. She had shown no symptoms of ill health, met with no particular difficulty in conducting business, and no agitation, anxiety or gloom, had been noticed in her conduct. We had no reason to suppose that during that day she had expected anything particular to occur, any more than the rest of us. After the close of our customary labours, and evening lecture, she dismissed us to retire to bed, exactly in her usual manner. The next morning the bell rung we sprang from our bed, hurried on our clothes as usual, and proceeded to the community-room in double line, to commence the morning exercises. There, to our surprise, we found Bishop Lartigue; but the Superior was nowhere to be seen. The Bishop soon addressed us, instead of her, and informed us, that a lady near him, whom he presented to us, was now the Superior of the Convent, and enjoined upon us the same respect and obedience which we had paid to her predecessor.

The lady he introduced to us was one of our oldest nuns, Saint Du ——, a very large, fleshy woman, with swelled limbs, which rendered her very slow in walking, and often gave her great distress. Not a word was dropped from which we could conjecture the cause of this change, nor of the fate of the old Superior. I took the first opportunity to inquire of one of the nuns, whom I dared talk to, what had become of her; but I found them as ignorant as myself, though suspicious that she had been murdered by the orders of the Bishop. Never did I obtain any light on her mysterious disappearance. I am confident, however, that if the Bishop wished to get rid of her privately and by foul means, he had ample opportunities and power at his command. Jane Ray, as usual, could not allow such an occurrence to pass by without intimating her own suspicions more plainly than any other of the nuns would have dared to do. She spoke out one day, in the community-room, and said, "I'm going to have a hunt in the cellar for my old Superior."

"Hush, Jane Ray!" exclaimed some of the nuns, "you'll be punished."

"My mother used to tell me," replied Jane, "never to be afraid of the face of a man."

It cannot be thought strange that we were superstitious. Some were more easily terrified than others, by unaccountable sights and sounds; but all of us believed in the power and occasional appearance of spirits, and were ready to look for them at almost any time. I have seen several instances of alarm caused by such superstition, and have experienced it myself more than once. I was one day sitting mending aprons, beside one of the old nuns, in a community-room, while the litanies were repeating; as I was very easy to laugh, Saint Ignace or Agnes, came in, walked up to her with much agitation, and began to whisper in her ear. She usually talked but little, and that made me more curious to know what was the matter with her. I overheard her say to the old nun, in much alarm, that in the cellar from which she had just returned, she had heard the most dreadful groans that ever came from any being. This was enough to give me uneasiness. I could not account for the appearance of an evil spirit in any part of the Convent, for I had been assured that the only one ever known there, was that of the nun who had died with an unconfessed sin, and that others were kept at a distance by the holy water that was rather profusely used in different parts of the nunnery. Still, I presumed that the sounds heard by Saint Ignace must have proceeded from some devil, and I felt great dread at the thought of visiting the cellar again. I determined to seek further information of the terrified nun; but when I addressed her on the subject, at recreation-time, the first opportunity I could find, she replied, that I was always trying to make her break silence, and walked off to another group in the room, so that I could obtain no satisfaction.

It is remarkable that in our nunnery, we were almost entirely cut off from the means of knowing anything, even of each other. There were many nuns whom I know nothing of to this day, after having been in the same rooms with them every day and night for many months. There was a nun, whom I supposed to be in the Convent, and whom I was anxious to learn something about from the time of my entrance as a novice; but I never was able to learn anything concerning her, not even whether she was in the nunnery or not, whether alive or dead. She was the daughter of a rich family, residing at Point aux Trembles, of whom I had heard my mother speak before I entered the Convent. The name of her family I think was Lafayette, and she was thought to be from Europe. She was known to have taken the black veil; but as I was not acquainted with the name of the Saint she had assumed, and I could not describe her in "the world," all my inquiries and observations proved entirely in vain. I had heard before my entrance into the Convent, that one of the nuns had made her escape from it during the last war, and, once inquired about her of the Superior. She admitted that such was the fact; but I was never able to learn any particulars concerning her name, origin, or manner of escape.

CHAPTER XVIII

Disappearance of Nuns—St. Pierre—Gags—My temporary Confinement in a Cell—The Cholera Season—How to avoid it— Occupation in the Convent during the Pestilence—Manufacture of Wax Candles—The Election Riots—Alarm among the Nuns— Preparations for defence—Penances.

I am unable to say how many nuns disappeared while I was in the Convent. There were several. One was a young lady called St. Pierre, I think, but am not certain of her name. There were two nuns by this name. I had known her as a novice with me. She had been a novice about two years and a half before I became one. She was rather large without being tall and had rather dark hair and eyes. She disappeared unaccountably, and nothing was said of her except what I heard in whispers from a few of the nuns, as we found moments when we could speak unobserved.

Some told me they thought she must have left the Convent; and I might have supposed so, had I not some time afterward found some of her things lying about, which she would, in such a case, doubtless have taken with her. I never had known any thing more of her than what I could observe or conjecture. I had always, however, the idea that her parents or friends were wealthy, for she sometimes received clothes and other things, which were very rich.

Another nun, named Saint Paul, died suddenly; but as in other cases, we knew so little, or rather were so entirely ignorant of the cause and circumstances that we could only conjecture; and being forbidden to converse freely on that or any other subject, thought but little about it. I have mentioned that a number of veiled nuns thus mysteriously disappeared during my residence among them. I cannot, perhaps, recall them all, but I am confident there were as many as five, and I think more. All that we knew in such cases was, that one of our number who had appeared as usual when last observed, was nowhere to be seen, and never was again. Mad Jane Ray, on several such occasions, would indulge in her bold, and, as we thought, dangerous remarks. She had intimated that some of those, who had been for a time in the Convent, were by some means removed to make way for new ones; and it was generally the fact, that the disappearance of one and the introduction of another into our community, were nearly at the same time. I have repeatedly heard Jane Ray say, with one of her significant looks, "When you appear, somebody else disappears!"

84

It is unpleasant enough to distress or torture one's self; but there is something worse in being tormented by others, especially where they resort to force, and show a pleasure in compelling you, and leave you no hope of escape, or opportunity to resist. I had seen the gags repeatedly in use, and sometimes applied with a roughness which seemed rather inhuman; but it is one thing to see and another thing to feel. There were some of the old nuns who seemed to take pleasure in oppressing those who fell under their displeasure. They were ready to recommend or resort to compulsory measures, and ever ready to run for the gags. These were kept in one of the community-rooms, in a drawer between two closets; and there a stock of about fifty of them was always in deposite. Sometimes a number of nuns would prove refractory at a time; and I have seen battles commenced in which several appeared on both sides. The disobedient were, however, soon overpowered: and to prevent their screams from being heard beyond the walls, gagging commenced immediately. I have seen half a dozen lying, gagged and bound at once.

I have been subjected to the same state of involuntary silence more than once; for sometimes I became excited to a state of desperation by the measures used against me, and then conducted in a manner perhaps not less violent than some others. My hands had been tied behind me, and a gag put into my mouth, sometimes with such force and rudeness as to lacerate my lips and cause the blood to flow freely.

Treatment of this kind is apt to teach submission, and many times I have acquiesced under orders received, or wishes expressed, with a fear of a recurrence to some severe measures.

One day I had incurred the anger of the Superior in a greater degree than usual, and it was ordered that I should be taken to one of the cells. I was taken by some of the nuns, bound and gagged, carried down the stairs in the cellar, and laid upon the floor. Not long afterward I induced one of the nuns to request the Superior to come down and see me; and on making some acknowledgment I was released. I will, however, relate this story rather more in detail.

On that day I had been engaged with Jane Ray, in carrying into effect a plan of revenge upon another person, when I fell under the vindictive spirit of some of the old nuns, and suffered severely. The Superior ordered me to the cells, and a scene of violence commenced which I will not attempt to describe, nor the precise circumstances which led to it. Suffice it to say, that after exhausting my strength, by resisting as long as I could against several nuns, I had my hands drawn behind my back, a leathern band passed first round my thumbs, then round my hands, and then round my waist,

85

and fastened. This was drawn so tight that it cut through the flesh of my thumbs, making wounds, the scars of which still remain. A gag was then forced into my mouth, not indeed so violently as it sometimes was, but roughly enough; after which I was taken by main force, and carried down into the cellar, across it almost to the opposite extremity, and brought to the last of the second range of cells on the left hand. The door was opened, and I was thrown in with violence, and left alone, the door being immediately closed and bolted on the outside. The bare ground was under me, cold and hard as if it had been beaten down even. I lay still, in the position in which I had fallen, as it would have been difficult for me to move, confined as I was, and exhausted by my exertions; and the shock of my fall, and my wretched state of desperation and fear, disinclined me from any further attempt. I was in almost total darkness, there being nothing perceptible except a slight glimmer of light which came in through the little window far above me.

How long I remained in that condition I can only conjecture. It seemed to me a long time, and must have been two or three hours. I did not move, expecting to die there, and in a state of distress which I cannot describe, from the tight bandage about my hands, and the gag holding my jaws apart at their greatest extension. I am confident I must have died before morning, if, as I then expected, I had been left there all night. By-and-by, however, the bolt was drawn, the door opened, and Jane Ray spoke to me in a tone of kindness. She had taken an opportunity to slip into the cellar unnoticed on purpose to see me. She unbound the gag, and took it out of my mouth, and told me she would do any thing to get me out of my dungeon. If she had had the bringing of me down, she would not have thrust me so brutally, and she would be revenged on those who had. She offered to throw herself upon her knees before the Superior and beg her forgiveness. To this I would not consent; but told her to ask the Superior to come to me, as I wished to speak to her. This I had no idea she would condescend to do; but Jane had not been gone long before the Superior came, and asked if I had repented in the sight of God for what I had done. I replied in the affirmative; and after a lecture of some length on the pain I had given the Virgin Mary by my conduct, she asked whether I was willing to ask pardon of all the nuns for the scandal I had caused them by my behaviour. To this I made no objection; and I was then released from my prison and my bonds, went up to the community-room, and kneeling before all the sisters in succession begged the forgiveness and prayers of each.

Among the marks which I still bear of the wounds received from penances and violence, are the scars left by the belt with which

I repeatedly tortured myself, for the mortification of my spirit. These are most distinct on my side; for although the band, which was four or five inches in breadth, and extended round the waist, was stuck full of sharp iron points in all parts, it was sometimes crowded most against my side, by rocking in my chair, and the wounds were usually deeper there than anywhere else.

My thumbs were several times cut severely by the tight drawing of the band used to confine my arms, and the scars are still visible upon them.

The rough gagging which I several times endured wounded my lips very much; for it was common, in that operation, to thrust the gag hard against the teeth, and catch one or both the lips, which were sometimes cut. The object was to stop the screams made by the offender as soon as possible; and some of the old nuns delighted in tormenting us. A gag was once forced into my mouth which had a large splinter upon it, and this cut through my under lip, in front, leaving to this day a scar about half an inch long. The same lip was several times wounded, as well as the other; but one day worse than ever, when a narrow piece was cut off from the left side of it, by being pinched between the gag and the under fore-teeth; and this has left an inequality in it which is still very observable.

One of the most shocking stories I heard of events that had occurred in the nunnery before my acquaintance with it, was the following, which was told me by Jane. What is uncommon, I can fix the date when I heard it. It was on New-Year's day, 1834. The ceremonies, customary in the early part of that day, had been performed; after mass, in the morning, the Superior had shaken hands with all the nuns, and given us her blessing, for she was said to have received power from heaven to do so only once a year, and then on the first day of the year. Besides this, cakes, raisins, &c. are distributed to the nuns on that day.

While in the community-room, I had taken a seat just within the cupboard-door, where I often found a partial shelter from observation with Jane, when a conversation incidentally began between us. Our practice often was, to take places there beside one of the old nuns, awaiting the time when she would go away for a little while and leave us partially screened from the observation of others. On that occasion, Jane and I were left for a time alone; when after some discourse on suicide, she remarked, that three nuns once killed themselves in the Convent. This happened, she said, not long after her reception, and I knew, therefore, that it was several years before, for she had been received a considerable time before I had become a novice. Three young ladies, she informed me, took the veil together, or very near the same time, I am not certain which. I know they have four robes in the Convent, to be worn during the ceremony of taking the veil; but I have never seen more than one of them used at a time.

Two of the new nuns were sisters, and the other their cousin. They had been received but a few days, when information was given one morning that they had been found dead in their beds, amid a profusion of blood. Jane Ray said, she saw their corpses, and that they appeared to have killed themselves, by opening veins in their arms with a knife they had obtained, and all had bled to death together. What was extraordinary, Jane Ray added, that she had heard no noise, and that she believed nobody had suspected that any thing was wrong during the night. Saint Hypolite, however, had stated, that she found them in the morning, after the other nuns had gone to prayers, lying lifeless in their beds.

For some reason or other, their death was not made public; but their bodies, instead of being exhibited in full dress in the chapel, and afterward interred with solemnity beneath it, were taken unceremoniously into the cellar, and thrown into the hole I have so often mentioned.

There were a few instances, and only a few, in which we knew any thing that was happening in the world; and even then our knowledge did not extend out of the city. I can recall but three occasions of this kind. Two of them were when the cholera prevailed in Montreal; and the other was the election riots. The appearance of the cholera, in both seasons of its ravages, gave us abundance of occupation. Indeed, we were more borne down by hard labor at those times, than ever before or afterward during my stay. The Pope had given early notice that the burning of wax candles would afford protection from the disease, because so long as any person continued to burn one, the Virgin Mary would intercede for him. No sooner, therefore, had the alarming disease made its appearance in Montreal, than a long wax candle was lighted in the Convent for each of the inmates, so that all parts of it in use were artificially illuminated day and night. Thus a great many candles were kept constantly burning, which were to be replaced from those manufactured by the nuns. But this was a trifle. The Pope's message having been promulgated in the Grey Nunnery, the Congregational Nunnery, and to Catholics at large, through the pulpits, an extraordinary demand was created for wax candles, to supply which we were principally depended upon. All who could be employed in making them were therefore set at work, and I among the rest, assisted in different departments, and witnessed all.

Numbers of the nuns had been long familiar with the business; for a very considerable amount of wax had been annually manufactured in the Convent; but now the works were much extended, and other occupations in a great degree laid aside. Large quantities of wax were received in the building, which was said to have been imported from England; kettles were placed in some of the working-rooms, in which it was clarified by heat over coal fires, and when prepared, the process of dipping commenced. The wicks which were quite long, were placed hanging upon a reel, taken up and dipped in succession, until, after many slow revolutions of the reel, the candles were of the proper size. They were then taken to a part of the room where tables were prepared for rolling them smooth. This is done by passing a roller over them, until they became even and polished, after which they are laid by for sale. These processes caused a constant bustle in several of the rooms; and the melancholy reports from without, of the ravages of the cholera, with the uncertainty of what might be the result with us, notwithstanding the promised intercession of the Virgin, and the brilliant lights constantly burning in such numbers around us, impressed the scenes I used to witness very deeply on my mind. I had very little doubt myself of the strict truth of the story we had heard of the security conferred upon those who burnt candles, and yet I sometimes had serious fears arise in my mind. These thoughts, however, I did my utmost to regard as great sins, and evidences of my own want of faith.

It was during that period that I formed a partial acquaintance with several Grey nuns, who used to come frequently for supplies of candles for their Convent. I had no opportunity to converse with them, except so far as the purchase and sale of the articles they required. I became familiar with their countenances and appearances, but was unable to judge of their characters or feelings. Concerning the rules and habits prevailing in the Grey Nunnery; I therefore remained as ignorant as if I had been a thousand miles off; and they had no better opportunity to learn anything of us beyond what they could see around them in the room where the candles were sold.

We supplied the Congregational Nunnery also with wax candles, as I before remarked; and in both those institutions, it was understood a constant illumination was kept up. Citizens were also frequently running in to buy candles, in great and small quantities, so that the business of storekeeping was far more laborious than common.

We were confirmed in our faith in the intercession of the Virgin, when we found that we remained safe from the cholera; and it is a remarkable fact, that not one case of that disease existed in the nunnery, during either of the seasons in which it proved so fatal in the city.

When the election riots prevailed in Montreal, the city was thrown into general alarm; we heard some reports, from day to day, which made us anxious for ourselves. Nothing, however, gave me any serious thoughts until I saw uncommon movements in some parts of the nunnery, and ascertained, to my own satisfaction, that there was a large quantity of gunpowder stored in some secret place within the walls, and that some of it was removed, or prepared for use, under the direction of the Superior.

I have mentioned several penances, in different parts of this narrative, which we sometimes had to perform. There is a great variety of them; and, while some, though trifling in appearance, became very painful, by long endurance, or frequent repetition; others are severe in their nature, and would never be submitted to unless through fear of something worse, or a real belief in efficacy to remove guilt. I will mention here such as I recollect, which can be named without offending a virtuous ear; for some there were, which, although I have been compelled to submit to, either by misled conscience, or the fear of severe punishments, now that I am better able to judge of my duties, and at liberty to act, I would not mention or describe.

Kissing the floor, is a very common penance; kneeling and kissing the feet of the other nuns, is another: as are kneeling on hard peas, and walking with them in the shoes. We had repeatedly to walk on our knees through the subterranean passage, leading to the Congregational Nunnery; and sometimes to eat our meals with a rope round our necks. Sometimes we were fed only with such things as we most disliked. Garlic was given to me on this account, because I had a strong antipathy against it. Eels were repeatedly given to some of us, because we felt an unconquerable repugnance to them, on account of reports we had heard of their feeding on dead carcasses, in the river St. Lawrence. It was no uncommon thing for us to be required to drink the water in which the Superior had washed her feet. Sometimes we were required to brand ourselves with a hot iron, so as to leave scars; at other times to whip our naked flesh with several small rods, before a private altar, until we drew blood. I can assert, with the perfect knowledge of the fact, that many of the nuns bear the scars of these wounds.

One of our penances was to stand for a length of time, with our arms extended, in imitation of the Saviour on the cross. The Chemin de la Croix, or Road to the Cross, is, in fact, a penance, though it consists of a variety of prostrations, with the repetition of many prayers, occupying two or three hours. This we had to perform frequently, going into the chapel, and falling before each chapelle in succession, at each time commemorating some particular act or circumstance reported of the Saviour's progress to the place of his crucifixion. Sometimes we were obliged to sleep on the floor in the winter, with nothing over us but a single sheet; and sometimes to chew a piece of window-glass to a fine powder, in the presence of the Superior.

We had sometimes to wear leathern belts stuck full of sharp metallic points round our waists, and the upper part of our arms, bound on so tight that they penetrated the flesh, and drew blood.

Some of the penances was so severe, that they seemed too much to be endured; and when they were imposed, the nuns who were to suffer them, sometimes showed the most violent repugnance. They would often resist, and still oftener express their opposition by exclamations and screams.

Never, however, was any noise heard from them, for a long time for there was a remedy always ready to be applied in cases of the kind. The gag which was put into the month of the unfortunate Saint Francis, had been brought from a place where there were forty or fifty others, of different shapes and sizes. These I have seen in their depository, which is a drawer between two closets, in one of the community-rooms. Whenever any loud noise was made, one of these instruments was demanded, and gagging commenced at once. I have known many, many instances, and sometimes five or six nuns gagged at once. Sometimes they would become so much excited before they could be bound and gagged, that considerable force was necessary to be exerted; and I have seen the blood flowing from months into which the gag had been thrust with violence.

Indeed I ought to know something on this department of nunnery discipline: I have had it tried upon myself, and I can bear witness that it is not only most humiliating and oppressive, but often extremely painful. The month is kept forced open, and the straining of the jaws at their utmost stretch, for a considerable time, is very distressing.

One of the worst punishments which I ever saw inflicted, was that with a cap; and yet some of the old nuns were permitted to inflict it at their pleasure. I have repeatedly known them to go for a cap, when one of our number had transgressed a rule, sometimes though it were a very unimportant one. These caps were kept in a cupboard in the old nuns' room, whence they were brought when wanted.

They were small, made of a reddish looking leather, fitted closely to the head, and fastened under the chin with a kind of buckle. It was the common practice to tie the nun's hands behind and gag her before the cap was put on, to prevent noise and resistance. I never saw it worn by any for one moment, without throwing them into severe sufferings. If permitted, they would scream in a most shocking manner; and they always writhed as much as their confinement would allow. I can speak from personal knowledge of this punishment, as I have endured it more than once; and yet I have no idea of the cause of the pain. I never examined one of the caps, nor saw the inside, for they are always brought and taken away quickly; but although the first sensation was that of coolness, it was hardly put on my head before a violent and indescribable sensation began, like that of a blister, only much more insupportable; and this continued until it was removed. It would produce such an acute pain as to throw us into convulsions, and I think no human being could endure it for an hour. After this punishment we felt its effects through the system for many days. Having once known what it was by experience, I held the cap in dread, and whenever I was condemned to suffer the punishment again, felt ready to do any thing to avoid it. But when tied and gagged, with the cap on my head again, I could only sink upon the floor, and roll about in anguish until it was taken off.

This was usually done in about ten minutes, sometimes less, but the pain always continued in my head for several days. I thought that it might take away a person's reason if kept on a much longer time. If I had not been gagged, I am sure I should have uttered awful screams. I have felt the effects for a week. Sometimes fresh cabbage leaves were applied to my head to remove it. Having had no opportunity to examine my head, I cannot say more.

This punishment was occasionally resorted to for very trifling offences, such as washing the hands without permission; and it was generally applied on the spot, and before the other nuns in the community-room.

CHAPTER XIX

The Priests of the District of Montreal have free access to the Black Nunnery—Crimes committed and required by them—The Pope's command to commit indecent Crimes—Characters of the Old and New Superiors—The timidity of the latter—I began to be employed

92

in the Hospitals—Some account of them—Warning given me by a sick Nun—Penance by Hanging.

I have mentioned before, that the country, as far down as Three Rivers, is furnished with priests by the Seminary of Montreal; and that these hundred and fifty men are liable to be occasionally transferred from one station to another. Numbers of them are often to be seen in the streets of Montreal, as they may find a home in the Seminary.

They are considered as having an equal right to enter the Black Nunnery whenever they please; and then, according to our oaths, they have complete control over the nuns. To name all the works of shame of which they are guilty in that retreat, would require much time and space, neither would it be necessary to the accomplishment of my object, which is, the publication of but some of their criminality to the world, and the development, in general terms, of scenes thus far carried on in secret within the walls of that Convent, where I was so long an inmate.

Secure against detection by the world, they never believed that an eyewitness would ever escape to tell of their crimes, and declare some of their names before the world; but the time has come, and some of their deeds of darkness must come to the day. I have seen in the nunnery, the priests from more, I presume, than a hundred country places, admitted for shameful and criminal purposes: from St. Charles, St. Denis, St. Mark's St. Antoine, Chambly, Bertier, St. John's, &c. &c.

How unexpected to them will be the disclosures I make! Shut up in a place from which there has been thought to be but one way of egress, and that the passage to the grave, they considered themselves safe in perpetrating crimes in our presence, and in making us share in their criminality as often as they chose, and conducted more shamelessly than even the brutes. These debauchees would come in without ceremony, concealing their names, both by night and by day, where the cries and pains of the injured innocence of their victims could never reach the world, for relief or redress for their wrongs; without remorse or shame, they would glory in torturing, in the most barbarous manner, the feelings of those under their power; telling us, at the same time, that this mortifying of the flesh was religion, and pleasing to God.

We were sometimes invited to put ourselves to voluntary sufferings in a variety of ways, not for a penance, but to show our devotion to God. A priest would sometimes say to us—

"Now, which of you have love enough for Jesus Christ to stick a pin through your cheeks?"

Some of us would signify our readiness, and immediately thrust one through up to the head. Sometimes he would propose that we should repeat the operation several times on the spot; and the cheeks of a number of nuns would be bloody.

There were other acts occasionally proposed and consented to, which I cannot name in a book. Such the Superior would sometimes command us to perform; many of them things not only useless, and unheard of, but loathsome and indecent in the highest possible degree. How they could ever have been invented I never could conceive. Things were done worse than the entire exposure of the person, though this was occasionally required of several at once, in the presence of priests.

The Superior of the Seminary would sometimes come and inform us, that he had received orders from the Pope, to request that those nuns who possessed the greatest devotion and faith, should be requested to perform some particular deeds, which he named or described in our presence, but of which no decent or moral person could ever endure to speak. I cannot repeat what would injure any ear, not debased to the lowest possible degree. I am bound by a regard to truth, however, to confess, that deluded women were found among us, who would comply with those requests.

There was a great difference between the characters of our old and new Superior, which soon became obvious. The former used to say she liked to walk, because it would prevent her from becoming corpulent. She was, therefore, very active, and constantly going about from one part of the nunnery to another, overseeing us at our various employments. I never saw in her any appearance of timidity: she seemed, on the contrary, bold and masculine, and sometimes much more than that, cruel and cold-blooded, in scenes calculated to overcome any common person. Such a character she had exhibited at the murder of Saint Francis.

The new Superior, on the other hand, was so heavy and lame, that she walked with much difficulty, and consequently exercised a less vigilant oversight of the nuns. She was also of a timid disposition, or else had been overcome by some great fright in her past life; for she was apt to become alarmed in the night, and never liked to be alone in the dark. She had long performed the part of an old nun, which is that of a spy upon the younger ones, and was well known to us in that character, under the name of Ste. Margarite. Soon after her promotion to the station of Superior, she appointed me to sleep in her apartment, and assigned me a sofa to lie upon. One night while, I was asleep, she suddenly threw herself upon me, and exclaimed in great alarm, "Oh! mon Dieu! mon Dieu! Qu'est que ça?" Oh, my God! my God! What is that? I jumped up and looked about the room, but saw nothing, and endeavoured to convince her that there was nothing extraordinary there. But she insisted that a ghost had come and held her bed-curtain, so that she could not draw it. I examined it, and found that the curtain had been caught by a pin in the valance, which had held it back; but it was impossible to tranquillize her for some time. She insisted on my sleeping with her the rest of the night, and I stretched myself across the foot of her bed, and slept there till morning.

During the last part of my stay in the Convent, I was often employed in attending in the hospitals. There are, as I have before mentioned, several apartments devoted to the sick, and there is a physician of Montreal, who attends as physician to the Convent. It must not be supposed, however, that he knows anything concerning the private hospitals. It is a fact of great importance to be distinctly understood, and constantly borne in mind, that he is never, under any circumstances, admitted into the private hospital-rooms. Of those he sees nothing more than any stranger whatever. He is limited to the care of those patients who are admitted from the city into the public hospital, and one of the nuns' hospitals, and these he visits every day. Sick poor are received for charity by the institution, attended by some of the nuns, and often go away with the highest ideas of their charitable characters and holy lives. The physician himself might perhaps in some cases share in the delusion.

I frequently followed Dr. Nelson through the public hospital, at the direction of the Superior, with pen, ink, and paper in my hands, and wrote down the prescriptions which he ordered for the different patients. These were afterwards prepared and administered by the attendants. About a year before I left the Convent, I was first appointed to attend the private sick-rooms, and was frequently employed in that duty up to the day of my departure. Of course, I had opportunities to observe the number and classes of patients treated there; and in what I am to say on the subject, I appeal with perfect confidence to any true and competent witness to confirm, my words, whenever such a witness may appear.

It would be vain for any body who has merely visited the Convent from curiosity, or resided in it as a novice, to question my declarations. Such a person must necessarily be ignorant of even the existence of the private rooms, unless informed by some one else. Such rooms however, there are, and I could relate many things which have passed there during the hours I was employed in them, as I have stated.

One night I was called to sit up with an old nun, named Saint Clare, who, in going down-stairs, had dislocated a limb, and lay in a sick-room adjoining an hospital. She seemed to be a little out of her head a part of the time, but appeared to be quite in possession of her reason most of the night. It was easy to pretend that she was delirious; but I considered her as speaking the truth, though I felt reluctant to repeat what I heard her say, and excused myself from mentioning it even at confession, on the ground that the Superior thought her deranged.

What led her to some of the most remarkable parts of her conversation, was a motion I made, in the course of the night, to take the light out of her little room into the adjoining apartment, to look once more at the sick persons there. She begged me not to leave her a moment in the dark, for she could not bear it. "I have witnessed so many horrid scenes," said she, "in this Convent, that I want somebody near me constantly, and must always have a light burning in my room. I cannot tell you," she added, "what things I remember, for they would frighten you too much. What you have seen are nothing to them. Many a murder have I witnessed; many a nice young creature has been killed in this nunnery. I advise you to be very cautions—keep everything to yourself—there are many here ready to betray you."

What it was that induced the old nun to express so much kindness to me I could not tell, unless she was frightened at the recollection of her own crimes, and those of others, and felt grateful for the care I took of her. She had been one of the night-watches, and never before showed me any particular kindness. She did not indeed go into detail concerning the transactions to which she alluded, but told me that some nuns had been murdered under great aggravations of cruelty, by being gagged, and left to starve in the cells, or having their flesh burnt off their bones with red-hot irons.

It was uncommon to find compunction expressed by any of the nuns. Habit renders us insensible to the sufferings of others, and careless about our own sins. I had become so hardened myself, that I find it difficult to rid myself of many of my former false principles and views of right and wrong.

I was one day set to wash some of the empty bottles from the cellar, which had contained the liquid that was poured into the cemetery there. A number of these had been brought from the corner where so many of them were always to be seen, and placed at the head of the cellar stairs, and there we were required to take them and wash them out. We poured in water and rinsed them; a few drops, which got upon our clothes, soon made holes in them. I think the liquid was called vitriol, or some such name; and I heard some persons say, that it would soon destroy the flesh, and even the bones of the dead. At another time, we were furnished with a little of the liquid, which was mixed with a quantity of water, and used in dying some cloth black, which was wanted at funerals in the chapels. Our hands were turned very black by being dipped in it, but a few drops of some other liquid were mixed with fresh water and given us to wash in, which left our skin of a bright red.

The bottles of which I spoke were made of very thick, dark-coloured glass, large at the bottom, and, from recollection, I should say held something less than a gallon.

I was once much shocked, on entering the room for the examination of conscience, at seeing a nun hanging by a cord from a ring in the ceiling, with her head downward. Her clothes had been tied round with a leathern strap, to keep them in their place, and then she had been fastened in that situation, with her head at some distance from the floor. Her face had a very unpleasant appearance, being dark-coloured and swollen by the rushing in of the blood; her hands were tied and her mouth stopped with a large gag. This nun proved to be no other than Jane Ray, who for some fault had been condemned to this punishment.

This was not, however, a solitary case; I heard of numbers who were "hung," as it was called, at different times; and I saw Saint Hypolite and Saint Luke undergoing it. This was considered a most distressing punishment; and it was the only one which Jane Ray could not endure, of all she had tried.

Some of the nuns would allude to it in her presence, but it usually made her angry. It was probably practised in the same place while I was a novice; but I never heard or thought of such a thing in those days. Whenever we wished to enter the room for examination of conscience, we had to ask leave; and after some delay were permitted to go, but always under a strict charge to bend the head forward, and keep the eyes fixed upon the floor.

CHAPTER XX

More visits to the imprisoned Nuns—Their fears—Others temporarily put into the Cells—Reliques—The Agnus Dei—The Priests' private Hospital, or Holy Retreat—Secret Rooms in the Eastern Wing—Reports of Murders in the Convent—The Superior's

I often seized an opportunity, when I safely could, to speak a cheering or friendly word to one of the poor prisoners, in passing their cells, on my errands in the cellars. For a time I supposed them to be sisters; but I afterward discovered that this was not the case. I found that they were always under the fear of suffering some punishment, in case they should be found talking with a person not commissioned to attend them. They would often ask, "Is not somebody coming?"

I could easily believe what I heard affirmed by others, that fear was the severest of their sufferings. Confined in the dark, in so gloomy a place, with the long and spacious arched cellar stretching off this way and that, visited now and then by a solitary nun, with whom they were afraid to speak their feelings, and with only the miserable society of each other; how gloomy thus to spend day after day, months, and even years, without any prospect of liberation, and liable every moment to any other fate to which the Bishop or Superior might condemn them! But these poor creatures must have known something of the horrors perpetrated in other parts of the building, and could not have been ignorant of the hole in the cellar, which was not far from their cells, and the use to which it was devoted. One of them told me, in confidence, she wished they could get out. They must also have been often disturbed in their sleep, if they ever did sleep, by the numerous priests who passed through the trapdoor at no great distance. To be subject to such trials for a single day would be dreadful; but these nuns had them to endure for years.

I often felt much compassion for them, and wished to see them released; but at other times, yielding to the doctrine perpetually taught us in the Convent, that our future happiness would be proportioned to the sufferings we had to undergo in this world, I would rest satisfied that their imprisonment was a real blessing to them. Others, I presume, participated with me in such feelings. One Sunday afternoon, after we had performed all our ceremonies, and were engaged as usual, at that time, with backgammon and other amusements, one of the young nuns exclaimed, "Oh, how headstrong are those wretches in the cells— they are as bad as the day they were first put in!"

This exclamation was made, as I supposed, in consequence of some recent conversation with them, as I knew her to be particularly acquainted with the older one.

98

Some of the vacant cells were occasionally used for temporary imprisonment. Three nuns were confined in them, to my knowledge, for disobedience to the Superior, as she called it. They did not join the rest in singing in the evening, being exhausted by the various exertions of the day. The Superior ordered them to sing, and as they did not comply, after her command had been twice repeated, she ordered them away to the cells.

They were immediately taken down into the cellar, placed in separate dungeons, and the doors shut and barred upon them. There they remained through that night, the following day, and second night, but were released in time to attend mass on the second morning.

The Superior used occasionally to show something in a glass box, which we were required to regard with the highest degree of reverence. It was made of wax, and called an Agnus Dei. She used to exhibit it to us when we were in a state of grace; that is, after confession and before sacrament. She said it had been blessed in the very dish in which our Saviour had eaten. It was brought from Rome. Every time we kissed it, or even looked at it, we were told it gave a hundred days release from purgatory to ourselves, or if we did not need it, to our next of kin in purgatory, if not a Protestant. If we had no such kinsman, the benefit was to go to the souls in purgatory not prayed for.

Jane Ray would sometimes say to me, "Let's kiss it—some of our friends will thank us for it."

I have been repeatedly employed in carrying dainties of different kinds to the little private room I have mentioned, next beyond the Superior's sitting-room, in the second story, which the priests made their "Holy Retreat." That room I never was allowed to enter. I could only go to the door with a waiter of refreshments, set it down upon a little stand near it, give three raps on the door, and then retire to a distance to await orders. When any thing was to be taken away, it was placed on the stand by the Superior, who then gave three raps for me, and closed the door.

The Bishop I saw at least once when he appeared worse for wine, or something of the kind. After partaking of some refreshments in the Convent, he sent for all the nuns, and, on our appearance, gave us his blessing, and put a piece of poundcake on the shoulder of each of us, in a manner which appeared singular and foolish.

There are three rooms in the Black Nunnery which I never entered. I had enjoyed much liberty, and had seen, as I supposed, all parts of the building, when one day I observed an old nun go to a corner of an apartment near the northern end of the western wing, push the end of her scissors into a crack in the panelled wall, and pull out a door. I was much surprised, because I had never conjectured that any door was there; and it appeared when I afterward examined the place, that no indication of it could be discovered on the closest scrutiny. I stepped forward to see what was within, and saw three rooms opening into each other; but the nun refused to admit me within the door, which she said led to rooms kept as depositories.

She herself entered and closed the door, so that I could not satisfy my curiosity; and no occasion presented itself. I always had a strong desire to know the use of these apartments: for I am sure they must have been designed for some purpose of which I was intentionally kept ignorant, otherwise they would never have remained unknown to me so long. Besides, the old nun evidently had some strong reasons for denying me admission, though she endeavoured to quiet my curiosity.

The Superior, after my admission into the Convent, had told me that I had access to every room in the building; and I had seen places which bore witness to the cruelties and the crimes committed under her commands or sanction; but here was a succession of rooms which had been concealed from me, and so constructed as if designed to be unknown to all but a few. I am sure that any person, who might be able to examine the wall in that place, would pronounce that secret door a surprising piece of work. I never saw any thing of the kind which appeared to me so ingenious and skilfully made. I told Jane Ray what I had seen, and she said, at once, "We will get in and see what is in there." But I suppose she never found an opportunity.

I naturally felt a good deal of curiosity to learn whether such scenes, as I had witnessed in the death of Saint Francis, were common or rare, and took an opportunity to inquire of Jane Ray. Her reply was—

"Oh, yes; and there were many murdered while you was a novice, whom you heard nothing about."

This was all I ever learnt on the subject; but although I was told nothing of the manner in which they were killed, I supposed it to be the same which I had seen practised, viz. by smothering.

I went into the Superior's parlour one day for something, and found Jane Ray there alone, looking into a book with an appearance of interest. I asked her what it was, but she made some trifling answer, and laid it by, as if unwilling to let me take it. There are two bookcases in the room; one on the right as you enter the door, and the other opposite, near the window and sofa. The former contains the lecture-books and other printed volumes, the latter seemed to

100

be filled with note and account books. I have often seen the keys in the bookcases while I have been dusting the furniture, and sometimes observed letters stuck up in the room; although I never looked into one, or thought of doing so, as we were under strict orders not to touch any of them, and the idea of sins and penances was always present with me.

Some time after the occasion mentioned, I was sent into the Superior's room, with Jane, to arrange it; and as the same book was lying out of the case, she said "Come, let us look into it." I immediately consented, and we opened it, and turned over several leaves. It was about a foot and a half long, as nearly as I can remember, a foot wide, and about two inches thick, though I cannot speak with particular precision, as Jane frightened me almost as soon as I touched it, by exclaiming, "There you have looked into it, and if you tell of me, I will of you."

The thought of being subjected to a severe penance, which I had reason to apprehend, fluttered me very much; and although I tried to overcome my fears, I did not succeed very well. I reflected, however, that the sin was already committed, and that it would not be increased if I examined the book. I, therefore, looked a little at several pages, though I still felt a good deal of agitation. I saw, at once, that the volume was the record of the entrance of nuns and novices into the Convent, and of the births that had taken place in the Convent. Entries of the last description were made in a brief manner, on the following plan: I do not give the names or dates as real, but only to show the form of entering them.

Saint Mary delivered of a son, March 16,1834.
Saint Clarice "daughter, April 2,"
Saint Matilda "daughter, April, 80,"

No mention was made in the book of the death of the children, though I well knew not one of them could be living at that time. Now I presume that the period the book embraced, was about two years, as several names near the beginning I knew; but I can form only a rough conjecture of the number of infants born, and murdered of course, records of which it contained. I suppose the book contained at least one hundred pages, that one fourth were written upon, and that each page contained fifteen distinct records. Several pages were devoted to the list of births. On this supposition there must have been a large number, which I can easily believe to have been born there in the course of two years.

What were the contents of the other books belonging to the same case with that which I looked into, I have no idea, having never dared to touch one of them; I believe, however, that Jane Ray was well acquainted with them, knowing, as I do, her intelligence and prying disposition. If she could be brought to give her testimony, she would doubtless unfold many curious particulars now unknown.

I am able, in consequence of a circumstance which appeared accidental, to state with confidence the exact number of persons in the Convent one day of the week in which I left it. This may be a point of some interest, as several secret deaths had occurred since my taking the veil, and many burials had been openly made in the chapel.

I was appointed, at the time mentioned, to lay out the covers for all the inmates of the Convent, including the nuns in the cells. These covers, as I have said before, were linen bands, to be bound around the knives, forks, spoons, and napkins, for eating. These were for all the nuns and novices, and amounted to two hundred and ten. As the number of novices was then about thirty, I know that there must have been at that time about one hundred and eighty veiled nuns.

I was occasionally troubled with a desire of escaping from the nunnery, and was much distressed whenever I felt so evil an imagination rise in my mind. I believed that it was a sin, and did not fail to confess at every opportunity, that I felt discontent. My confessors informed me that I was beset by an evil spirit, and urged me to pray against it. Still, however, every now and then, I would think, "Oh, if I could get out!"

At length one of the priests, to whom I had confessed this sin, informed me, for my comfort, that he had begun to pray to Saint Anthony, and hoped his intercession would, by-and-by, drive away the evil spirit. My desire of escape was partly excited by the fear of bringing an infant to the murderous hands of my companions, or of taking a potion whose violent effects I too well knew.

One evening, however, I found myself more filled with the desire of escape than ever; and what exertions I made to dismiss the thought, proved entirely unavailing. During evening prayers, I became quite occupied with it; and when the time for meditation arrived, instead of falling into a doze as I often did, although I was a good deal fatigued, I found no difficulty in keeping awake. When this exercise was over, and the other nuns were about to retire to the sleeping-room, my station being in the private sickroom for the night, I withdrew to my post, which was the little sitting-room adjoining it.

Here, then, I threw myself upon the sofa, and, being alone, reflected a few moments on the manner of escaping which had occurred to me. The physician had arrived a little before, at half-past eight; and I had now to accompany him, as usual, from bed to bed, with pen, ink, and paper, to write down his prescriptions for the direction of the old nun, who was to see them administered. What I wrote that evening, I cannot now recollect, as my mind was uncommonly agitated; but my customary way was to note down briefly his orders in this manner:

1 d salts, St. Matilde. 1 blister, St. Geneviere, &c. &c.

I remember that I wrote three such orders that evening, and then, having finished the rounds, I returned for a few minutes to the sitting-room.

There were two ways of access to the street from those rooms: first, the more direct, from the passage adjoining the sick-room, down stairs, through a door, into the nunnery-yard, and through a wicket-gate; that is the way by which the physician usually enters at night, and he is provided with a key for that purpose.

It would have been unsafe, however, for me to pass out that way, because a man is kept continually in the yard, near the gate, who sleeps at night in a small hut near the door, to escape whose observation would be impossible. My only hope, therefore, was, that I might gain my passage through the other way, to do which I must pass through the sick-room, then through a passage, or small room, usually occupied by an old nun; another passage and staircase leading down to the yard, and a large gate opening into the cross street. I had no liberty ever to go beyond the sick-room, and knew that several of the doors might be fastened. Still, I determined to try; although I have often since been astonished at my boldness in undertaking what would expose me to so many hazards of failure, and to severe punishment if found out.

It seemed as if I acted under some extraordinary impulse, which encouraged me to do what I should hardly at any other moment have thought of undertaking. I had sat but a short time upon the sofa, however, before I rose, with a desperate determination to make the experiment. I therefore walked hastily across the sick-room, passed into the nun's room, walked by her in a great hurry, and almost without giving her time to speak or think, said—"A message!" and in an instant was through the door and in the next passage. I think there was another nun with her at the moment; and it is probable that my hurried manner, and prompt intimation that I was sent on a pressing mission, to the Superior, prevented them from entertaining any suspicion of my intention. Besides, I had the written orders of the physician in my hand, which may have tended to mislead them; and it was well known to some of the nuns, that I had twice left the Convent and returned from choice; so that I was probably more likely to be trusted to remain than many of the others.

The passage which I had now reached had several doors, with all which I was acquainted; that on the opposite side opened into a community-room, where I should probably have found some of the old inns at that hour, and they would certainly have stopped me. On the left, however, was a large door, both locked and barred; but I gave the door a sudden swing, that it might creak as little as possible, being of iron. Down the stairs I hurried, and making my way through the door into the yard, stepped across it unbarred the great gate, and was at liberty!

CHAPTER XXI

At liberty—Doubtful what to do—Found refuge for the night— Disappointment—My first day opt of the Convent—Solitude— Recollections, fears, and plans.

I have but a confused idea of the manner in which I got through some of the doors; several of them, I am confident, were fastened, and one or two I fastened behind me.[6] But I was now in the street, and what was to be done next? I had got my liberty; but where should I go? It was dark, I was in great danger, go which way I would: and for a moment, I thought I had been unwise to leave the Convent. If I could return unobserved, would it not be better? But summoning resolution, I turned to the left, and ran some distance up the street; then reflecting that I had better take the opposite direction, I returned under the same Convent walls, and ran as fast down to St. Paul's street, and turning up towards the north, exerted all my strength, and fled for my life. It was a cold evening, but I stopped for nothing, having recollected the house where I had been put to board for a short time, by the priest Roque, when prepared to enter the Convent as a novice, and resolved to seek a lodging there for the night. Thither I went. It seemed as if I flew rather than ran. It was by that time so dark, that I was able to see distinctly through

---

[6] Before leaving the nunnery grounds, I ran round the end of the building, stood a moment in hesitation whether I had not better return, then hastening back to the other side, ran to the gate, opened it, and went out.

the low windows by the light within; and had the pleasure to find that she was alone with her children. I therefore went boldly to the door, was received with readiness, and entered to take up my lodging there once more.

Here I changed my nun's dress for one less likely to excite observation; and having received a few dollars in addition to make up the difference, I retired to rest, determined to rise early and take the morning steamboat for Quebec. I knew that my hostess was a friend of the Superior, as I have mentioned before, and presumed that it would not be long before she would give information against me. I knew, however, that she could not gain admittance to the Convent very early, and felt safe in remaining in the house through the night.

But after I had retired I found it impossible to sleep, and the night appeared very long. In the morning early, I requested that a son of the woman might accompany me to the steamboat, but learnt to my regret that it would not go before night. Fearing that I might fall into the hands of the priests, and be carried back to the nunnery, and not knowing where to go, I turned away, and determined to seek some retired spot immediately. I walked through a part of the city, and some distance on the Lachine road, when finding a solitary place, I seated myself in much distress of mind, fearful and anxious, beyond my power, of description. I could not think myself safe anywhere in the neighbourhood of Montreal; for the priests were numerous, and almost all the people were entirely devoted to them. They would be very desirous of finding me, and, as I believed, would make great exertions to get me again in their hands.

It was a pleasant spot where I now found myself; and as the weather was not uncomfortable in the daytime, I had nothing to trouble me except my recollections and fears. As for the want of food, that gave me not the slightest uneasiness, as I felt no inclination whatever to eat. The uncertainty and doubts I continually felt, kept me in a state of irresolution the whole day. What should I do? Where should I go? I had not a friend in the world to whom I could go with confidence; while my enemies were numerous, and, it seemed to me, all around me, and ready to seize me. I thought of my uncle, who lived at the distance of five miles; and sometimes I almost determined to set off immediately for his house. I had visited it often when a child, and had been received with the utmost kindness. I remembered that I had been a great favourite of his; but some considerations would arise which discouraged me from looking for safety in that direction. The steamboat was to depart in a few hours. I could venture to pass through the city once more by twilight; and if once arrived at

105

Quebec, I should be at a great distance from the nunnery, in a large city, and among a larger proportion of Protestant inhabitants. Among them I might find friends, or, at least, some sort of protection; and I had no doubt that I could support myself by labor.

Then I thought again of the place I had left; the kindness and sympathy, small though they were, which I had found in some of my late companions in the Convent; the awful mortal sin I had committed in breaking my vows; and the terrible punishment I should receive if taken as a fugitive and carried back. If I should return voluntarily, and ask to be admitted again: what would the Superior say, how would she treat me? Should I be condemned to any very severe penance? Might I not, at least, escape death? But then there was one consideration that would now and then occur to me, which excited the strongest determination never to return. I was to become a mother, and the thought of witnessing the murder of my own child was more than I could bear.

Purgatory was doubtless my portion; and perhaps hell for ever—such a purgatory and hell as are painted in the Convent: but there was one hope for me yet.

I might confess all my deadly sins sometime before I died, and a Bishop could pardon the worst of them.

This was good Catholic doctrine, and I rested upon it with so much hope, that I was not quite driven to despair.

In reflections like these, I spent the whole day, afraid to stray from the secluded spot to which I had retreated, though at different times forming momentary plans to leave it, and go in various directions. I ate not a morsel of food, and yet felt no hunger. Had I been well provided, I could have tasted nothing in such a state of mind. The afternoon wasted away, the sun set, and darkness began to come on: I rose and set off again for the city. I passed along the streets unmolested by any one; and reached it a short time before the boat was ready to start.

CHAPTER XXII

Start for Quebec—Recognised—Disappointed again—Not permitted to land—Return to Montreal—Landed and passed through the city before day—Lachine Canal—Intended close of my life.

Soon after we left the shore, the captain, whom I had previously seen, appeared to recognise me.

He came up and inquired if I was not the daughter of my mother, mentioning her name. I had long been taught and accustomed to deceive; and it may be supposed that in such a case I did not hesitate to deny the truth, hoping that I might avoid being known, and fearing to be defeated in my object. He however persisted that he knew me, and said he must insist on my returning with him to Montreal, adding that I must not leave his boat to land at Quebec. I said but little to him, but intended to get on shore if possible, at the end of our journey—a thing I had no doubt I might effect.

When we reached Quebec, however I found, to my chagrin, that the ladies' maid carefully locked the cabin-door while I was in, after the ladies had left it, who were six or eight in number.

I said little, and made no attempts to resist the restriction put upon me; but secretly cherished the hope of being able, by watching an opportunity, to slip on shore at tea-time, and lose myself among the streets of the city. Although a total stranger to Quebec, I longed to be at liberty there, as I thought I could soon place myself among persons who would secure me from the Catholics, each of whom I now looked upon as an enemy.

But I soon found that my last hopes were blighted: the maid, having received, as I presumed, strict orders from the captain, kept me closely confined, so that escape was impossible. I was distressed, it is true, to find myself in this condition; but I had already become accustomed to disappointments, and therefore perhaps sunk less under this new one, than I might otherwise have done. When the hour for departure arrived, I was therefore still confined in the steamboat, and it was not until we had left the shore that I was allowed to leave the cabin. The captain and others treated me with kindness in every respect, except that of permitting me to do what I most desired. I have sometimes suspected, that he had received notice of my escape from some of the priests, with a request to stop my flight, if I should go on board his boat. His wife is a Catholic, and this is the only way in which I can account for his conduct: still I have not sufficient knowledge of his motives and intentions to speak with entire confidence on the subject.

My time passed heavily on board of the steamboat, particularly on my passage up the river towards Montreal. My mind was too much agitated to allow me to sleep, for I was continually meditating on the scenes I had witnessed in the Convent, and anticipating with dread such as I had reason to think I might soon be called to pass through. I bought for a trifle while on board, I hardly know why, a small medallion with a head upon it, and the name of Robertson, which I hung on my neck. As I sat by day with nothing to do, I occasionally sunk into a doze for a few minutes, when I usually waked with a start from some frightful dream. Sometimes I thought I was running away from the priests, and closely pursued, and sometimes had no hope of escape. But the most distressing of my feelings were those I suffered in the course of the night. We stopped some time at Berthier, where a number of prisoners were taken on board, to be carried up the river; and this caused much confusion, and added to my painful reflections.

My mind became much agitated, worse than it had been before; and what between waking fears, and sleeping visions, I spent a most wretched night. Sometimes I thought the priests and nuns had me shut up in a dungeon; sometimes they were about to make away with me in a most cruel manner. Once I dreamed that I was in some house, and a coach came up to the door, into which I was to be put by force; and the man who seized me, and was putting me in, had no head.

When we reached Montreal on Saturday morning, it was not daylight; and the captain, landing, set off as I understood, to give my mother information that I was in his boat. He was gone a long time, which led me to conjecture that he might have found difficulty in speaking with her; but the delay proved very favourable to me, for perceiving that I was neither locked up nor watched, I hastened on shore, and pursued my way into the city. I felt happy at my escape: but what was I then to do? Whither could I go? Not to my mother: I was certain I could not remain long with her, without being known to the priests.

My friendlessness and utter helplessness, with the dread of being murdered in the Convent, added to thoughts of the shame which must await me if I lived a few months, made me take a desperate resolution, and I hurried to put it into effect.

My object was to reach the head of the Lachine Canal, which is near the St. Lawrence, beyond the extremity of the southern suburbs. I walked hastily along St. Paul's street, and found all the houses still shut; then turning to the old Recollet Church, I reached Notre-Dame street, which I followed in the direction I wished to go.

The morning was chilly, as the season was somewhat advanced: but that was of no importance to me. Day had appeared, and I desired to accomplish the object on which I was now bent, before the light should much increase. I walked on, therefore, but the morning had broken bright before I arrived at the Canal; and then I found to my disappointment that two Canadians were at work on the hank, getting water, or doing something else.

I was by the great basin where the boats start, and near the large canal storehouse. I have not said what was my design; it was to drown myself.

Fearing the men would rescue me, I hesitated for some time, hoping they would retire: but finding that they did not, I grew impatient. I stood looking on the water; it was nearly on a level with the banks, which shelved away, as I could perceive, for some distance, there being no wind to disturb the surface. There was nothing in the sight which seemed frightful or even forbidding to me; I looked upon it as the means of the easiest death, and longed to be buried below. At length finding that the men were not likely to leave the place, I sprung from the bank, and was in an instant in the cold water. The shock was very severe. I felt a sharp freezing sensation run through me, which almost immediately rendered me insensible; and the last thing I can recollect was, that I was sinking in the midst of water almost as cold as ice, which wet my clothes, and covered me all over.

CHAPTER XXIII

Awake among strangers—Dr. Robertson—Imprisoned as a vagrant—Introduction to my mother—Stay in her house—Removal from it to Mrs. McDonald's—Return to my mother's—Desire to get to New York—Arrangements for going.

How long I remained in the canal I knew not; but in about three minutes, as I conjectured, I felt a severe blow on my right side; and opening my eyes I saw myself surrounded by men, who talked a great deal, and expressed much anxiety and curiosity about me. They enquired of me my name, where I lived, and why I had thrown myself into the water: but I would not answer a word. The blow which I had felt, and which was probably the cause of bringing me for a few moments to my senses, I presume was caused by my falling, after I was rescued, upon the stones, which lay thickly scattered near the water. I remember that the persons around me continued to press me with questions, and that I still remained silent. Some of them having observed the little medallion on my neck, and being able to read, declared I was probably the daughter of Dr. Robertson, as it bore the name; but to this, I also gave no answer, and sunk again into a state of unconsciousness.

When my senses once more returned, I found myself lying in a bed covered up warm, in a house, and heard several persons talking of the mass, from which they had just returned. I could not imagine where I was, for my thoughts were not easily collected, and every thing seemed strange around me. Some of them, on account of the name on the little medallion, had sent to Dr. Robertson, to inform him that a young woman had been prevented from drowning herself in the basin, who had a portrait on her neck, with his family name stamped upon it; and he had sent word, that although she could be no relation of his, they had better bring her to his house, as he possibly might be able to learn who she was. Preparations were therefore made to conduct me thither; and I was soon in his house. This was about midday, or a little later.

The doctor endeavored to draw from me some confession of my family: but I refused; my feelings would not permit me to give him any satisfaction. He offered to send me to my home if I would tell him where I lived; but at length, thinking me unreasonable and obstinate, began to threaten to send me to jail.

In a short time I found that the latter measure was determined on, and I was soon put into the hands of the jailer, Captain Holland, and placed in a private room in his house.

I had formerly been acquainted with his children, but had such strong reasons for remaining unknown, that I hoped they would not recognise me; and, as we had not met for several years I flattered myself that such would be the case. It was, at first, as I had hoped; they saw me in the evening, but did not appear to suspect who I was. The next morning, however, one of them asked me if I were not sister of my brother, mentioning his name; and though I denied it, they all insisted that I must be, for the likeness, they said, was surprisingly strong. I still would not admit the truth; but requested they would send for the Rev. Mr. Esson, a Presbyterian clergyman in Montreal, saying I had something to say to him. He soon made his appearance and I gave him some account of myself and requested him to procure my release from confinement, as I thought there was no reason why I should be deprived of my liberty.

Contrary to my wishes, however, he went and informed my mother. An unhappy difference had existed between us for many years concerning which I would not speak, were it not necessary to allude to it to render some things intelligible which are important to my narrative. I am willing to bear much of the blame: for my drawing part of her pension had justly irritated her. I shall not attempt to justify or explain my own feelings with respect to my mother, whom I still regard at least in some degree as I ought. I will merely say, that I thought she indulged in partialities and antipathies in her family during my childhood; and that I attribute my entrance into the nunnery, and the misfortunes I have suffered, to my early estrangement from home, and my separation from the family. I had neither, seen her nor heard from her in several years; and I knew not whether she had even known of my entrance into the Convent, although I now learnt, that she still resided where she formerly did.

It was therefore with regret that I heard that my mother had been informed of my condition; and that I saw an Irishwoman, an acquaintance of hers, come to take me to the house. I had no doubt that she would think I had disgraced her, by being imprisoned, as well as by my attempt to drown myself; and what would be her feelings towards me, I could only conjecture.

I accompanied the woman to my mother's, and found nearly such a reception as I had expected. Notwithstanding our mutual feelings were much as they had been, she wished me to stay with her, and kept me in one of her rooms for several weeks, and with the utmost privacy, fearing that my appearance would lead to questions, and that my imprisonment would become known. I soon satisfied myself that she knew little of what I had passed through, within the few past years; and did not think it prudent to inform her, for that would greatly have increased the risk of my being discovered by the priests. We were surrounded by those who went frequently to confession, and would have thought me a monster of wickedness, guilty of breaking the most solemn vows, and a fugitive from a retreat which is generally regarded there as a place of great sanctity, and almost like a gate to heaven. I well knew the ignorance and prejudices of the poor Canadians, and understood how such a person as myself must appear in their eyes. They felt as I formerly had, and would think it a service to religion, and to God, to betray the place of my concealment if by chance they should find, or even suspect it. As I had become in the eyes of Catholics, "a spouse of Jesus Christ," by taking the veil, my leaving the Convent must appear to them a forsaking of the Saviour.

As things were, however, I remained for some time undisturbed. My brother, though he lived in the house, did not know of my being there for a fortnight.

When he learnt it, and came to see me, he expressed much kindness towards me: but I had not seen him for several years, and had seen so much evil, that I knew not what secret motives he might have, and thought it prudent to be reserved. I, therefore, communicated to him nothing of my history or intentions, and rather repulsed his advances. The truth is, I had been so long among nuns and priests, that I thought there was no sincerity or virtue on earth.

What were my mother's wishes or intentions towards me, I was not informed: but I found afterwards, that she must have made arrangements to have me removed from her house, for one day a woman came to the door with a cariole, and on being admitted to see me, expressed herself in a friendly manner, spoke of the necessity of air and exercise for my health, and invited me to take a ride. I consented, supposing we should soon return: but when we reached St. Antoine suburbs, she drove up to a house which I had formerly heard to be some kind of refuge, stopped, and requested me to alight. My first thought was, that I should be exposed to certain detection, by some of the priests whom I presumed officiated there; as they had all known me in the nunnery. I could not avoid entering; but I resolved to feign sickness, hoping thus to be placed out of sight of the priests.

The result was according to my wishes: for I was taken to an upper room, which was used as an infirmary, and there permitted to remain. There were a large number of women in the house; and a Mrs. M'Donald, who has the management of it, had her daughters in the Ursuline Nunnery at Quebec, and her son in the college. The nature of the establishment I could not fully understand: but it seemed to me designed to become a nunnery at some future time.

I felt pretty safe in the house; so long as I was certain of remaining in the infirmary; for there was nobody there who had ever seen me before. But I resolved to avoid, if possible, ever making my appearance below, for I felt that I could not do it without hazard of discovery.

Among other appendages of a Convent which I observed in that place, was a confessional within the building, and I soon learnt, to my dismay, that Father Bonin, one of the murderers of Saint Francis, was in the habit of constant attendance as priest and confessor. The recollections which I often indulged in of scenes in the Hotel Dieu, gave me uneasiness and distress: but not knowing where to go to seek greater seclusion, I remained in the infirmary week after week, still affecting illness in the best manner I could. At length I found that I was suspected of playing off a deception with regard to the state of my health; and at the close of a few weeks, I became satisfied that I could not remain longer without making my appearance below stairs. I at length complied with the wishes I heard expressed, that I would go into the community-room, where those in health were accustomed to assemble to work, and then some of the women began to talk of my going to confession. I merely expressed unwillingness at first; but when they pressed the point, and began to insist, my fear of detection overcame every other feeling, and I plainly declared that I would not go. This led to an altercation, when the mistress of the house pronounced me incorrigible, and said she would not keep me for a hundred pounds a year. She, in fact, became so weary of having me there, that she sent to my mother to take me away.

My mother, in consequence, sent a cariole for me, and took me again into her house; but I became so unhappy in a place where I was secluded and destitute of all agreeable society, that I earnestly requested her to allow me to leave Canada. I believe she felt ready to have me removed to a distance, that she might not be in danger of having my attempt at self-destruction, and my confinement in prison made public.

There was a fact which I had not disclosed, and of which all were ignorant: viz., that which had so much influence in exciting me to leave the Convent, and to reject every idea of returning to it.

When conversing with my mother about leaving Canada, I proposed to go to New York. She inquired why I wished to go there. I made no answer to that question: for, though I had never been there, and knew scarcely anything about the place, I presumed that I should find protection from my enemies, as I knew it was in a Protestant country. I had not thought of going to the United States before, because I had no one to go with me, nor money enough to pay my expenses; but then a plan presented itself to my mind, by which I thought I might proceed to New York in safety.

There was a man who I presumed would wish to have me leave Canada, on his own account; and that was the man I had so precipitately married while residing at St. Denis. He must have had motives, as I thought, for wishing me at a distance. I proposed therefore that he should be informed that I was in Montreal, and anxious to go to the States; and such a message was sent to him by a woman whom my mother knew.[7] She had a little stand for the sale of some articles, and had a husband who carried on some similar kind of business at the Scotch mountain. Through her husband, as I suppose, she had my message conveyed, and soon informed me that arrangements were made for my commencing my journey, under the care of the person to whom it had been sent.

---

[7] Mrs. Tarbert, or M'Gan. See her affidavit. What house she refers to I cannot conjecture.

CHAPTER XXIV

Singular concurrence of circumstances, which enabled me to get to the United States—Intentions in going there—Commence my journey—Fears of my companion—Stop at Whitehall—Injury received in a canal boat—Arrival at New York—A solitary retreat.

It is remarkable that I was able to stay so long in the midst of Catholics without discovery, and at last obtain the aid of some of them in effecting my flight. There is probably not a person in Montreal, who would sooner have betrayed me into the power of priests than that woman, if she had known my history.

She was a frequent visitor at the Convent and the Seminary, and had a ticket which entitled her every Monday to the gift of a loaf of bread from the former. She had an unbounded respect for the Superior and the priests, and seized every opportunity to please them. Now the fact that she was willing to take measures to facilitate my departure from Montreal, afforded sufficient evidence to me of her entire ignorance of myself, in all respects in which I could wish her to be ignorant; and I confided in her, because I perceived that she felt no stronger motive, than a disposition to oblige my mother.

Should any thing occur to let her into the secret of my being a fugitive from the Black Nunnery, I knew that I could not trust to her kindness for an instant. The discovery of that fact would transform her into a bitter and deadly enemy. She would at once regard me as guilty of mortal sin, an apostate, and a proper object of persecution. And this was a reflection I had often reason to make, when thinking of the numerous Catholics around me. How important, then, the keeping of my secret, and my escape before the truth should become known, even to a single person near me.

I could realize, from the dangers through which I was brought by the hand of God, how difficult it must be, in most cases, for a fugitive from a nunnery to obtain her final freedom from the power of her enemies. Even if escaped from a Convent, so long as she remains among Catholics, she is in constant exposure to be informed against; especially if the news of her escape is made public, which fortunately was not the fact in my case.

If a Catholic comes to the knowledge of any fact calculated to expose such a person, he will think it his duty to disclose it at confession; and then the whole fraternity will be in motion to seize her.

How happy for me that not a suspicion was entertained concerning me, and that not a whisper against me was breathed into the ear of a single priest at confession!

Notwithstanding my frequent appearance in the street, my removals from place to place, and the various exposures I had to discovery, contrary to my fears, which haunted me even in my dreams, I was preserved; and as I have often thought, for the purpose of making the disclosures which I have made in this volume. No power but that of God, as I have frequently thought, could ever have led me in safety through so many dangers.

I would not have my readers imagine, however, that I had at that period any thought of making known my history to the world. I wished to plunge into the deepest possible obscurity; and next to the fear of falling again into the hands of the priests and Superior, I shrunk most from the idea of having others acquainted with the scenes I had passed through. Such a thought as publishing never entered my mind till months after that time. My desire was, that I might meet a speedy death in obscurity, and that my name and my shame might perish on earth together. As for my future doom, I still looked forward to it with gloomy apprehensions: for I considered myself as almost, if not quite, removed beyond the reach of mercy. During all the time which had elapsed since I left the Convent, I had received no religious instruction, nor even read a word in the scriptures; and, therefore, it is not wonderful that I should still have remained under the delusions in which I had been educated.

The plan arranged for the commencement of my journey was this: I was to cross the St. Lawrence to Longueil, to meet the man who was to accompany me. The woman who had sent my message into the country, went with me to the ferry, and crossed the river, where, according to the appointment, we found my companion. He willingly undertook to accompany me to the place of my destination, and at his own expense; but declared, that he was apprehensive we should be pursued. To avoid the priests, who he supposed would follow us, he took an indirect route, and during about twelve days, or nearly that, which we spent on the way, passed over a much greater distance than was necessary. It would be needless, if it were possible, to mention all the places we visited. We crossed Carpenter's ferry, and were at Scotch-mountain and St. Alban's; arrived at Champlain by land, and there took the steamboat, leaving it again at Burlington.

As we were riding towards Charlotte, my companion entertained fears, which, to me, appeared ridiculous; but it was impossible for me to reason him out of them, or to hasten our journey. Circumstances which appeared to me of no moment whatever, would influence, and sometimes would make him change his whole plan and direction. As we were one day approaching Charlotte, for instance, on inquiring of a person on the way, whether there were any Canadians there, and being informed there were not a few, and that there was a Roman Catholic priest residing there, he immediately determined to avoid the place, and turned back, although we were then only nine miles distant from it.

During several of the first nights after leaving Montreal, he suffered greatly from fear; and on meeting me in the morning, repeatedly said: "Well, thank God, we are safe so far!" When we arrived at Whitehall, he had an idea we should run a risk of meeting priests, who he thought, were in search of us, if we went immediately on; and insisted that we had better stay there a little time, until they should have passed. In spite of my anxiety to proceed, we accordingly remained there about a week; when we entered a canal-boat to proceed to Troy.

An unfortunate accident happened to me while on our way. I was in the cabin, when a gun, which had been placed near me, was started from its place by the motion of the boat, caused by another boat running against it, and striking me on my left side, threw me some distance. The shock was violent, and I thought myself injured, but hoped the effects would soon pass off. I was afterwards taken with vomiting blood; and this alarming symptom several times returned; but I was able to keep up.

We came without any unnecessary delay from Troy to New York, where we arrived in the morning, either on Thursday or Friday, as I believe: but my companion there disappeared without informing me where he was going, and I saw him no more. Being now, as I presumed, beyond the reach of my enemies, I felt relief from the fear of being carried back to the nunnery, and sentenced to death or the cells: but I was in a large city where I had not a friend. Feeling overwhelmed with my miserable condition, I longed for death; and yet I felt no desire to make another attempt to destroy myself.

On the contrary, I determined to seek some solitary retreat, and await God's time to remove me from a world in which I had found so much trouble, hoping and believing that it would not be long.

Not knowing which way to go to find solitude, I spoke to a little boy, whom I saw on the wharf, and told, him I would give him some money if he would lead me into the "bush". (This is the common word by which, in Canada, we speak of the woods or forests.) When he understood what I meant, he told me that there was no bush about New York; but consented to lead me to the most

116

lonely place he knew of. He accordingly set off, and I followed him, on a long walk to the upper part of the city, and beyond, until we reached the outskirts of it. Turning off from the road, we gained a little hollow, where were a few trees and bushes, a considerable distance from any house; and there, he told me, was the loneliest place with which he was acquainted. I paid him for his trouble out of the small stock of money I had in my possession, and let him go home, desiring him to come the next day, and bring me something to eat, with a few pennies which I gave him.

CHAPTER XXV

Reflections and sorrow in solitude—Night—Fears—Exposure to rain—Discovered by strangers—Their unwelcome kindness—Taken to the Bellevue Almshouse.

There I found myself once more alone, and truly it was a great relief to sit down and feel that I was out of the reach of priests and nuns, and in a spot where I could patiently wait for death, when God might please to send it, instead of being abused and tormented according to the caprices and passions of my persecutors.

But then again returned most bitter anticipations of the future. Life had no attractions for me, for it must be connected with shame; but death under any circumstances, could not be divested of horrors, so long as I believed in the doctrines relating to it which had been inculcated upon me.

The place where I had taken up, as I supposed, my last earthly abode, was pleasant in clear and mild weather; and I spent most of my time in as much peace as the state of my mind would permit. I saw houses, but no human beings, except on the side of a little hill near by, where were some men at work, making sounds like those made in hammering stone. The shade around me was so thick that I felt assured of being sufficiently protected from observation if I kept still; and a cluster of bushes offered me shelter for the night. As evening approached, I was somewhat alarmed by the sound of voices near me, and I found that a number of labourers were passing that way from their work. I went in a fright to the thickest of the bushes, and lay down, until all again was still, and then ventured out to take my seat again on the turf.

117

Darkness now came gradually on; and with it fears of another description. The thought struck me that there might be wild beasts in that neighborhood, ignorant as I then was of the country; and the more I thought of it, the more I became alarmed. I heard no alarming sound, it is true; but I knew not how soon some prowling and ferocious beast might come upon me in my defenceless condition, and tear me in pieces. I retired to my bushes, and stretched myself under them upon the ground: but I found it impossible to sleep; and my mind was almost continually agitated by thoughts on the future or the past.

In the morning the little boy made his appearance again, and brought me a few cakes which he had purchased for me. He showed much interest in me, inquired why I did not live in a house; and it was with difficulty that I could satisfy him to let me remain in my solitary and exposed condition. Understanding that I wished to continue unknown, he assured me that he had not told even his mother about me; and I had reason to believe that he faithfully kept my secret to the last. Though he lived a considerable distance from my hiding-place, and, as I supposed, far down in the city, he visited me almost every day, even when I had not desired him to bring me any thing. Several times I received from him some small supplies of food for the money I had given him. I once gave him a half-dollar to get changed; and he brought me back every penny of it, at his next visit.

As I had got my drink from a brook or pool, which was at no great distance, he brought me a little cup one day to drink out of; but this I was not allowed to keep long, for he soon after told me that his mother wanted it, and he must return it. He several times arrived quite out of breath, and when I inquired the reason, calling him as I usually did, "Little Tommy" he said it was necessary for him to run, and to stay but a short time, that he might be at school in good season. Thus he continued to serve me, and keep my secret, at great inconvenience to himself, up to the last day of my stay in that retreat; and I believe he would have done so for three months if I had remained there. I should like to see him again and hear his broken English.

I had now abundance of time to reflect on my lost condition; and many a bitter thought passed through my mind, as I sat on the ground, or strolled about by day, and lay under the bushes at night.

Sometimes I reflected on the doctrines I had heard at the nunnery, concerning sins and penances, Purgatory and Hell; and sometimes on my late companions, and the crimes I had witnessed in the Convent.

Sometimes I would sit and seriously consider how I might

118

best destroy my life; and sometimes would sing a few of the hymns with which I was familiar; but I never felt willing or disposed to pray, as I supposed there was no hope of mercy for me.

One of the first nights I spent in that houseless condition was stormy; and though I crept under the thickest of the bushes, and had more protection against the rain than one might have expected, I was almost entirely wet before morning; and, it may be supposed, passed a more uncomfortable night than usual. The next day I was happy to find the weather clear, and was able to dry my garments by taking off one at a time, and spreading them on the bushes. A night or two after, however, I was again exposed to a heavy rain, and had the same process afterward to go through with: but what is remarkable, I took no cold on either occasion; nor did I suffer any lasting injury from all the exposures I underwent in that place. The inconveniences I had to encounter, also, appeared to me of little importance, not being sufficient to draw off my mind from its own troubles; and I had no intention of seeking a more comfortable abode, still looking forward only to dying as soon as God would permit, alone and in that spot.

One day, however, when I had been there about ten days, I was alarmed at seeing four men approaching me. All of them had guns, as if out on a shooting excursion. They expressed much surprise and pity on finding me there, and pressed me with questions. I would not give them any satisfactory account of myself, my wants, or intentions, being only anxious that they might withdraw. I found them, however, too much interested to render me some service to be easily sent away; and after some time, thinking there would be no other way, I pretended to go away not to return. After going some distance, and remaining some time, thinking they had probably left the place, I returned; but to my mortification found they had concealed themselves to see whether I would come back. They now, more urgently than before, insisted on my removing to some other place, where I might be comfortable. They continued to question me; but I became distressed in a degree I cannot describe, hardly knowing what I did. At last I called the oldest gentleman aside, and told him something of my history. He expressed great interest for me, offered to take me anywhere I would tell him, and at last insisted that I should go with him to his own house. All these offers I refused; on which one proposed to take me to the Almshouse, and even to carry me by force if I would not go willingly.

To this I at length consented; but some delay took place, and I

119

became unwilling, so that with reluctance I was taken to that institution, which was about half a mile distant.[8]

CHAPTER XXVI

Reception at the Almshouse—Message from Mr. Conroy, a Roman priest in New York—His invitations to a private interview—His claims, propositions, and threats—Mr. Kelly's message—Effects of reading the Bible.

I was now at once made comfortable, and attended with kindness and care. It is not to be expected in such a place, where so many poor and suffering people are collected and duties of a difficult nature are to be daily performed by those engaged in the care of the institution, that petty vexations should not occur to individuals of all descriptions.

But in spite of all, I received kindness and sympathy from several persons around me, to whom I feel thankful.

I was standing one day at the window of the room number twenty-six, which is at the end of the hospital building, when I saw a spot I once visited in a little walk I took from my hiding-place. My feelings were different now in some respects, from what they had been; for, though I suffered much from my fears of future punishment, for the sin of breaking my Convent vows, I had given up the intention of destroying my life.

After I had been some time in the Institution, I found it was reported by some about me, that I was a fugitive nun; and it was not long after, that an Irish woman, belonging to the Institution, brought me a secret message, which caused me some agitation.

I was sitting in the room of Mrs. Johnson, the matron, engaged in sewing, when that Irish woman, employed in the Institution, came in and told me that Mr. Conroy was below, and had sent to see me. I was informed that he was a Roman priest, who often visited the house, and he had a particular wish to see me at

---

[8] See the affidavit of Mr. Hilliker, in Appendix. The letter to which he refers I had forgotten to mention. It contains a short account of the crimes I had witnessed in the nunnery, and was written on paper which "little Tommy" had bought for me.

that time; having come, as I believe, expressly for that purpose, I showed unwillingness to comply with such an invitation, and did not go. The woman told me further, that he sent me word that I need not think to avoid him, for it would be impossible for me to do so. I might conceal myself as well as I could, but I should be found and taken. No matter where I went, or what hiding-place I might choose, I should be known; and I had better come at once. He knew who I was; and he was authorized to take me to the Sisters of Charity, if I should prefer to join them. He would promise that I might stay with them if I chose, and be permitted to remain in New York. He sent me word farther, that he had received full power and authority over me from the Superior of the Hotel Dieu Nunnery of Montreal, and was able to do all that she could do; as her right to dispose of me at her will had been imparted to him by a regular writing received from Canada. This was alarming information for me, in the weakness in which I was at that time. The woman added, that the same authority had been given to all the priests; so that, go where I might, I should meet men informed about me and my escape, and fully empowered to seize me wherever they could, and convey me back to the Convent, from which I had escaped.

Under these circumstances, it seemed to me that the offer to place me among the Sisters of Charity, with permission to remain in New York, was mild and favourable. However, I had resolution enough to refuse to see the priest Conroy.

Not long afterward, I was informed by the same messenger, that the priest was again in the building, and repeated his request. I desired one of the gentlemen connected with the Institution, that a stop might be put to such messages, as I wished to receive no more of them. A short time after, however, the woman told me that Mr. Conroy wished to inquire of me whether my name was not St. Eustace while a nun, and if I had not confessed to Priest Kelly in Montreal. I answered, that it was all true; for I had confessed to him a short time while in the nunnery. I was then told again that the priest wanted to see me, and I sent back word that I would see him in the presence of Mr. Tappan, or Mr. Stevens; which, however, was not agreed to; and I was afterwards informed, that Mr. Conroy, the Roman priest, spent an hour in a room and a passage where I had frequently been; but through the mercy of God; I was employed in another place at that time, and had no occasion to go where I should have met him. I afterwards repeatedly heard, that Mr. Conroy continued to visit the house, and to ask for me; but I never saw him. I once had determined to leave the Institution, and go to the Sisters of Charity; but circumstances occurred which gave me time for further reflection; and I was saved from the destruction to which I should have been exposed.

121

As the period of my accouchment approached, I sometimes thought that I should not survive it; and then the recollection of the dreadful crimes I had witnessed in the nunnery would come upon me very powerfully, and I would think it a solemn duty to disclose them before I died. To have a knowledge of those things, and leave the world without making them known, appeared to me like a great sin: whenever I could divest myself of the impression made upon me, by the declarations and arguments of the Superior, nuns, and priests, of the duty of submitting to every thing, and the necessary holiness of whatever the latter did or required.

The evening but one before the period which I anticipated with so much anxiety, I was sitting alone, and began to indulge in reflections of this kind. It seemed to me that I must be near the close of my life, and I determined to make a disclosure at once. I spoke to Mrs. Ford, a woman whose character I respected, a nurse in the hospital, in number twenty-three. I informed her that I had no expectation of living long, and had some things on my mind which I wished to communicate before it should be too late. I added, that I should prefer to tell them to Mr. Tappan, the chaplain, of which she approved, as she considered it a duty to do so under those circumstances. I had no opportunity, however, to converse with Mr. T. at that time, and probably my purpose, of disclosing the facts already given in this book, would never have been executed but for what subsequently took place. It was alarm which had led me to form such a determination; and when the period of trial had been safely passed, and I had a prospect of recovery, anything appeared to me more likely than that I should make this exposure.

I was then a Roman Catholic, at least a great part of my time; and my conduct, in a great measure, was according to the faith and motives of a Roman Catholic. Notwithstanding what I knew of the conduct of so many of the priests and nuns, I thought that it had no effect on the sanctity of the Church, or the authority or effects of the acts performed by the former at the mass, confession, &c. I had such a regard for my vows as a nun, that I considered my hand as well as my heart irrevocably given to Jesus Christ, and could never have allowed any person to take it. Indeed, to this day, I feel an instinctive aversion to offering my hand, or taking the hand of another person, even as an expression of friendship. I also thought that I might soon return to the Catholics, although fear and disgust held me back. I had now that infant to think for, whose life I had happily saved by my timely escape from the nunnery; and what its fate might be, in case it should ever fall into the power of the priests I could not tell.

I had, however, reason for alarm. Would a child destined to

destruction, like the infants I had seen baptized and smothered, be allowed to go through the world unmolested, a living memorial of the truth of crimes long practised in security, because never exposed? What pledges could I get to satisfy me, that I, on whom her dependence must be, would be spared by those who I had reason to think were then wishing to sacrifice me? How could I trust the helpless infant in hands which had hastened the baptism of many such, in order to hurry them to the secret pit in the cellar? Could I suppose that Father Phelan, Priest of the Parish Church of Montreal, would see his own child growing up in the world, and feel willing to run the rink of having the truth exposed? What could I expect, especially from him, but the utmost rancor, and the most determined enmity against the innocent child and its abased and defenceless mother?

Yet, my mind would sometimes still incline in the opposite direction, and indulge the thought, that perhaps the only way to secure heaven to as both, was to throw ourselves back into the hands of the Church, to be treated as she pleased. When, therefore, the fear of immediate death was removed, I renounced all thoughts of communicating the substance of the facts in this volume. It happened, however, that my danger was not passed. I was soon seized with very alarming symptoms; then my desire to disclose my story revived.

I had before had an opportunity to speak in private with the chaplain; but, as it was at a time when I supposed myself out of danger, I had deferred for three days my proposed communication, thinking that I might yet avoid it altogether. When my symptoms, however, became more alarming, I was anxious for Saturday to arrive, the day which I had appointed; and when I had not the opportunity on that day, which I desired, I thought it might be too late. I did not see him till Monday, when my prospects of surviving were very gloomy; and I then informed him that I wished to communicate to him a few secrets, which were likely otherwise to die with me. I then told him, that while a nun, in the convent of Montreal, I had witnessed the murder of a nun, called Saint Francis, and of at least one of the infants which I have spoken of in this book. I added some few circumstances, and I believe disclosed, in general terms, some of the other crimes I knew of in that nunnery.

My anticipations of death proved to be unfounded; for my health afterward improved, and had I not made the confessions on that occasion, it is very possible I never might have made them. I, however, afterward, felt more willing to listen to instruction, and experienced friendly attentions from some of the benevolent persons around me, who, taking an interest in me on account of my darkened understanding, furnished me with the Bible, and were ever ready to counsel me when I desired it.

I soon began to believe that God might have intended that his creatures should learn his will by reading his word, and taking upon them the free exercise of their reason, and acting under responsibility to him.

It is difficult for one who has never given way to such arguments and influences as those to which I had been exposed, to realize how hard it is to think aright after thinking wrong. The Scriptures always affect me powerfully when I read them; but I feel that I have but just begun to learn the great truths, in which I ought to have been early and thoroughly instructed. I realize, in some degree, how it is, that the Scriptures render the people of the United States so strongly opposed to such doctrines as are taught in the Black and the Congregational Nunneries of Montreal. The priests and nuns used often to declare, that of all heretics, the children from the United States were the most difficult to be converted; and it was thought a great triumph when one of them was brought over to "the true faith." The first passage of Scripture that made any serious impression upon my mind, was the text on which the chaplain preached on the Sabbath after my introduction into the house—"Search the Scriptures."

I made some hasty notes of the thoughts to which it gave rise in my mind, and often recurred to the subject. Yet I sometimes questioned the justice of the views I began to entertain, and was ready to condemn myself for giving my mind any liberty to seek for information concerning the foundations of my former faith.

CHAPTER XXVII

Proposition to go to Montreal and testify against the priests— Commencement of my journey—Stop at Troy, Whitehall, Burlington, St. Alban's, Plattsburgh, and St. John's—Arrival at Montreal—Reflections on passing the Nunnery, &c.

About a fortnight after I had made the disclosures mentioned in the last chapter, Mr. Hoyt called at the Hospital to make inquiries about me. I was introduced to him by Mr. Tappan. After some conversation, he asked me if I would consent to visit Montreal, and give my evidence against the priests and nuns before a court. I immediately expressed my willingness to do so, on condition that I should be protected. It immediately occurred to me, that I might enter the nunnery at night, and bring out the nuns in the cells, and possibly Jane Ray, and that they would confirm my testimony. In a short time, arrangements were made for our journey, I was furnished with clothes; and although my strength was but partially restored, I set off in pretty good spirits.

Our journey was delayed for a little while, by Mr. Hoyt's waiting to get a companion. He had engaged a clergyman to accompany us, as I understood, who was prevented from going by unexpected business. We went to Troy in a steamboat; and, while there, I had several interviews with some gentlemen who were informed of my history, and wished to see me. They appeared to be deeply impressed with the importance of my testimony; and on their recommendation it was determined that we should go to St. Alban's, on our way to Montreal, to get a gentleman to accompany us, whose advice and assistance, as an experienced lawyer, were thought to be desirable to us in prosecuting the plan we had in view: viz. the exposure of the crimes with which I was acquainted.

We travelled from Troy to Whitehall in a canal packet, because the easy motion was best adapted to my state of health. We met on board the Rev. Mr. Sprague of New York, with whom Mr. Hoyt was acquainted, and whom he tried to persuade to accompany us to Montreal. From Whitehall to Burlington we proceeded in a steamboat; and there I was so much indisposed, that is was necessary to call a physician. After a little rest, we set off in the stage for St. Alban's; and on arriving, found that Judge Turner was out of town. We had to remain a day or two before he returned; and then he said it would be impossible for him to accompany us. After some deliberation, it was decided that Mr. Hunt should go to Montreal with us, and that Judge Turner should follow and join us there as soon as his health and business would permit.[9]

We therefore crossed the lake by the ferry to Plattsburgh, where, after some delay, we embarked in a steamboat, which took us to St. John's. Mr. Hunt, who had not reached the ferry early enough to cross with us, had proceeded on to ——, and there got on board the steamboat in the night. We went on to Laprairie with little delay, but finding that no boat was to cross the St. Lawrence at that place during the day, we had to take another private carriage to Longeuil, whence we rowed across to Montreal by three men, in a small boat.

---

[9] Mr. Hunt was recommended as a highly respectable lawyer; to whose kindness, as well as that of Judge Turner, I feel myself under obligations.

I had felt quite bold and resolute when I first consented to go to Montreal, and also during my journey: but when I stepped on shore in the city, I thought of the different scenes I had witnessed there, and of the risks I might run before I should leave it. We got into a caleche, and rode along towards the hotel where we were to stop. We passed up St. Paul's street; and, although it was dusk, I recognised every thing I had known. We came at length to the nunnery; and then many recollections crowded upon me. First, I saw a window from which I had sometimes looked at some of the distant houses in that street; and I wondered whether some of my old acquaintances were employed as formerly. But I thought if I were once within those walls, I should be in the cells for the remainder of my life, or perhaps be condemned to something still more severe. I remembered the murder of St. Francis, and the whole scene returned to me as if it had just taken place; the appearance, language, and conduct of the persons most active in her destruction. Those persons were now all near me, and would use all exertions they safely might, to get me again into their power.

And certainly they had greater reason to be exasperated against me, than against that poor helpless nun, who had only expressed a wish to escape.[10]

---

[10] My gloomy feelings however did not always prevail. I had hope of obtaining evidence to prove my charges. I proposed to my companions to be allowed to proceed that evening to execute the plan I had formed when a journey to Montreal had first been mentioned. This was to follow the physician into the nunnery, conceal myself under the red calico sofa in the sitting-room, find my way into the cellar after all was still, release the nuns from their cells, and bring them out to confirm my testimony. I was aware that there were hazards of my not succeeding, and that I must forfeit my life if detected—but I was desperate; and feeling as if I could not long live in Montreal, thought I might as well die one way as another, and that I had better die in the performance of a good deed. I thought of attempting to bring out Jane Ray—but that seemed quite out of the question, as an old nun is commonly engaged in cleaning a community-room, through which I should have to pass; and how could I hope to get into, and out of the sleeping-room unobserved? I could not even determine that the imprisoned nuns would follow me out—for they might be afraid to trust me. However, I determined to try, and presuming my companions had all along understood and approved my plan, told them I was ready to go at once. I was chagrined and mortified more than I can express, when they objected, and almost refused to permit me. I insisted and urged the importance of the step—but they represented its extreme rashness. This conduct of theirs, for a time diminished my confidence to them, although everybody else has approved of it.

When I found myself safely in Goodenough's hotel, in a retired room, and began to think alone, the most gloomy apprehensions filled my mind. I could not eat, I had no appetite, and I did not sleep all night. Every painful scene that I ever passed through seemed to return to my mind; and such was my agitation, I could fix my thoughts upon nothing in particular. I had left New York when the state of my health was far from being established; and my strength, as may be presumed, was now much reduced by the fatigue of travelling. I shall be able to give but a faint idea of the feelings with which I passed that night, but must leave it to the imagination of my readers. Now once more in the neighborhood of the Convent, and surrounded by the nuns and priests, of whose conduct I had made the first disclosures ever made, surrounded by thousands of persons devoted to them, and ready to proceed to any outrage, as I feared, whenever their interference might be desired, there was abundant reason for my uneasiness.

I now began to realize that I had some attachment to life remaining. When I consented to visit the city, and furnish the evidence necessary to lay open the iniquity of the Convent, I had felt, in a measure, indifferent to life; but now, when torture and death seemed at hand, I shrunk from it. For myself, life could not be said to be of much value. How could I be happy with such things to reflect upon as I had passed through? and how could I enter society with gratification? But my infant I could not abandon, for who would care for it if its mother died.

I was left alone in the morning by the gentlemen who had accompanied me, as they went to take immediate measures to open the intended investigation. Being alone I thought of my own position in every point of view, until I became more agitated than ever. I tried to think what persons I might safely apply to as friends; and though still undecided what to do, I arose, thinking it might be unsafe to remain any longer exposed, as I imagined myself, to be known and seized by my enemies.

I went from the hotel,[11] hurried along, feeling as if I were on my way to some asylum, and thinking I would first go to the house where I had several times previously found a temporary refuge. I

---

[11] It occurred to me, that I might have been seen by some person on landing, who might recognise me if I appeared in the streets in the same dress; and I requested one of the female servants to lend me some of hers. I obtained a hat and shawl from her with which I left the house. When I found myself in Notre Dame street, the utmost indecision what to do, and the thought of my friendless condition almost overpowered me.

did not stop to reflect that the woman was a devoted Catholic and a friend to the Superior; but thought only of her kindness to me on former occasions, and hastened along Notre Dame street. But I was approaching the Seminary; and a resolution was suddenly formed to go and ask the pardon and intercession of the Superior. Then the character of Bishop Lartigue seemed to present an impassable obstacle; and the disagreeable aspect and harsh voice of the man as I recalled him, struck me with horror. I recollected him as I had known him when engaged in scenes concealed from the eye of the world. The thought of him made me decide not to enter the Seminary. I hurried, therefore, by the door; and the great church being at hand, my next thought was to enter there. I reached the steps, walked in, dipped my finger into the holy water, crossed myself, turned to the first image I saw, which was that of Saint Magdalen, threw myself upon my knees, and began to repeat prayers with the utmost fervour. I am certain that I never felt a greater desire to find relief from any of the Saints; but my agitation hardly seemed to subside during my exercise, which continued, perhaps, a quarter of an hour or more. I then rose from my knees, and placed myself under the protection of St. Magdalen and St. Peter by these words: "Je me mets sous vôtre protection"—(I place myself under your protection;) and added, "Sainte Marie, mère du bon pasteur, prie pour moi"—(Holy Mary, mother of the good shepherd, pray for me.)

I then resolved to call once more at the house where I had found a retreat after, my escape from the nunnery, and proceeded along the streets in that direction. On my way, I had to pass a shop kept by a woman[12] I formerly had an acquaintance with. She happened to see me passing, and immediately said, "Maria is that you? Come in."

I entered, and she soon proposed to me to let her go and tell my mother that I had returned to the city. To this I objected. I went with her, however, to the house of one of her acquaintances near by where I remained some time, during which she went to my mother's and came with a request from her, that I would have an interview with her, proposing to come up and see me, saying that she had something very particular to say to me. What this was, I could not with any certainty conjecture. I had my suspicions that it might be something from the priests, designed to get me back into their power, or, at least, to suppress my testimony.

---

[12] This was Mrs. Tarbert.

I felt an extreme repugnance to seeing my mother, and in the distressing state of apprehension and uncertainty in which I was, could determine on nothing, except to avoid her. I therefore soon left the house, and walked on without any particular object. The weather was then very unpleasant, and it was raining incessantly. To this I was very indifferent, and walked on till I had got to the suburbs, and found myself beyond the windmills. Then I returned, and passed back through the city, still not recognised by anybody.

I once saw one of my brothers, unless I was much mistaken, and thought he knew me. If it was he, I am confident he avoided me, and that was my belief at the time, as he went into a yard with the appearance of much agitation. I continued to walk up and down most of the day, fearful of stopping anywhere, lest I should be recognised by my enemies, or betrayed into their power. I felt all the distress of a feeble, terrified woman, in need of protection, and, as I thought, without a friend in whom I could safely confide. It distressed me extremely to think of my poor babe; and I had now been so long absent from it, as necessarily to suffer much inconvenience.

I recollected to have been told, in the New York Hospital, that laudanum would relieve distress both bodily and mental, by a woman who had urged me to make a trial of it. In my despair, I resolved to make an experiment with it, and entering an apothecary's shop asked for some. The apothecary refused to give me any; but an old man who was there, told me to come in, and inquired where I had been, and what was the matter with me, seeing that I was quite wet through. I let him know that I had an infant, and on his urging me to tell more, I told him where my mother lived. He went out, and soon after returned accompanied by my mother, who told me she had my child at home, and pressed me to go to her house and see it, saying she would not insist on my entering, but would bring it out to me.

I consented to accompany her; but on reaching the door, she began to urge me to go in, saying I should not be known to the rest of the family, but might stay there in perfect privacy. I was resolved not to comply with this request, and resisted all her entreaties, though she continued to urge me for a long time, perhaps half an hour. At length she went in, and I walked away, in a state no less desperate than before. Indeed, night was now approaching, the rain continued, and I had no prospect of food, rest, or even shelter. I went on till I reached the parade-ground, unnoticed, I believe, by anybody, except one man, who asked where I was going, but to whom I gave no answer. I had told my mother, before she had left me, that she might find me in the parade-ground. There I stopped in a part of the open ground where there was no probability of my being observed, and stood thinking of the many distressing things which harassed me; suffering, indeed, from exposure to wet and cold, but indifferent to them as evils of mere trifling importance, and expecting that death would soon ease me of my present sufferings. I had hoped that my mother would bring my babe to me there; but as it was growing late, I gave up all expectation of seeing her.

At length she came, accompanied by Mr. Hoyt, who, as I afterward learnt, had called on her after my leaving the hotel, and, at her request, had intrusted my child to her care. Calling again after I had left her house, she had informed him that she now knew where I was, and consented to lead him to the spot. I was hardly able to speak or to walk, in consequence of the hardships I had undergone; but being taken to a small inn, and put under the care of several women, I was made comfortable with a change of clothes and a warm bed.[13]

---

[13] I afterward learnt, that the two gentlemen who accompanied me from the States, had been seeking me with great anxiety all day. I persisted in not going to my mother's, and that was the reason why we applied to strangers for a lodging. For some time it appeared doubtful whether I should find any refuge for the night, as several small inns in the neighbourhood proved to be full. At length, however, lodgings were obtained for me in one, and I experienced kindness from the females of the house, who put me into a warm bed, and by careful treatment soon rendered me more comfortable. I thought I heard the voice of a woman, in the course of the evening, whom I had seen about the nunnery, and ascertained that I was not mistaken. I forgot to mention, that, while preparing to leave this house the next day, Mrs. Tarbert came in and spoke with me. She said, that she had just come from the government-house, and asked, "What are all those men at your mother's for? what is going on there?" I told her I could not tell. She said, "Your mother wants to speak with you very much." I told her I would not go to her house, for I feared there was some plan to get me into the hands of the priests. The inn in which I was, is one near the government-house, in a block owned by the Baroness de Montenac, or the Baroness de Longeuil, her daughter. I think it must be a respectable house, in spite of what Mrs. Tarbert says in her affidavit. Mrs. Tarbert is the woman spoken of several times in the "Sequel," without being named; as I did not know how to spell her name till her affidavit came out.

CHAPTER XXVIII

Received into a hospitable family—Fluctuating feelings—Visits from several persons—Father Phelan's declarations against me in his church—Interviews with a Journeyman Carpenter—Arguments with him.

In the morning I received an invitation to go to the house of a respectable Protestant, an old inhabitant of the city, who had been informed of my situation; and although I felt hardly able to move, I proceeded thither in a cariole, and was received with a degree of kindness, and treated with such care, that I must ever retain a lively gratitude towards the family.

On Saturday I had a visit from Dr. Robertson, to whose house I had been taken soon after my rescue from drowning. He put a few questions to me, and soon withdrew.

On Monday, after the close of mass, a Canadian man came in, and entered into conversation with the master of the house in an adjoining room. He was, as I understood, a journeyman carpenter, and a Catholic, and having heard that a fugitive nun was somewhere in the city, began to speak on the subject in French. I was soon informed that Father Phelan had just addressed his congregation with much apparent excitement about myself; and thus the carpenter had received his information. Father Phelan's words, according to what I heard said by numerous witnesses at different times, must have been much like the following:—

"There is a certain nun now in this city, who has left our faith, and joined the Protestants. She has a child, of which she is ready to swear I am the father. She would be glad in this way to take away my gown from me. If I knew where to find her, I would put her in prison. I mention this to guard you against being deceived by what she may say. The devil has such a hold upon people now-a-days, that there is danger that some might believe her story."

Before he concluded his speech, as was declared, he burst into tears, and appeared to be quite overcome. When the congregation had been dismissed, a number of them came round him, and he told some of them, that I was Antichrist; I was not a human being, as he was convinced, but an evil spirit, who had got among the Catholics, and been admitted into the nunnery, where I had learnt the rules so that I could repeat them. My appearance, he declared, was a fulfilment of prophecy, as Antichrist is foretold to be coming, in order to break down, if possible, the Catholic religion.

131

The journeyman carpenter had entered the house where I lodged under these impressions, and had conversed some time on the subject, without any suspicion that I was near. After he had railed against me with much violence, as I afterwards learned, the master of the house informed him that he knew something of the nun, and mentioned that she charged the priests of the Seminary with crimes of an awful character; in reply to which the carpenter expressed the greatest disbelief.

"You can satisfy yourself," said the master of the house, "if you will take the trouble to step up stairs: for she lives in my family."

"I see her!" he exclaimed—"No, I would not see the wretched creature for any thing. I wonder you are not afraid to have her in your house—she will bewitch you all—the evil spirit!"

After some persuasion, however, he came into the room where I was sitting, but looked at me with every appearance of dread and curiosity; and his exclamations, and subsequent conversation, in Canadian French, were very ludicrous.

"Eh bien," he began on first seeing me, "c'est ici la malheureuse?" [Well, is this the poor creature?] But he stood at a distance, and looked at me with curiosity and evident fear. I asked him to sit down, and tried to make him feel at his ease, by speaking in a mild and pleasant tone. He soon became so far master of himself, as to enter into conversation. "I understood," said he, "that she has said very hard things against the priests. How can that be true?" "I can easily convince you," said I, "that they do what they ought not, and commit crimes of the kind I complain of. You are married, I suppose?" He assented. "You confessed, I presume, on the morning of your wedding day?" He acknowledged that he did. "Then did not the priest tell you at confession, that he had had intercourse with your intended bride, but that it was for her sanctification, and that you must never reproach her with it?"

This question instantly excited him, but he did not hesitate a moment to answer it. "Yes," replied he; "and that looks black enough." I had put the question to him, because I knew the practice to which I alluded had prevailed at St. Denis while I was there, and believed it to be universal, or at least very common in all the Catholic parishes of Canada. I thought I had reason to presume, that every Catholic, married in Canada, had had such experience, and that an allusion to the conduct of the priest in this particular, must compel any of them to admit that my declarations were far from being incredible. This was the effect on the mind of the simple mechanic; and from that moment he made no more serious questions concerning my truth and sincerity, during that interview.

Further conversation ensued, in the course of which I

132

expressed the willingness which I have often declared, to go into the Convent and point out things which would confirm, to any doubting person, the truth of my heaviest accusations against the priests and nuns. At length he withdrew, and afterwards entered, saying that he had been to the Convent to make inquiries concerning me. He assured me that he had been told that although I had once belonged to the nunnery, I was called St. Jacques, and not St. Eustace; and that now they would not own or recognize me. Then he began to curse me, but yet sat down, as if disposed for further conversation. It seemed, as if he was affected by the most contrary feelings, and in rapid succession. One of the things he said, was to persuade me to leave Montreal. "I advise you," said he, "to go away to-morrow." I replied that I was in no haste, and might stay a month longer.

Then he fell to cursing me once more: but the next moment broke out against the priests, calling them all the names he could think of. His passion became so high against them, that he soon began to rub himself, as the low Canadians, who are apt to be very passionate, sometimes do, to calm their feelings, when they are excited to a painful degree. After this explosion he again became quite tranquil, and turning to me in a frank and friendly manner, said: "I will help you in your measures against the priests: but tell me, first—you are going to print a book, are you not?" "No," said I, "I have no thoughts of that."

Then he left the house again, and soon returned, saying he had been in the Seminary, and seen a person who had known me in the nunnery, and said I had been only a novice, and that he would not acknowledge me now. I sent back word by him, that I would show one spot in the nunnery that would prove I spoke the truth. Thus he continued to go and return several times, saying something of the kind every time, until I became tired of him. He was so much enraged once or twice during some of the interviews, that I felt somewhat alarmed; and some of the family heard him swearing as he went down stairs: "Ah, sacre—that is too black!"

He came at last, dressed up like a gentleman, and told me he was ready to wait on me to the nunnery. I expressed my surprise that he should expect me to go with him alone, and told him I had never thought of going without some protector, still assuring, that with any person to secure my return, I would cheerfully go all over the nunnery, and show sufficient evidence of the truth of what I alleged.

My feelings continued to vary: I was sometimes fearful, and sometimes so courageous as to think seriously of going into the Recollet church during mass, with my child in my arms, and calling

133

upon the priest to own it. And this I am confident I should have done, but for the persuasions used to prevent me.[14]

CHAPTER XXIX

A Milkman—An Irishwoman—Difficulty in having my Affidavit taken—Legal objection to it when taken.

Another person who expressed a strong wish to see me, was an Irish milkman. He had heard, what seemed to have been pretty generally reported, that I blamed none but the Irish priests. He put the question, whether it was a fact that I accused nobody but Father Phelan. I told him that it was not so; and this pleased him so well, that he told me if I would stay in Montreal, I should have milk for myself and my child as long as I lived. It is well known that strong antipathies have long existed between the French and Irish Catholics in the city.

The next day the poor Irishman returned, but in a very different state of mind. He was present at church in the morning, he said, when Father Phelan told the congregation that the nun of whom he had spoken before, had gone to court and accused him; and that he, by the power he possessed, had struck her powerless as she stood before the judge, so that she sunk helpless on the floor. He expressed, by the motion of his hands, the unresisting manner in which she had sunk under the mysterious influence, and declared that she would have died on the spot, but that he had chosen to keep her alive that she might retract her false accusation. This, he said, she did, most humbly, before the court; acknowledging that she had been paid a hundred pounds as a bribe.

The first words of the poor milkman, on revisiting me, therefore, were like these: "That's to show you what power the priest has! Didn't he give it to you in the court? It is to be hoped you will leave the city now." He then stated what he had heard Father Phelan say, and expressed his entire conviction of its truth, and the extreme

---

[14] I did not make up my mind (so far as I remember), publicly to proclaim who was the father of my child, unless required to do so, until I learnt that Father Phelan had denied it.

joy he felt on discovering, as he supposed he had, that his own priest was innocent, and had gained such a triumph over me.

A talkative Irish woman also made her appearance, among those who called at the house, and urged for permission to see me. Said she, "I have heard dreadful things are told by a nun you have here, against the priests; and I have to convince myself of the truth. I want to see the nun you have got in your house." When informed that I was unwell, and not inclined at present to see any more strangers, she still showed much disposition to obtain an interview. "Well, ain't it too bad," she asked, "that there should be any reason for people to say such things against the priests?" At length she obtained admittance to the room where I was, entered with eagerness, and approached me.

"Arrah," she exclaimed, "God bless you—is this you? Now sit down, and let me see the child. And is it Father Phelan's, God bless you? But they say you tell about murders; and I want to know if they are all committed by the Irish priests." "Oh no," replied I, "by no means." "Then God bless you," said she. "If you will live in Montreal, you shall never want. I will see that neither you nor your child ever want, for putting part of the blame upon the French priests. I am going to Father Phelan, and I shall tell him about it. But they say you are an evil spirit. I want to know whether it is so or not." "Come here," said I, "feel me, and satisfy yourself. Besides, did you ever hear of an evil spirit having a child?"

I heard from those about me, that there was great difficulty in finding a magistrate willing to take my affidavit I am perfectly satisfied that this was owing to the influence of the priests to prevent my accusations against them from been made public. One evening a lawyer, who had been employed for the purpose, accompanied me to a French justice with an affidavit ready prepared in English, for his signature, and informed him that he wished him to administer to me the oath. Without any apparent suspicion of me, the justice said, "Have you heard of the nun who ran away from the Convent, and has come back to the city, to bear witness against the priests?" "No matter about that now," replied the lawyer hastily; "I have no time to talk with you—you will take this person's oath now or not?" He could not read a word of the document, because it was not in his own language, and soon placed his signature to the bottom. It proved, however, that we had gained nothing by this step, for the lawyer afterward informed us, that the laws required the affidavit of a nun or minor to be taken before a superior magistrate.

CHAPTER XXX

Interview with the Attorney General of the Province—Attempt to abduct me—More interviews—A mob excited against me—Protected by two soldiers—Convinced that an investigation of my charges could not be obtained—Departure from Montreal—Closing reflections.

Those who had advised to the course to be pursued, had agreed to lay the subject before the highest authorities. They soon came to the conviction that it would be in vain to look for any favour from the Governor, and resolved to lay it before the Attorney General as soon as he should return from Quebec. After waiting for some time, he returned; and I was informed, in a few days, that he had appointed an interview on the following morning. I went at the time with a gentleman of the city, to the house of Mr. Grant, a distinguished lawyer. In a short time a servant invited us to walk up stairs, and we went; but after I had entered a small room at the end of the parlour, the door was shut behind me by Mr. Ogden, the Attorney General. A chair was given me, which was placed with the back towards a bookcase, at which a man was standing, apparently looking at the books; and besides the two persons I have mentioned, there was but one more in the room,[15] Mr. Grant, the master of the house. Of the first part of the interview I shall not particularly speak.

The two legal gentlemen at length began a mock examination of me, in which they seemed to me to be actuated more by a curiosity no way commendable, than a sincere desire to discover the truth, writing down a few of my answers. In this, however, the person behind me took no active part. One of the questions put to me was, "What are the colours of the carpet in the Superior's room?"

I told what they were, when they turned to him, and inquired whether I had told the truth. He answered only by a short grunt of assent, as if afraid to speak, or even to utter a natural tone; and at the same time, by his hastiness, showed that he was displeased that my answer was correct. I was asked to describe a particular man I had seen in the nunnery, and did so. My examiner partly turned round with some remark or question which was answered in a similar spirit. I turned and looked at the stranger, who was

---

[15] Unless another was concealed—as I suspected.

evidently skulking to avoid my seeing him, and yet listening to every word that was said. I saw enough in his appearance to become pretty well satisfied that I had seen him before; and something in his form or attitude reminded me strongly of the person, whose name had been mentioned. I was then requested to repeat some of the prayers used in the nunnery, and repeated part of the office of the Virgin, and some others.

At length, after I had been in the little room, as I should judge, nearly an hour, I was informed that the examination had been satisfactory, and that I might go.

I then returned home; but no further step was taken by the Attorney General, and he refused, as I understood, to return my affidavit, which had been left in his hands to act upon.

Besides the persons I have mentioned, I had interviews with numbers of others. I learnt from some, that Father Phelan addressed his congregation a second time concerning me, and expressly forbade them to speak to me if they should have an opportunity, on pain of excommunication. It was also said, that he prayed for the family I lived with, that they might be converted.

I repeated to several different persons my willingness to go into the nunnery, and point out visible evidences of the truth of my statements; and when I was told, by one man, who said he had been to the priests, that I had better leave the city, or I would be clapped into prison, I made up my mind that I should like to be imprisoned a little while, because then, I thought I could not be refused a public examination.

Some Canadians were present one day, when the mistress of the house repeated, in my presence, that I was ready to go into the nunnery if protected, and, if I did not convince others of the truth of my assertions, that I would consent to be burned.

"O yes, I dare say," replied one of the men—"the devil would take her off—she knows he would. He would take care of her—we should never be able to get her—the evil spirit!"

A woman present said—"I could light the fire to burn you, myself."

A woman of Montreal, who has a niece in the nunnery, on hearing of what I declared about it, said that if it was true she would help tear it down.

Among those who came to see me, numbers were at first as violent as any I have mentioned, but after a little conversation, became mild and calm. I have heard persons declare, that it would be no harm to kill me, as I had an evil spirit.

One woman told me, that she had seen Father Phelan in the street, talking with a man, to whom he said, that the people were coming to tear down the house in which I stayed, intending afterward to set fire to it in the cellar. This story gave me no serious alarm, for I thought I could see through it evidence of an intention to frighten me, and make me leave the city.[16] I was under great apprehensions, however, one day, in consequence of an accidental discovery of a plan laid to take me off by force. I had stepped into the cellar to get an iron-holder, when I heard the voices of persons in the street above, and recognised those of my mother and the Irish woman her friend. There was another woman with them.

"You go in and lay hold of her," said one voice.

"No, you are her mother—you go in and bring her out—we will help you."

I was almost overcome with dread of falling into their hands, believing that they would deliver me up to the Superior. Hastening into a room, I got behind a bed, told the lady of the house the cause of my fear, and calling to a little girl to bring me my child, I stood in a state of violent agitation. Expecting them in the house every instant, and fearing my infant might cry, and so lead them to the place of my concealment, I put my hand upon its mouth to keep it quiet.

It was thought desirable to get the testimony of the mistress of the house where I spent the night after my escape from the nunnery, as one means of substantiating my story. I had been there the day before my visit to the house of Mr. Grant, accompanied by a friend, and on my first inquiring of her about my nunnery dress, she said she had carried it to the Superior; speaking with haste, as if she apprehended I had some object very different from what I actually had. It now being thought best to summon her as a witness before a magistrate, and not knowing her whole name, we set off again towards her house to make inquiry.

On our way we had to pass behind the parade. I suddenly heard an outcry from a little gallery in the rear of a house which fronts another way, which drew my attention. "There's the nun!" exclaimed a female, after twice clapping her hands smartly together, "There's the nun, there's the nun!"

I looked up, and whom should I see but the Irishwoman, who had taken so active a part, on several occasions in my affairs, on

---

[16] I felt very confident, from some circumstances, that this woman had been sent to bring such a story by Father Phelan; and such evidence of his timidity rather emboldened me. I was in another room when she came, and heard her talking on and abusing me; then coming out, I said, "How dare you say I do not speak the truth?" "God bless you," said she, "sit down and tell me all."

account of her friendship for my mother—the same who had accompanied me to Longeuil in a boat, when I set out for New York, after making arrangements for my journey. She now behaved as if exasperated against me to the utmost; having, as I had no doubt, learnt the object of my journey to Montreal since I had last spoken with her, and having all her Catholic prejudices excited. She screamed out: "There's the nun that's come to swear against our dear Father Phelan. Arrah, lay hold, lay hold upon her! Catch her, kill her, pull her to pieces."

And so saying she hurried down to the street, while a number of women, children, and some men, came running out, and pursued after me. I immediately took to flight, for I did not know what they might do; and she, with the rest, pursued us, until we reached two soldiers, whom we called upon to protect us. They showed a readiness to do so; and when they learnt that we were merely going to a house beyond, and intended to return peaceably, consented to accompany us. The crowd, which might rather be called a mob, thought proper not to offer us any violence in the presence of the soldiers, and after following us a little distance, began to drop off, until all had disappeared. One of the soldiers, however, soon after remarked, that he observed a man following us, whom he had seen in the crowd, and proposed that instead of both of them going before us, one should walk behind, to guard against any design he might have. This was done; and we proceeded to a house near the one where I had found a refuge, and after obtaining the information we sought, returned, still guarded by the soldiers.

All our labour, in this, however, proved unavailing; for we were unable to get the woman to appear in court.

At length it was found impossible to induce the magistrates to do any thing in the case; and arrangements were made for my return to New York. While in the ferry-boat, crossing from Montreal to Laprairie, I happened to be standing near two little girls, when I overheard, the following conversation.

"Why do you leave Montreal so soon?"

"I had gone to spend a week or two; but I heard that Antichrist was in the city, and was afraid to be there. So I am going right home. I would not be in Montreal while Antichrist is there. He has come to destroy the Catholic religion." I felt quite happy when I found myself once more safe in New York; and it has only been since my return from Montreal, and the conviction I had there formed, that it was in vain for me to attempt to get a fair investigation into the Hotel Dieu Nunnery, that I seriously thought of publishing a book. Under some disadvantages this volume has been prepared, and unfortunately its publication has been delayed

139

to a season when it will be difficult to transmit it promptly to all parts of the country. I am sure, however, that in spite of all, no material errors will be found in it uncorrected, though many, very many, facts and circumstances might have been added which would have proved interesting. Indeed I am persuaded, from the experience I have already had, that past scenes, before forgotten, will continue to return to my memory, the longer I dwell upon my convent life, and that many of these will tend to confirm, explain, or illustrate some of the statements now before the public.

But before I close this volume, I must be indulged in saying a word of myself. The narrative through which the reader has now passed, he must not close and lay aside as if it were a fiction; neither would I wish him to forget the subject of it as one worthy only to excite surprise and wonder for a moment.

CONCLUSION

It is desired that the author of this volume may be regarded, not as a voluntary participator in the very guilty transactions which are described; but receive sympathy for the trials which she has endured, and the peculiar situation in which her past experience, and escape from the power of the Superior of the Hotel Dieu Nunnery, at Montreal, and the snares of the Roman priests in Canada, have left her.

My feelings are frequently distressed, and agitated, by the recollection of what I have passed through; and by night, and by day, I have little peace of mind, and few periods of calm and pleasant reflection. Futurity also appears uncertain. I know not what reception this little work may meet with; and what will be the effect of its publication here, or in Canada, among strangers, friends, or enemies. I have given the world the truth, so far as I have gone, on subjects of which I am told they are generally ignorant; and I feel perfect confidence, that any facts which may yet be discovered, will confirm my words, whenever they can be obtained. Whoever shall explore the Hotel Dieu Nunnery, at Montreal, will find unquestionable evidence that the descriptions of the interior of that edifice, given in this book, were furnished by one familiar with them; for whatever alterations may be attempted, there are changes which no mason or carpenter can make and effectually conceal; and therefore, there must be plentiful evidence in that institution of the truth of my description.

There are living witnesses, also, who ought to be made to speak, without fear of penances, tortures, and death; and possibly their testimony, at some future time, may be added to confirm my statements. There are witnesses I should greatly rejoice to see at liberty; or rather there were. Are they living now? or will they be permitted to live after the Priests and Superior have seen this book? Perhaps the wretched nuns in the cells have already suffered for my sake—perhaps Jane Ray has been silenced for ever, or will be murdered, before she has an opportunity to add her most important testimony to mine.

But speedy death, in respect only to this world, can be no great calamity to those who lead the life of a nun. The mere recollection of it always makes me miserable. It would distress the reader, should I repeat the dreams with which I am often terrified at night; for I sometimes fancy myself pursued by my worst enemies; frequently I seem as if shut up again in the Convent; often I imagine myself present at the repetition of the worst scenes that I have hinted at or described. Sometimes I stand by the secret place of interment in the cellar; sometimes I think I can hear the shrieks of helpless females in the hands of atrocious men; and sometimes almost seem actually to look again upon the calm and placid countenance of Saint Francis, as she appeared when surrounded by her murderers.

I cannot banish the scenes and characters of this book from my memory. To me it can never appear like an amusing fable, or lose its interest and importance, the story is one which is continually before me, and must return fresh to my mind, with painful emotions, as long as I live. With time, and Christian instruction, and the sympathy and example of the wise and good, I hope to learn submissively to bear whatever trials are appointed for me, and to improve under them all.

Impressed as I continually am with the frightful reality of the painful communications that I have made in this volume, I can only offer to all persons who may doubt or disbelieve my statements, these two things:—

Permit me to go through the Hotel Dieu Nunnery, at Montreal, with some impartial ladies and gentlemen, that they may compare my account with the interior parts of that building, into which no persons but the Roman Bishop and the priests,[17] are ever admitted; and if they do not find my description true, then discard

---

[17] I should have added, and such persons as they introduce.

me as an impostor. Bring me before a court of justice—there I am willing to meet Lartigue, Dufresne, Phelan, Bonin, and Richards, and their wicked companions, with the Superior, and any of the nuns, before ten thousand men.

MARIA MONK
New York, 11th January, 1836

THE TRUTH
OF THE
"AWFUL DISCLOSURES BY MARIA MONK"
DEMONSTRATED

1. *Early means used to discredit the took. Different of objectors.*—It was anticipated that persons who know little or nothing of the changeless spirit and uniform practices of the Papal ecclesiastics, would doubt or deny the statements which Maria Monk has given of the Hotel Dieu Nunnery at Montreal. The delineations, if true, are so loathsome and revolting, that they exhibit the principles of the Roman priesthood, and the corruption of the monastic system, as combining a social curse, which must be extinguished for the welfare of mankind.

From the period when the intimations were first published in the Protestant Vindicator, that a Nun had escaped from one of the Convents in Canada, and that a narrative of the secrets of that prison-house for females was preparing for the press; attempts have occasionally been made to prejudice the public judgment, by fulsome eulogies of the Roman Priests and Nuns, as paragons of immaculate perfection; and also by infuriated denunciations and calumnies of all persons, who seriously believe that every human institution which directly violates the constitution of nature, and the express commands of God, must necessarily be immoral.

The system of seclusion and celibacy adopted in Convents is altogether unnatural, and subverts all the appointments of Jehovah in reference to the duties and usefulness of man; while the

142

impenetrable secrecy, which is the cement of the gloomy superstructure, not only extirpates every incentive to active virtue, but unavoidably opens the flood-gates of wickedness, without restraint or remorse, because it secures entire impunity.

Since the publication of the "Awful Disclosures," much solicitude has been felt for the result of the exhibitions which they present us: but it is most remarkable, that the incredulity is confined almost exclusively to Protestants, or at least, to those who pretend not to be Papists. The Roman Priests are too crafty to engage directly in any controversy respecting the credibility of Maria Monk's narrative. As long as they can induce the Roman Catholics privately to deny the statements, and to vilify Christians as the inventors of falsehoods concerning "the Holy Church and the Holy Priests!" so long will they laugh at the censures of the Protestants; and as long as they can influence the Editors of political papers vociferously to deny evangelical truth, and to decry every attempt to discover the secrets of the Romish priestcraft as false and uncharitable, so long will the Jesuits ridicule and despise that incredulity which is at once so blinding, deceitful, and dangerous.

The volume entitled "Awful Disclosures by Maria Monk," has been assailed by two classes of Objectors. Some persons affirm that they cannot, and that they will not believe her narrative, because it is so improbable. Who is to judge of the standard of improbabilities? Assuredly not they who are ignorant of the whole subject to which those improbabilities advert. Now it is certain, that persons who are acquainted with Popery, are generally convinced, and readily agree, that Maria Monk's narrative, is very much assimilated to the abstract view which a sound judgment, enlightened by the Holy Scriptures, would form of that antichristian system, as predicted by the prophet Daniel, and the apostles, Peter, Paul, and John.

2. *The question of Probability.*—But the question of probabilities may be tested by another fact; and that is the full, unshaken conviction, and the serious declaration of many persons who have lived in Canada, that Maria Monk's allegations against the Roman Priests and Nuns in that province, are precisely the counterpart of their ordinary character, spirit, and practice. There are many persons now residing in the city of New York, who long dwelt in Montreal and Quebec; and who are thoroughly acquainted with the situation of affairs among the Canadian Papists—and such of them as are known, with scarcely a dissenting voice, proclaim the same facts which every traveller, who has any discernment or curiosity, learns when he makes the northern summer tour. It is

also indubitable, that intelligent persons in Canada generally, especially residents in Montreal and Quebec, who have no inducement either to falsify or to conceal the truth, uniformly testify, that the nunneries in those cities are notorious places of resort for the Roman Priests for habitual and unrestrained licentiousness; that, upon the payment of the stipulated price to the Chaplain, other persons, in the disguise of Priests, are regularly admitted within the Convents for the same infamous purpose; and that many Infants and Nuns, in proportion to the aggregate amount of the whole body of females, are annually murdered and buried within their precincts. All this turpitude is as assuredly believed by the vast majority of the enlightened Protestants, as well as by multitudes of even the Papists in Montreal and Quebec, as their own existence; and judging from their declarations, they have no more doubt of the fact, than they have of the summer's sunshine, and the winter's frost and snow. Of what value, therefore, is the cavil of ignorance respecting improbabilities?

But it is also objected, that the British government would not tolerate such a system of enormous wickedness. To which it is replied, that the inordinate licentiousness of the Roman Priests and Nuns in Canada, is demonstrated to be of long standing by the archives of that Province, as may be seen in Smith's History of Canada; year 1733, Chapter 5, p. 194.

The author of that work is Secretary of the Province; and his narrative was compiled immediately from the public documents, which are under his official guardianship and control. He thus writes:—"The irregularities and improper conduct of the Nuns of the General Hospital had been the subject of much regret and anxiety. Contrary to every principle of their institution, they frequently accepted of invitations to dinners and suppers, and mixed in society, without considering the vows which restricted them to their Convent. The king of France directed a letter, Maurepas' letter of April 9, 1733, to be written to the Coadjutor of Quebec, by the minister having the department of the Marine; importing that the king was much displeased with the Nuns—that regularity and order might be restored by reducing the nuns to the number of twelve, according to their original establishment—and that, as the management and superintendence of the community had been granted to the Governor, Prelate, and Intendant, the Coadjutor should take the necessary measures to prevent them from repeating conduct so indecent and improper."

The entire affair seems to have been this; that the Nuns of Quebec at that period preferred the gallant military officers, and their bewitching festivities, to the coarser and less diversified indulgences of the Jesuits; upon which the latter murmured, and resolved to hinder the soldiers from intruding into their fold, and among the cloistered females, to visit whom they claimed as their own peculiar privilege, inseparably attached to their priestly character and ecclesiastical functions. It is infallibly certain that after a lapse of 100 years, neither the Jesuits nor the Nuns in Canada, are in the smallest particle reformed.

The British government, by the treaty made upon the surrender of that province to them, guarantied to the Papal Ecclesiastics, both male and female, their prior exemptions and special immunities. Many of the officers of the Government in Canada, who have long resided there, are anxious to see the nunneries and their adjuncts totally extirpated; and it may be safely asserted that they know the character given of those institutions by Maria Monk is a graphical picture of their continuous doings.

The British government, for the purpose of retaining their supremacy over the province, have not only connived at those irregularities, but have always enjoined that the public sanction should be given to their puerile shows, and their pageant, pompous processions by the attendance of the civil and military officers upon them, and by desecrating the Lord's day with martial music, &c. In this particular affair, the executive officers of the Provincial Government are fully apprised of all the substantial facts in the case; for an affidavit of the principal circumstances was presented to Mr. Ogden, the Attorney General of Canada, and to Mr. Grant, another of the King's counsellors: and afterward Maria Monk did undergo an examination by those gentlemen, in the house of Mr. Grant, at Montreal, in the presence of Mr. Comte, one of the superior order of priests of that city; and of another Priest, believed to be either Phelan or Dufresne, who was concealed behind the sofa.

It is also incontrovertible, that the nominal Papists in Canada, who, in reality, are often infidels, notwithstanding their jocose sneers, and affected contempt, do generally believe every title of Maria Monk's narrative. This is the style in which they talk of it. They first, according to custom, loudly curse the authors; for to find a Papist infidel who does not break the third commandment, is as difficult as to point out a moral Roman Priest or a chaste Nun. They first swear at the author, and then, with a hearty laugh, add the following illustration:—"Everybody knows that the Priests are a jolly set of fellows, who live well, and must have license, or they would be contrary to nature. They have the privilege of going into the nunneries, and they would be great fools if they did not use and enjoy it!" Such is the exact language which is adopted among the Canadians; and such are the precise words which have been used by

Canadian gentlemen in New York, when criticising Maria Monk's volume. It affords stronger proof than a direct attestation.

The other class of persons who verily believe the "Awful Disclosures," are the religious community in Canada. We think that scarcely a well-informed person can be discovered in Montreal or Quebec, who does not feel assured, that the interior of the Hotel Dieu Nunnery is most faithfully depicted by Maria Monk. Many persons are now inhabitants of New York who formerly resided in Montreal, some of whom have been upon terms of familiar intimacy for years with those Roman Priests, who are specified as the principal actors in the scenes depicted in that book; and they most solemnly declare, that they have no doubt of the truth of Maria Monk's narrative.

Mr. Samuel B. Smith, who has been not only a Roman Priest, but has had several cages of nuns under his sole management, questioned Maria Monk expressly respecting those affairs, customs and ceremonies, which appertain only to nunneries, because they cannot be practiced by any other females but those who are shut up in those dungeons; and, after having minutely examined her, he plainly averred that it was manifest she could not have known the things which she communicated to him unless she had been a nun; not merely a scholar, or a temporary resident, or even a novice, but a nun, who had taken the veil, in the strictest sense of the appellative. This testimony is of the more value, because the conclusion does not depend upon any conflicting statements, of partial or prejudicial witnesses, but upon a fact which is essential to the system of monachism; that no persons can know all the secrets of nunneries, but the Chaplain, the Abbess, and their accomplices in that "mystery of iniquity." Mr. Smith's declaration in one other respect is absolutely decisive. He has declared not only that Maria Monk has been a nun, but also that the descriptions which she gives are most minutely accurate.

Mr. Smith also testifies that the account which Maria Monk gives of the proceedings of the priests, the obscene questions which they ask young females, and their lewd practices with them at auricular confession, are constantly exemplified by the Roman Priests; and he also confirms her statements, by the testimony of his own individual experience, and actual personal acquaintance with the Canadian nunneries, as well as with those in the United States, and especially of that at Monroe, Michigan, which was dissolved by Mr. Fenwick, on account of scandalous impurity, several years ago.

Mrs. ——, a widow lady now in New York, who formerly was a Papist in Montreal, and was recently converted to Christianity, solemnly avers, that the Priest Richards himself, conducted her

146

from the Seminary through the subterraneous passage to the nunnery, and describes the whole exactly in accordance with the statement of Maria Monk.

Mr. Lloyd, who was in business a number of years adjacent to the nunnery, and who is intimately acquainted with those priests, their characters, principles, and habits, avows his unqualified conviction of the truth of the "Awful Disclosures."

Mr. Hogan, who was eighteen months in the Jesuit Seminary at Montreal, and in constant intercourse and attendance upon Lartigue and his accomplices, unequivocally affirms, that Maria Monk's complex description of those Priests are most minutely and accurately true.

One hundred other persons probably can be adduced, who, during their residence in Canada, or on their tours to that province, by inquiries ascertained that things in accordance with Maria Monk's delineations are the undoubted belief of each class of persons, and of every variety of condition, and in all places which they visited in Lower Canada.

Mr. Greenfield, the father of the gentleman who owns the two steamboats on the river St. Lawrence, called the Lady of the Lake, and the Canadian Eagle, who is a citizen of New York, avows his unqualified assent to all Maria Monk's statements, and most emphatically adds—"Maria Monk has not disclosed one tenth part of the truth respecting the Roman Priests and Nuns in Canada."

Fifty other persons from that province, now residing in New York, likewise attest the truth of the "Disclosures."

At Sorel, Berthier, and Three Rivers, the usual stopping-places for the steamboats on the River St. Lawrence, the Priests, if they have any cause to be at the wharf, may be seen accompanied by one or more children, their "Nephews," as the Priests facetiously denominate their offspring; and if any person on the steamboat should be heard expatiating upon the piety, the temperance, the honesty, or the purity of Roman Priests and Nuns, he would be laughed at outright, either as a natural or an ironical jester; while the priest himself would join in the merriment, as being a "capital joke."

We are assured by the most indisputable authority in Montreal, that the strictly religious people in that city do generally credit Maria Monk's statements without hesitation; and the decisive impression of her veracity can never be removed. If it were possible at once to reform the nunneries, and to transform them from castles of ignorance, uncleanness, and murder, where all their arts are concealed in impervious secrecy, into abodes of wisdom, chastity, and benevolence to every recess of which all persons, at every hour, might have unrestricted admission—that would not change the past; it would leave them indelibly branded with the emphatical title applied to the nunnery at Charlestown, "FILTHY, MURDEROUS DENS."

3. *Who are those who deny the truth of the book? Case of Father Conroy. Father Conroy's deception.*

In addition to the objections from improbability, another series of opposition consists of flat, broad denials of the truth of Maria Monk's "Awful Disclosures." This mode of vanquishing direct charges is even more invalid than the former futile cavilling. It is also remarkable, when we remember who are the persons that deny the statements made by Maria Monk. Are they the Roman Priests implicated? Not at all. They are too crafty. The only persons who attempt to hint even a suspicion of the truth of the secrets divulged in the "Awful Disclosures," are editors of Newspapers: some of whom are ever found on the side of infidelity and vice; men always reproaching religion; and directly calumniating, or scornfully ridiculing the best Christians in the land; and profoundly ignorant of Popery and Jesuitism, and the monastic system.

It is true that Priest Conroy of New York, has contradicted in general terms the truth of the statement respecting himself, and his attempt to abduct Maria Monk from the Almshouse. But what does he deny? He is plainly charged, in the "Awful Disclosures," with a protracted endeavor, by fraud or by force to remove Maria Monk from that institution. Now that charge involves a flagrant misdemeanor, or it is a wicked and gross libel. Let him answer the following questions:

Did he not frequently visit the house, and lurk about at various times, for longer and shorter periods, expressly to have an interview with Maria Monk?

Did he not state that he was acquainted with her by the name she bore in the nunnery, Sainte Eustace.

Did he not declare that he was commissioned by Lartigue, Phelan, Dufresne, Kelly, and the Abbess of the Hotel Dieu Nunnery at Montreal, to obtain a possession of her, that she might be sent back to the abode of the Furies?

Did he not offer her any thing she pleased to demand, provided she would reside with the Ursulines of this city?

Did he not also declare that he would have her at all risks, and that she could not escape him?

Did he not persevere in this course of action, until he was positively assured that she would not see him, and that the Priest Conroy should not have access to Maria Monk?

Was not the priest Kelly, from Canada, in New York at that

period, prompting Conroy; and did not that same Kelly come on here expressly to obtain possession of Maria Monk, that he might carry her back to the Hotel Dieu Nunnery, there to murder her, as his accomplices have smothered, poisoned, and bled to death other victims of their beastly licentiousness?

All these questions are implied in Maria Monk's statement, and they involve the highest degree of crime against the liberty, rights, and life of Maria Monk, and the laws of New York, and the charge is either true or false. Why does not the Priest Conroy try it? Why does he not demonstrate that he is calumniated, by confronting the Authoress and Publishers of the book before an impartial jury. We are assured that the Executive committee of the New York Protestant Association will give ten dollars to any Lawyer, whom Mr. Conroy will authorize to institute a civil suit for libel, payable at the termination of the process. Will he subject the question to that scrutiny? Never. He would rather follow the example of his fellow priests, and depart from New York. Many of the Maynooth Jesuits, after having fled from Ireland for their crimes, to this country, to avoid the punishments due to them for the repetition of them in the United States, and to elude discovery, have assumed false names and gone to France; or in disguise have joined their dissolute companions in Canada.

It is also a fact, that the Priest, named Quarter, with one of his minions, did visit the house where Maria Monk resides, on the 13th day of February, 1836; and did endeavor to see her alone, under the false pretext of delivering to her a packet from her brother in Montreal; and as an argument for having an interview with her without company, one of the two impostors did protest that he had a parcel from John Monk; which "he had sworn not to deliver except into the hands of his sister in person." Now what object had Mr. Quarter in view; and what was his design in going to her residence between nine and ten o'clock at night, under a lying pretence? Mr. Quarter comes from Canada. He knows all the Priests of Montreal. For what purpose did he assume a fictitious character, and utter base and wilful falsehoods, that, he might have access to her, with another man, when Maria Monk, as they hoped, would be without a protector? For what ignoble design did he put an old Truth Teller into a parcel, and make his priest-ridden minion declare that it was a very valuable packet of letters from John Monk? That strange contrivance requires explanation. Did Priest Quarter believe that Maria Monk was in Montreal? Did he doubt her personal identity? Does not that fact alone verity that all the Roman Priests are confederated? Does it not prove that her delineations are correct? Does it not evince that the Papal Ecclesiastics dread the disclosures?

149

4. *The great ultimate test which the nature of this case demands. Challenge of the New York Protestant Association.*—It is readily admitted, that the heinous charges which are made by Maria Monk against the Roman priests cannot easily be rebutted in the usual form of disproving criminal allegations. The denial of those Priests is good for nothing, and they cannot show an alibi. But there is one mode of destroying Maria Monk's testimony, equally prompt and decisive, and no other way is either feasible, just, or can be efficient. That method is the plan proposed by the New York Protestant Association.

The Hotel Dieu Nunnery is in Montreal. Here is Maria Monk's description of its interior apartments and passages. She offers to go to Montreal under the protection of a committee of four members of the New York Protestant Association, and in company with four gentlemen of Montreal, to explore the Nunnery; and she also voluntarily proposes that if her descriptions of the interior of the Hotel Dieu Nunnery are not found to be true, she will surrender herself to Lartigue and his confederates to torture her in what way they may please, or will bear the punishment of the civil laws as a base and wilful slanderer of the Canadian Jesuit Ecclesiastics.

When Lartigue, Bonin, Dufresne, Phelan, Richards, and their fellows, accede to this proposition, we shall hesitate respecting Maria Monk's veracity; until then, by all impartial and intelligent judges, and by enlightened Protestants and Christians, the "Awful Disclosures" will be pronounced undeniable facts. The scrutiny, however, respecting Maria Monk's credibility comprises two general questions, to which we shall succinctly reply.

I. *Was Maria Monk a Nun in the Hotel Dieu Convent at Montreal?*—In ordinary cases, to dispute respecting a circumstance of that kind would be deemed a most strange absurdity; and almost similar to an inquiry into a man's personal identity when his living form is before your eyes. Maria Monk says she was a nun, presents you a book descriptive of the Convent in which she resided, and leaves the fact of her abode there to be verified by the minute accuracy of her delineations of arcana, with which only the visiting Roman Priests and the imprisoned nuns are acquainted. That test, neither Lartigue nor the Priests will permit to be applied; and therefore, so far, Maria Monk's testimony cannot directly be corroborated. It is however not a little remarkable, that no one of all the persons so boldly impeached by her of the most atrocious crimes, has, even whispered a hint that she was not a nun; while the priest Conroy has confirmed that fact far more certainly than if he had openly asserted its truth.

5. *The Testimony of Mrs. Monk considered.*—The only

evidence against that fact is her mother. Now it is undeniable, that her mother is a totally incompetent witness. She is known in Montreal to be a woman of but little principle; and her oath in her daughter's favour would be injurious to her; for she is so habitually intemperate, that it is questionable whether she is ever truly competent to explain any matters which come under her notice. Truth requires this declaration, although Maria, with commendable filial feelings, did not hint at the fact. Besides, during a number of years past, she has exhibited a most unnatural aversion, or rather animosity, to her daughter; so that to her barbarous usage of Maria when a child, may be imputed the subsequent scenes through which she has passed. When appealed to respecting her daughter, her uniform language was such as this—"I do not care what becomes of her, or who takes her, or where she goes, or what is done to her, provided she keeps away from me." It is also testified by the most unexceptionable witnesses in Montreal, that when Maria Monk went to that city in August, 1835, and first made known her case, that Mrs. Monk repeatedly declared, that her daughter had been a Nun; and that she had been in the Nunneries at Montreal a large portion of her life. She also avowed, that the offer of bribery that had been made unto her, had been made, not by Protestants, to testify that her daughter Maria had been an inmate of the Hotel Dieu Nunnery; but by the Roman Priests, who had promised her one hundred dollars, if she would make an affidavit that Maria had not been in that nunnery at all; and would also swear to any other matters which they dictated. Now there is little room for doubt, that the affidavit to the truth of which she finally swore was thus obtained; for she has not capacity to compose such a narrative, nor has she been in a state of mind, for a number of years past, to understand the details which have thus craftily been imposed upon the public in her name. When she had no known inducement to falsify the fact in August, 1835, before the Priests became alarmed, then she constantly affirmed that her daughter had been a Nun; but after Lartigue and his companions were assured that her daughter's narrative would appear, then the mother was probably bribed, formally to swear to a wilful falsehood; for it is most probable, that she either did not see, or from intoxication could not comprehend, the contents of the paper to which her signature is affixed. Her habitual intemperance, her coarse impiety, her long-indulged hatred and cruelty towards her daughter, and her flat self-contradictions, with her repeated and public declarations, that she had been offered a large sum of money by the Montreal Priests, thus to depreciate her daughter's allegations, and to attest upon oath precisely the contrary to that which she had previously declared, to

151

persons whose sole object was to ascertain the truth—all those things demonstrate that Mrs. Monk's evidence is of no worth; and yet that is all the opposite evidence which can be adduced.

6. *Testimony in favour of the book.*—Mr. Miller the son of Adam Miller, a well known teacher at St. John's, who has known Maria Monk from her childhood, and who is now a resident of New York, solemnly attests, that in the month of August, 1833, he made inquiries of Mrs. Monk respecting her daughter Maria, and that Mrs. Monk informed him that Maria was then a Nun! that she had taken the veil previous to that conversation, and that she had been in the nunnery for a number of years. Mr. Miller voluntarily attests to that fact. He was totally ignorant of Maria Monk's being out of the Nunnery at Montreal, until he saw her book, and finally by searching out her place of abode, renewed the acquaintance with her which had existed between them from the period when she attended his father's school in her childhood. See the affidavit of William Miller.

When Maria Monk made her escape, as she states, from the Hotel Dieu Nunnery, she took refuge in the house of a woman named Lavalliere in Elizabeth street, Montreal, the second or third door from the corner of what is commonly called "the Bishop's Church." Madame Lavalliere afterward admitted, that Maria Monk did arrive at her house at the time specified, in the usual habiliments of a Nun, and made herself known as an eloped Nun; that she provided her with other clothing; and that she afterward carried the Nun's garments to the Hotel Dieu Nunnery.

After her escape, Maria Monk narrates that she went on board a steamboat for Quebec, intending thereby to avoid being seized and again transferred to the Nunnery, that she was recognised by the Captain, was kept under close watch during the whole period of the stay of that boat at Quebec, and merely by accident escaped the hands of the Priests, by watching for an unexpected opportunity to gain the shore during the absence of the Captain, and the momentary negligence of the female attendant in the cabin. The woman was called Margaret ——, the other name is forgotten. The name of the Master of the steamboat is probably known and he has never pretended to deny that statement, that he did thus detain Maria Monk, would not permit her to go on shore at Quebec, and that he also conducted her back to Montreal; having suspected or ascertained that she was a Nun who had clandestinely escaped from a Convent.

7. *Corroborative evidence unintentionally furnished by the opponents of the book.*—After her flight from the steamboat, she was found early in the morning, in a very perilous situation, either

152

on the banks, or partly in Lachine Canal, and was committed to the public prison by Dr. Robertson, whence she was speedily released through the intervention of Mr. Esson, one of the Presbyterian ministers of Montreal. Upon this topic, her statement coincides exactly with that of Dr. Robertson.

But he also states—"Although incredulous as to the truth of Maria Monk's story, I thought it incumbent upon me to make some inquiry concerning it, and have ascertained where she has been residing a great part of the time she states having been an inmate of the Nunnery. During the summer of 1832, she was at service at William Henry; the winters of 1832-3, she passed in this neighborhood at St. Ours and St. Denis."

That is most remarkable testimony, because, although Papists may justly be admitted to know nothing of times and dates, unless by their Carnivals, their Festivals, their Lent, or their Penance—yet Protestant Magistrates might be more precise. Especially, as it is a certain fact, that no person at Sorel can be discovered, who is at all acquainted with such a young woman in service in the summer of 1832. It is true, she did reside at St. Denis or St. Ours, as the Roman Priests can testify; but not at the period specified by Dr. Robertson.

For the testimony of a decisive witness in favour of Maria Monk, see the statement of an old schoolmate in Appendix.

8. *Summary view of the evidence.*—Let us sum up this contradictory evidence respecting the simple fact, whether Maria Monk was a resident of the Hotel Dieu Nunnery or not?

Her mother says—"I denied that my daughter had ever been in a Nunnery." Dr. Robertson informed us—"I have ascertained where she has been residing a great part of the time she states having been an inmate of the Nunnery." That is all which can be adduced to contradict Maria Monk's statement.

This is a most extraordinary affair, that a young woman's place of abode cannot be accurately discovered during several years, when all the controversy depends upon the fact of that residence. Why did not Dr. Robertson specify minutely with whom Maria Monk lived at service at William Henry, in the summer of 1832?— Why did not Dr. Robertson exactly designate where, and with whom, she resided at St. Denis and St. Ours, in the winters of 1832 and 1833? The only answer to these questions is this—Dr. Robertson cannot. He obtained his contradictory information most probably from her mother, or from the Priest Kelly, and then embodied it in his affidavit to regain that favour and popularity with the Montreal Papists which he has so long lost. We are convinced that neither the evidence of Mrs. Monk, nor Dr. Robertson, would be of a feather's weight in a court of justice against the other witnesses, Mrs. ——, and Mr. William Miller.

Maria Monk asserts, that she was a resident of the Hotel Dieu Nunnery during the period designated by Dr. Robertson, which is familiarly denominated the Cholera summer. In her narrative she develops a variety of minute and characteristic details of proceedings in that Institution, connected with things which all persons in Montreal know to have actually occurred, and of events which it is equally certain did happen, and which did not transpire anywhere else; and which is impossible could have taken place at Sorel or William Henry; because there is no Nunnery there; and consequently her descriptions would be purely fabricated and fictitious.

But the things asserted are not inventions of imagination. No person could thus delineate scenes which he had not beheld; and therefore Maria Monk witnessed them; consequently, she was a member of that family community; for the circumstances which she narrates nowhere else occurred. At all events, it seems more reasonable to suppose that an individual can more certainly tell what had been his own course of life, than persons who, by their own admission, know nothing of the subject; and especially when her statements are confirmed by such unexceptionable witnesses. There are, however, two collateral points of evidence which strongly confirm Maria Monk's direct statements. One is derived from the very character of the acknowledgments which she made, and the period when they were first disclosed. "A death-bed," says the Poet, "is a detector of the heart." Now it is certain, that the appalling facts which she states, were not primarily made in a season of hilarity, or with any design to "make money" by them, or with any expectation that they would be known to any other person than Mr. Hilliker, Mr. Tappan, and a few others at Bellevue; but when there was no anticipation that her life would be prolonged, and when agonized with the most dreadful retrospection and prospects.

It is not possible to believe, that any woman would confess those facts which are divulged by Maria Monk, unless from dread of death and the judgment to come, or from the effect of profound Christian penitence. Feminine repugnance would be invincible. Thus, the alarm of eternity, her entrance upon which appeared to be so immediate, was the only cause of those communications; which incontestably prove, that Nunneries are the very nurseries of the most nefarious crimes, and the most abandoned transgressors.

The other consideration is this—that admitting the statements to be true, Maria Monk could not be unconscious of the malignity of Roman Priests, and of her own danger; and if her statements were fictitious, she was doubly involving herself in irreparable disgrace and ruin. In either case, as long as she was in New York she was personally safe; and as her disclosures had been restricted to very few persons, she might have withdrawn from the public institution, and in privacy have passed away her life, "alike unknowing and unknown." Lunacy itself could only have instigated a woman situated as she was, to visit Montreal, and there defy the power, and malice, and fury of the Roman Priests, and their myrmidons; by accumulating upon them charges of rape, infanticide, the affliction of the tortures of the Inquisition, and murders of cold-blooded ferocity in the highest degree, with all the atrocious concomitant iniquities which those prolific sins include.

Now it is certain, that she was not deranged; and she was not forced. She went deliberately, and of her own accord, to meet the Popish Priests upon the spot where their crimes are perpetrated, and the stronghold of their power. Whether that measure was the most prudent and politic for herself, and the most wise and efficient for the acquisition of the avowed object, may be disputed; but the exemplary openness and the magnanimous daring of that act cannot be controverted.

The narrative, pages 116 to 127, respecting the cholera and the election riots at Montreal, both which scenes happened at the period when Dr. Robertson says Maria Monk was at William Henry, or St. Denis, or St. Ours; could not have been described, at least that part of it respecting the wax candles, and the preparation for defence, except by a resident of the Nunnery.

It is a public, notorious fact, that "blessed candles" were made, and sold by the Nuns, and used at Montreal under the pretext to preserve the houses from the Cholera, and to drive it away; that those candles were directed so to be kept burning by the pretended injunction of the Pope; and that large quantities of the Nunnery candles were dispersed about Montreal and its vicinity, which were fixed at a high price; and whoever suffered by the Cholera, the Nuns and their Masters, the Priests, could truly say—"By this craft we have our wealth." Acts 19:25. It is obvious, that a young Papist woman at service at William Henry, could know no more of those matters, than if she had been at Labrador; for the incidental remark with which that part of the narrative commences, is one of those apparently superfluous intimations, which it is evident a person who was writing a fiction would not introduce; and yet it is so profoundly characteristic of a Canadian Convent, that its very simple artlessness at once obliterates Dr. Robertson's affidavit. "There were a few instances, and only a few, in which we knew any thing that was happening in the world; and even then our knowledge did not extend out of the city." We cannot be infallibly certain of Maria Monk's description of the interior of the Nunnery; but that unpremeditated remark, so minutely descriptive of the predominating ignorance among the Nuns of all terrestrial concerns exterior of the Convent, is satisfactory proof that the narrator was not sketching from fancy, but depicting from actual life.

From those testimonies, direct and unintentional, it is fully evident, that Maria Monk was a long resident, and is profoundly acquainted with the doings in the Hotel Dieu Convent at Montreal.

II. What collateral evidence can be adduced of the truth of the "Awful Disclosures" by Maria Monk?

1. One corroborative testimony is derived from the silence of the Roman Priests and their avowed partisans. Months have passed away since the first statements of those matters were made, and also the defence of the Priests, with the affidavits and other connected circumstances, were presented to the public in the Protestant Vindicator. One of the persons in Montreal, who was in favour of the Jesuits, Mr. Doucet, stated that "the Priests never take up such things; they allow their character to defend itself." There was a time when that contemptuous course would have sufficed, or rather, when to have spoken the truth of the Roman Priests would have cost a man his life, and overwhelmed his family in penury, disgrace, and anguish. The Canadian Jesuits may be assured that time has passed away, never more to return. They must take up this thing; for their characters cannot defend themselves; and every enlightened man in Canada knows, that in a moral aspect, they cannot be defended.

Argument, denial, affidavits, if they could reach from Montreal to New York, and the oaths of every Papist and Infidel in Canada,—from Joseph Signay, the Popish Prelate of Quebec and Jean Jacques Lartigue, the Suffragan of Montreal, down to the most profligate of the half-pay military officers, among whom are to be found some of the dregs of the British army, all of them will avail nothing. They are not worth a puff of wind against the internal evidence of Maria Monk's book, in connexion with the rejection of the proposal of the New York Protestant Association, that the Nunnery shall undergo a strict and impartial examination. It is one of the remarkable evidences of the extraordinary delusion which blinds, or the infatuation which enchains the public mind, that men will not credit the corruptions and barbarities of Romanism. To account for this stupefaction among persons who are wide awake to every other system of deadly evil, is almost impossible. Popery necessarily extirpates the rights of man. It ever has destroyed the well-being of society. By it, all municipal law and domestic obligations are abrogated: It always subverts national prosperity and stability; and it is the invincible extinguisher of all true morality and genuine religion. Notwithstanding, men will give credence neither to its own avowed principles, character, and spirit; nor to the unavoidable effects which constantly have flowed from its operations and predominance.

In any other case but one exposing the abominations of Popery, such a volume as Maria Monk's "Awful Disclosures" would have been received without cavil; and immediate judicial measures would have been adopted, to ascertain the certainty of the alleged facts, and the extent and aggravation of their criminality. But now persons are calling for more evidence, when, if they reflected but for a moment, they would perceive, that the only additional evidence possible, is under the entire control of the very persons who are criminated; and to whom the admission of further testimony would be the accumulation of indelible ignominy.

The pretence, that it is contrary to their rules to allow strangers to explore the interior of a nunnery, only adds insult to crime. Why should a Convent be exempt from search, more than any other edifice? Why should Roman Priests be at liberty to perpetrate every deed of darkness in impenetrable recesses called nunneries? Why should one body of females, shut up in a certain species of mansion, to whom only one class of men have unrestricted access, be excluded from all public and legal supervision, more than any other habitation of lewd women, into which all men may enter? As citizens of the United States, we do not pretend to have any authoritative claim to explore a convent within the dominion of a foreign potentate. The Roman Priests of Canada, exercise a vast influence, and are completely intertwined with the Jesuits, in this republic. Therefore, when they remember the extinction of the nunneries at Monroe, Michigan, Charlestown, and Pittsburg; and when they recollect, that the delineations of Maria Monk, if they produce no effect in Canada, will assuredly render female convents in the United States very suspicious and insecure; if they have any solicitude for their confederates, they will intrepidly defy research, and dauntlessly accept the offer of the New York Protestant Association: that a joint committee of disinterested, enlightened and honorable judges, should fully investigate, and equitably decide upon the truth or falsehood of Maria Monk's averments. Their ominous silence, their affected contempt, and their audacious refusal, are calculated only to convince every impartial person, of even the smallest discernment, of the real state of things in that edifice; that the chambers of pollution are above, and that the dungeon of torture and death are below; and that they

157

dread the exposure of the theatre on which their horrible tragedies are performed.

It is also a fact publicly avowed by certain Montreal Papists themselves, and extensively told in taunt and triumph, that they have been employed as masons and carpenters by the Roman Priests, since Maria Monk's visit to Montreal in August, 1835, expressly to alter various parts of the Hotel Dieu Convent, and to close up some of the subterraneous passages and cells in that nunnery. This circumstance is not pretended even to be disputed or doubted; for when the dungeons under ground are spoken of before the Papists, their remark is this: "Eh bien! mais vous ne les trouverez pas, à present; on les a caché hors de vue. Very well, you will not find them there now; they are closed up, and out of sight." Why was the manoeuvre completed? Manifestly, that in urgent extremity, a casual explorer might be deceived, by the apparent proof that the avenues, and places of imprisonment and torture which Maria Monk describes are not discoverable. Now that circumstance might not even been suspected, if the Papist workmen themselves had not openly boasted of the chicanery by which the Priests, who employed them, expected to blind and deceive the Protestants. For in reference to the Romanists, a Popish Priest well knows that nothing more is necessary than for him to assert any absurdity, however gross or impossible, and attest it by the five crosses on his vestments, and his own superstitious vassal believes it with more assurance than his own personal identity. But the filling up and the concealment of the old apertures in the nunnery, by the order of the Roman Priests are scarcely less powerful corroborative proof of Maria Monk's delineations, than ocular and palpable demonstration.

2. Some of the circumstances attending Maria Monk's visit to Montreal, in August, 1835, add great weight in favour of the truth, which no cavils, skepticism, scorn, nor menaces, can counterbalance.

We will however state one very recent occurrence, because it seems to us, that it alone is almost decisive of the controversy. A counsellor of Quebec—his name is omitted merely from delicacy and prudential considerations—has been in New York since the publication of the "Awful Disclosures" His mind was so much influenced by the perusal of that volume, that he sought out the Authoress, and most closely searched into the credibility of her statements. Before the termination of the interview, that gentleman became so convinced of the truth of the picture which Maria Monk drew of the interior of the Canadian Nunneries, that he expressed himself to the following effect:—"My daughter, about 15 years of age, is in the Ursuline Convent at Quebec. I will return home immediately; and if I cannot remove her any other way, I will drag her out by the hair of her head, and raise a noise about their ears that shall not soon be quieted."

That gentleman did so return to Quebec, since which he has again visited New York; and he stated, that upon his arrival in Quebec, he went to the Convent, and instantly removed his daughter from the Ursuline Nunnery; from whom he ascertained, as far as she had been initiated into the mysteries, that Maria Monk's descriptions of Canadian Nunneries, are most minutely and undeniably accurate.

We have already remarked, that Mrs. ——, Mr. Lloyd, Mr. Hogan, and Mr. Smith, who was a Papist Priest, with scores of other persons who formerly resided in Montreal, all express their unqualified belief of the statements made by Maria Monk. Mr. Ogden's acquaintance with the facts, as Attorney General, and that of other officers of the Provincial Government, have also been noticed. The ensuing additional circumstances are of primary importance to a correct estimate of the value which should be attached to the crafty silence of the Roman Priests and the impudent denials of infidel profligates.

Mr. Bouthillier, one of the Montreal Magistrates, called at Mr. Johnson's house where Maria Monk stayed, in the month of August, 1835, when visiting Montreal.

He addressed her and said:—"There is some mystery about Novices—What is it? and asked how long a woman must be a novice before she can take the veil?" Having been answered, Mr. Bouthillier then desired Maria Monk to describe the Superior of the Hotel Dieu Nunnery. As soon as it was done, he became enraged, and said—"Vous dites un mensonge, vous en savez. You lie, you know you do?"—Mr. Bouthillier next inquired—"Was Mr. Tabeau in the Holy Retreat when you left the Convent?" She answered "Yes." To which he replied in French—"Anybody might have answered that question." Something having been said about the Hotel Dieu Nuns being confined to their convent, Mr. Bouthillier declared, that they were allowed to go about the streets. He was told that could not be the case, for it was a direct violation of the rules for Nuns to depart from the Hotel Dieu Nunnery. He replied—"Ce n'est pas vrai. That is not true," Mr. Bonthillier then became very angry, and applied to Maria Monk some very abusive epithets, for which a gentleman in the room reproved him. It was evident, that he lost his temper because he had lost his argument, and his hopes of controverting her statements.

On the Lord's day after Maria Monk's arrival in Montreal, and when the matter had become well known and much talked about, Phelan, the Priest, at the end of mass, addressed the Papists, who were assembled to hear mass, to this effect: "There is a certain nun in this city who has left our faith, and joined the Protestants. She has a child of which she is ready to swear I am the father. She wishes in this way to take my gown from me. If I knew where to find her, I would put her in prison. I mention this to guard you against being deceived by what she may say. The Devil now has such hold upon people that there is danger lest some might believe her story." He then pretended to weep, and appeared to be overcome with feeling. A number of the people gathered around him, and he said: "That nun is Antichrist. She is not a human being, but an evil spirit, who got among the Catholics, and was admitted into the nunnery, where she learned the rules." He also stated, that "in that nun, the prophecy respecting the coming of Antichrist is fulfilled, to break down the Catholic religion." Such was Phelan's address to the people. He declared that Maria Monk had been a nun. Now he knew her, for he saw her in Montreal, where she could not know him. It would have saved all further inquiry and research, if, instead of denouncing her after mass, he had merely assented to Maria Monk's proposition, to be confronted with those Roman Priests and nuns before impartial witnesses in the Hotel Dieu Convent.

One of the most impressively characteristic circumstances which occurred during Maria Monk's visit to Montreal in Aug. 1835, was an interview at Mr. Johnson's house with a carpenter who had heard Phelan's denunciation of Maria Monk after mass.

The heinous destruction of all domestic confidence and of all female purity, is known to be the constant and general practice, not only in Canada, but in all other Popish countries, and among Papists in every part of the world. For in truth it is only fulfilling the authentic dogmas of their own system. The following authoritative principles are divulged in the Corpus Juris Canonici, which contains the Decretals, Canons, &c. of the Popes and Councils; and other participants of the pretended Papal infallibility. "If the Pope fall into homicide or adultery, he cannot be accused, but is excused by the murders of Samson, and the adultery of David." Hugo, Glossa, distinc. 40 Chapter, Non vos.—"Likewise if any Priest is found embracing a woman, it must be presupposed and expounded that he doth it to bless her!"—Glossa, Caus. 12. Quest. 3. Chapter Absis. According to the Pope's bull he who does not believe those doctrines is accursed.

As that carpenter was completely overcome by the recollection of the Priest's information and caution about his marriage, he desisted from any further questions; but upon Maria Monk's declaration, that she was desirous to go into the convent, and prove all her accusations against the Priests and Nuns, he withdrew. Soon after he returned, and stated, that he had been to the Convent, to inquire respecting her; and that he had been informed, that she had once belonged to the Nunnery; but that they would not any longer own or recognise her. Afterwards he exhibited the most contradictory emotions, and first cursed Maria Monk; then reviled the Priests, applying to them all the loathsome epithets in the Canadian vocabulary. Subsequently, he went to make inquiries at the Seminary; and after his return to Mr. Johnson's house he declared, that the persons there had informed him, that Maria Monk had lived in the Nunnery, but not as a Nun; then he offered to assist her in her endeavours to expose the Priests; and finally disappeared, swearing aloud as he was retiring from the house; and apparently thinking over the conduct of the Priest to his wife before their marriage. "Oh, sacre!"—he repeated to himself—"c'est trop mechant!"

Similar facts to the above occurred frequently during the time of Maria Monk's visit to Montreal—in which strangers who called upon her, cursed and reviled her; then believed her statements and assented to them—and displayed all the natural excitement which was necessarily comprised in the working of their own belief and convictions of the iniquity of the Priests, and the dread resulting from their own superstitious vassalage, and the certainty of a heavy penance.

But in connexion with the preceding collateral evidence is another remarkable circumstance, which is this: the extensive knowledge which Maria Monk has obtained of the Canadian Jesuits. Those with whom she has been acquainted, she affirms that she could instantly identify. For that object, she has given a catalogue of those Priests whose names and persons are in some degree familiarly known to her. As the Priests are often changing their abodes, and many of them residents in Montreal until a vacancy occurs for them in the country parishes, in those particulars there may be a trifling mistake; but Maria Monk solemnly avers, that the Priests, whether dead or living, who are enumerated in the subsequent catalogue, either have dwelt or do yet reside in the places specified. When unexpectedly and closely examined in reference to the Priests of the same name, she particularly distinguished them, and pointed out the difference between them in their persons, gait, &c.; thus precluding all objection from the fact of there being more than one Priest with a similar appellative. This circumstance particularly is illustrated by the Priests named Marcoux, of whom she says there are three brothers or first

161

cousins—two called Dufresne, &c.: each of whom she graphically depicts. It is also certain, because she has done it in a great variety of instances, and in the presence of many different persons, all of whom are well acquainted with them, that she describes Lartigue; Dufresne; Richard; Phelan; Bonin; Comte; Bourget; McMahon; Kelly; Demers; Roux; Roque; Sauvage; Tabeau; Marcoux; Morin; Durocher; and all the Roman Priests around Montreal, with the utmost minuteness of accuracy; while the Chaplain of the Ursuline Nunnery at Quebec, Father Daulè, is as exactly depicted by her, as if her whole life had been passed under his surveillance. Some of the appellatives in the ensuing catalogue may not be correctly spelt. Scarcely any thing is more difficult than to acquire proper names in a foreign language; and especially where the pronunciation itself is provincial, as is the case with Canadian French; and when also those titles have to be transcribed from the mouth of a person who knows no more of orthoepy and orthography than a Canadian Nun. However, Maria Monk attests, that the Priests to whom she refers did reside at those places which she has designated, and that she has seen them all in the Hotel Dieu Nunnery—some of them very often, and others on a variety of occasions.

Nothing is more improbable, if not impossible, than that any Papist girl should have such an extensive acquaintance among Roman Priests. In Canada especially, where the large majority of females have little more correct knowledge of that which occurs out of their own district than of Herschel's astronomical discoveries, young women cannot be personally familiar with any Priests, in ordinary cases, except those who may have been "Curés" of the parish in which they reside, or of the immediate vicinity, or an occasional visitor during the absence, or sickness, or death of the resident Curate or Missionary. Notwithstanding, Maria Monk delineates to the life, the prominent features, the exact figure, and the obvious characteristic exterior habits and personal appearance of more than one hundred and fifty of those Priests, scattered about in all parts of Canada; Among others she particularly specifies the following men: but some of whom she notes as dead. Others she has named, but as her recollections of them are less distinct, they are not enumerated.

Jean Jacques Lartigue, Bishop of Telmese, Montreal. The Irish Priest McMahon, who has resided both in Montreal and Quebec. M. Dufrense, St. Nicholas. L. Cadieux, Vicar General, Three Rivers. F. F. Marcoux, Maskinonge. S. N. Dumoulin, Yamachiche. A. Leclerc, Yomaska. V. Fournier, Baie du Febre. J. Demers, St.

Gregoire. C. B. Courtain, Gentilly. T. Pepin, St. Jean.
Ignace Bourget, Montreal. The Priest Moor, Missionary.
J. C. Prince, Montreal. J. M. Sauvage, Montreal. J. Comte,
Montreal. J. H. A. Roux, Vicar General, Montreal. J.
Roque, Montreal. A. Malard, Montreal. A. L. Hubart,
Montreal. A. Satin, Montreal. J. B. Roupe, Montreal. Nic.
Dufresne, Montreal. J. Richard, Montreal. C. Fay,
Montreal. J. B. St. Pierre, Montreal. F. Bonin, P. Phelan,
Montreal. T. B. M'Mahon, Perce. J. Marcoux,
Caghuawaga. C. De Bellefeuille, Lake of two Mountains.
Claude Leonard, Montreal. F. Durocher, Lake of two
Mountains. G. Belmont, St. Francis. F. Demers, Vicar
General, St. Denis. J. O. Giroux, St. Benoit. J. B. St.
Germain, St. Laurent. J. D. Delisle, St. Cesaire. J. M.
Lefebvre, St. Genevieve. F. Pigeon, St. Philippe. A.
Duransau, Lachine. O. Chevrefils, St. Constant. Joseph
Quiblier, Montreal. Francis Humbert, Montreal. J.
Arraud, Montreal. O. Archambault, Montreal. J. Larkin,
Montreal. F. Sery, Montreal. R. Larre, Montreal. A.
Macdonald, Montreal. F. Larkin, Montreal. J.
Beauregard, Montreal. R. Robert, Montreal. J. Fitz
Patrick, Montreal. J. Toupin, Montreal. W. Baun,
Montreal. T. Filiatreault. Montreal. J. Brady, Montreal. P.
Trudel, St. Hyacinth. John Grant, St. Hyacinth. J. Delaire,
Chambly. J. Desautels, Chambly. P. D. Ricard, St.
Joachim. Jan. Leclaire, Isle Jesus. F. M. Turcot, St. Rose.
C. Larocque, Berthier, T. Brassard, St. Elizabeth. J. B.
Keller, St. Elizabeth. J. Ravienne, Lanorate. J. T. Gagno,
Valtrie. Gasford Guingner, St. Melanie. L. Nicholas
Jacques, St. Sulpice. J. Renucalde, St. Jaques. T. Can, St.
Esprit. C. J. Ducharme, St. Therese. J. Valliée, St.
Scholastique. J. J. Vinet, Arganteuil. M. Power,
Beauharnois. J. B. Labelle, Chateauguay. E. Bietz, St.
Constant. P. Bedard, St. Remi. C. Aubry, St. Athanase. L.
Vinet, Noyon. J. Roque, Noyon. J. Zeph, Carren. F.
Berauld, St. Valentia. A. Maresseau, Longueuil. P. Brunet,
——. J. Odelin, Rounilli. J. B. Dupuis, ——. L. Nau,
Rouville. A. O. Giroux, St. Marc. G. Marchesseau, ——. J.
B. Belanger, St. Ours. H. Marcotte, Isle du Pads. E.
Crevier, Yamaska. G. Arsonault, ——. Eusebe Durocher, —
—. D. Denis, St. Rosalie. F. X. Brunet, St. Damase. J.A.
Boisond, St. Pie. M. Quintal, St. Damase. L. Aubry, Points
Calire. P. Tetro, Beauharnois. B. Ricard, St. Constant. M.

163

Morin, Maskonche. J. Crevier, Blairfindie. P. Grenier, Charteaguay. A. Darocher, Pointe aux Trembles. P. Murcure, La Presentation. R. Gaulin, Dorchester. H. L. Girouard, St. Hyacinthe. J. Paquin, Blairfinde. E. Brassard, St. Polycarpe. J. Boissonnault, Riviere des Prairies. F. N. Blanchet, Soulanges. E. Lavoie, Blairfindie. J. B. Kelly, Sorel. E. Morriset, St. Cyprian. H. Hudon, Argenteuil. M. Brudet, St. Martin. P. P. Archambault, Vaudreuil. J. B. Boucher, La Prairie. J. Quevillion, St. Ours. A. Chaboillez, Longueuil. P. J. Delamothe, St. Scholastique. T. Lagard, St. Vincent. J. Durocher, St. Benoit. Antoine Tabeau, Vicar General, Montreal. J. F. Hebard, St. Ours. F. A. Trudeau, Montreal. M. J. Felix, St. Benoit. L. Lamothe, Bethier. J. Moirier, St. Anne. F. J. Deguise, Vicar General, Varennes. J. B. Bedard, St. Denis. R. O. Brunsau, Vercheres. F. Portier, Terrebonne. P. D. Ricard, Berthier. L. Gague, Lachenaie. Joseph Belanger, Chambly. M. Blanchet, St. Charles. P. M. Mignault, Chambly. F. Labelle, L'Assumption. F. Marcoux, St. Barthelemi. N. L. Amiot, Repentigny. J. B. Boucher, Chambly. P. Lafranc, St. Jean Baptiste. P. Robitaille, Monnie. F. De Bellefeullie, St. Vincent. M. Brassard, St. Elizabeth. P. Cousigny, St. Mathias. J. D. Daule, Quebec.

It is readily admitted, that any person could take one of the Ecclesiastical Registers of Lower Canada, and at his option mark any number of the Roman Priests in the catalogue, and impute to them any crime which he pleased. But if the accuser were closely examined, and among such a multitude of Priests, who in all their clothing are dressed alike, were called upon minutely to delineate them, it is morally impossible, that he could depict more than a hundred Priests dispersed from the borders of Upper Canada to Quebec, in as many different parishes, with the most perfect accuracy, unless he was personally and well acquainted with them.

Maria Monk, however, does most accurately describe all the Priests in the preceding catalogue, and repeats them at the expiration of weeks and months; and the question is this: how is it possible that she could have become acquainted with so many of that body, and by what means can she so precisely depict their external appearance?—The startling, but the only plausible answer which can be given to that question is this:—that she has seen them in the Nunnery, whither, as she maintains, most of them constantly resorted for licentious intercourse with the Nuns.

One other connected fact may here be introduced. Maria

Monk well knows the Lady Superior of the Charlestown Nunnery. That acquaintance could not have been made in the United States, because Saint Mary St. George as she called herself, or Sarah Burroughs, daughter of the notorious Stephen Burroughs, as is her real name, removed to Canada at the latter end of May, 1835; nor could it have been prior to the establishment of the Charlestown Nunnery, for at that period Maria Monk was a child, and was not in any Convent except merely as a scholar; and Mary St. George was at Quebec. How then did she become so familiar with that far-famed lady as to be able to describe her so exactly? The only answer is, that she derived her knowledge of the Charlestown Convent and of its Superior, from the intimations given, and from intercourse with that Nun in the Hotel Dieu Nunnery.

Young females often have been sent to the Nunneries in Canada under the fallacious hope of obtaining for them, a superior education; and very frequently, they are suddenly removed after being there but a short period; because the persons to whose partial guardianship they are committed perceive that they are in danger of being ensnared by the Chaplain and his female Syrens.

But there are two other particulars in American Nunneries, the toleration of which almost surpasses credibility.

In reference to girls, they are permitted to visit their friends, even when they reside in the vicinity of the Convent, only for an hour or two monthly—if their relatives are at a distance, they see them only during the annual vacation, and often remain in the Nunnery during that term. No correspondence is permitted between the mother, the guardian, the sister, or the friends of the young female in the Nunnery School, on either side, without the inspection of the argus-eyed agent of the Institution. Parental advice, filial complaints, and confidential communications are equally arrested; and only furnish to the Superiors of the establishment, artifices to thwart the Seniors, to entangle the Juniors, and effectually to cajole both parties. Consequently, it generally happens, that from one term to another, little or no intercourse exists between the youth and her relatives; and it is indubitable, that where any letters do nominally pass between them, they are forgeries; the real letters being surreptitiously detained. Those felonious regulations furnish ample scope for the initiation of girls just entering upon womanhood, into all the wickedness of the Nunnery; while the girls themselves are unconscious of the design, and the Nuns, those nefarious artificers of the iniquity, in subserviency to the Priests, in case of necessity, can exculpate themselves apparently from all participation in the treachery and crimes.

In the nunneries and conventual schools in the United States there is a sort of fairy land, talked about by the nuns to the elder girls. It is called the "Nuns' Island." That country is always described as an earthly paradise; and to girls who are manifestly fascinated by the witcheries of the nuns, and in whom moral sensibility has become blunted by the unmeaning superstitions which they witness, and which they mechanically perform, a visit to the "Nuns' Island," is always proposed as the greatest privilege, and the most costly reward, which can be given for constant obsequiousness to the nuns, and unreserved compliance with their requirements. The term "Nuns' Island," is thus used to express the nunneries in Canada, and probably some similar institutions in the United States, where they are not too difficult of access. At all events, girls just entering upon the character of women, after proper training, are finally gratified with a visit to the "Nuns' Island." They are taken to Montreal, and in the nunneries there are at once taught "the mystery of iniquity;" in all the living reality which Maria Monk describes. Those girls from the United States, who are represented as novices; in Maria Monk's "Awful Disclosures," were young ladies from the United States, who had been decoyed to visit the "Nuns' Island," and who, not being Papists, often were found very intractable; but posterior circumstances enforce the belief, that having found resistance vain, they had not returned to their school where they were duly qualified to continue the course into which they had been coerced, so as fully to elude all possibility of discovery and exposure. That mother who intrusts her daughter to a nunnery school, is chargeable with the high crime of openly conducting her into the chambers of pollution, and the path to irreligion, and the bottomless pit.

These combined circumstances satisfactorily prove that, the narrative of Maria Monk should be believed by all impartial persons; at least, until other evidence can be adduced, and the offer of exploring the Hotel Dieu Nunnery, by the New York Protestant Association, has been accepted and decided.

3. Additional evidence of the truth of Maria Monk's narrative is deduced from the exact conformity of the facts which she states concerning the Hotel Dieu Nunnery, when compared with the authoritative principles of the Jesuit Priesthood as recorded in their own duly sanctioned volumes. It is essential to remark, that of those books she knows nothing; that she has never seen one of them, and if she could grasp them, that they would impart no illumination to her mind, being in Latin; and yet in many momentous particulars, neither Lartigue nor any one of the Jesuit Priests now in Montreal, who was educated in France, could more minutely and accurately

furnish an exposition or practical illustration of the atrocious themes, than Maria Monk has unconsciously done.

Maria Monk's "Awful Disclosures," are reducible to three classes: intolerable sensuality; diversified murder; and most scandalous mendacity: comprehending flagrant, and obdurate, and unceasing violations of the sixth, seventh, and ninth commandments.

The ninth commandment: FALSEHOOD. Of this baseness, five specimens only shall suffice.

Sanchez, a very renowned author, in his work on "Morality and the Precepts of the Decalogue," part 2, book 3, chap. 6, no. 13, thus decides: "A person may take an oath that he has not done any certain thing, though in fact he has. This is extremely convenient, and is also very just, when necessary to your health, honour, and prosperity!" Charli, in his Propositions, no. 6, affirms that, "He who is not bound to state the truth before swearing, is not bound by his oath." Taberna in his vol. 2, part 2, tract 2, chap. 31, p. 288, asks: "Is a witness bound to declare the truth before a lawful judge?" To which he replies: "No, if his deposition will injure himself or his posterity." Laymann, in his works, book 4, tract 2, chap. 2, p. 73, proclaims: "It is not sufficient for an oath, that we use the formal words, if we had not the intention and will to swear, and do not sincerely invoke God as a witness." All those principles are sanctioned by Suarez in his "Precepts of Law," book 3, chap. 9, assertion 2, p. 473, where he says, "If any one has promised or contracted without intention to promise, and is called upon oath to answer, may simply answer, NO; and may swear to that denial."

The idea of obtaining truth, therefore, from a thorough-going Papist, upon any subject in which his "honour" is concerned—and every Papist's honour is indissolubly conjoined with "the Church"—is an absurdity so great, that it cannot be listened to with patience, while the above decisions are the authorised dogmas which the Roman Priests inculcate among their followers. How well the nuns of Montreal have imbibed those Jesuitical instructions, Maria Monk's "Awful Disclosures" amply reveal.

The Sixth Commandment: MURDER. The following miscellaneous decisions are extracted from the works of the regularly sanctioned Roman authors, of the very highest character and rank in that community.

In his famous volume called "Aphorisms," p. 178, Emmanuel Sa writes—"You may kill any person who may be able to put you to death—judge and witnesses—because it is self-defence."

Henriquez, in his "Sum of Moral Theology," vol. 1, book 14,

chap. 10, p. 859, decides that "a Priest is not criminal, if he kill the husband of a woman with whom he is caught in adultery."

Airault published a number of propositions. One of them says, that "a person may secretly kill another who attempts to destroy his reputation, although the facts are true which he published." The following must be cited in Latin. "An lieitium sit mulieri procurare abortum? Posset ilium excutere, ne honorem suum amittat, qui illi multo pretiosior est ipsa vita." "An liceat mulieri conjugatæ sumere pharmacum sterilitatis? Ita satius est ut hoc faciat, quam ut marito debitium conjugale recuset." Censures 319, 322, 327.

In his Moral Theology, vol. 4, book 32, sec. 2, problem 5, Escobar determines, that "it is lawful to kill an accuser whose testimony may jeopard your life and honour."

Guimenius promulged his seventh Proposition in these words: "You may charge your opponent with false crimes to destroy his credit; and you may also kill him."

Marin wrote a book called "Speculative and Moral Theology." In vol. 3, tract 23, disputation 8, sec. 5, no. 63, p. 448, are found the following sentences: "Licet procurare abortum, ne puella infametur." That doctrine is admitted, "to evade personal disgrace, and to conceal the infamy of Monks and Nuns." no. 67, p. 429. In no. 75, p. 430, of the same work, Marin writes: "Navarrus, Arragon, Bannez, Henriquez,, Sa, Sanchez, Palao, and others, all say, that a woman may use not only missione sanguinis, sed aliis medicamentis, etsi inde pereat foetus." With that doctrine also agrees Egidius, in his "Explication of the Decalogue," vol. 5, book 5, chap. 1, doubt 4; and Diana in his work upon Morality, part 6, tract 8, resolution 27, fully ratifies his sanction.

Gobatus published a work which he entitled, "Morality," and in vol. 2, part 2, tract 5, chap. 9, sec. 8, p. 318, is the following edifying specimen of Popish morals: "Persons may innocently desire to be drunk, if any great good will arise from it. A son who inherits wealth by his father's death, may rejoice that when he is intoxicated, he murdered his father." According to which combined propositions, a man may make himself drunk expressly to kill his parent, and yet be guiltless.

Busenbaum wrote a work denominated "Moral Theology." which was enlarged and explained by Lacroix. In vol. 1, p. 295, is the following position: "In all the cases where a man has a right to kill any person, another may do it for him." But we have already heard by Escobar that any "Roman Priest has a right to kill Maria Monk; and therefore any Papist may murder her for them."

Alagona, in his "Compend of the Sum of Theology," by Thomas Aquinas, question 94, p. 230, "Sums" up all the Romish system in this comprehensively blasphemous oracular adage. "By the command of God, it is lawful to murder the innocent, to rob, and to commit lewdness; and thus to fulfil his mandate, is our duty."

The seventh commandment.—In his Aphorisms, p. 80, and p. 259, Sa thus decides—"Copulari ante benedictionem, aut nullam aut leve peceatum est; quin etiam expedit, si multum isla differatur."— "Potest et femina quaeque et mas, pro turpi corporis usu, pretium, accipere et petere."

Hurtado issued a volume of "Disputations and Difficulties." At p. 476 is the following genuine Popish rule of life—"Carnal intercourse before marriage is not unlawful." So teaches that Jesuit oracle.

Dicastillo, in his work upon "Righteousness and other cardinal Virtues," p. 87, thus asks—"An puella, quae per vin opprimitur teneatur clamare et opem implorare ne violetur?" The answer is this—"Non videtur teneri impedire peccatum alterius—sed mere passive se habere."

Escobar, in his "Moral Theology," p. 326, 327, 328, of vol. 4, determines that "a man who abducts a woman from affection expressly to marry her, is guilty of mortal sin, but a Priest who forcibly violates her through lust, incurs no censure."

Tamburin unfolds the character of Romanism in his "Moral Theology," p. 186, in a lengthened discussion of the following characteristic inquiry—"Quantum pro usu corporis sui juste exigat mulier?"—The reply is, "de meretrice et de femina honesta sive conjugata, ant non."

Fegeli wrote a book of "Practical Questions;" and on p. 397, is the following—"Under what obligation is he who defiles a virgin?"— The answer is this—"Besides the obligation of penance, he incurs none; quia puella habet jus usum sui corporis concedendi."

Trachala published a volume which he facetiously entitled the "Laver of Conscience;" and at p. 96, he presents us with this astounding recipe to purify the conscience—"An Concubinarius sit absolvendus antequam concubinam dimittat?" To which he replies—"Si ilia concubina sit valde bona et utilis economa, et sic nullam aliam possit habere, esset absolvendus."

From the prior decisions, combined with numberless others which might be extracted from the works of the Romish authors, it is obvious, that the violations of the seventh commandment, are scarcely enumerated by the Papal priesthood among venial sins. Especially if we consider the definition of a prostitute by the highest Popish authority: for in the Decretals, Distinction 34, in the Gloss, is found this savory adage—"Meretrix est quae, admiserit plures quam

169

viginti tria hominum millia!" That is the infallible attestation to the truth of Maria Monk's "Awful Disclosures."

4. The antecedent narrative of the Hotel Dieu Nunnery, is confirmed by the universal and constant practice of Roman Priests in all Convents. Among the works of William Huntington, is a correspondence between himself and a young lady who was converted by his ministry. The seventh letter from Miss M. contains the following passage:—

"It is a shame for women to approach those confessionals. If they were never wise in scenes of iniquity before, the priest will instruct them, by asking the most filthy questions. I was confined to my bed three days from my first confession; and thought I would never go again, being so abashed by the abominations he had put in my head. I would just as soon recommend scalding water to cure Anthony's-fire, or a wet bed in an ice-house to cure an ague, as recommend a sinner to those accursed lies, Roman penance, and Auricular Confession."—The mental purity of Nuns consists in a life totally "contrary to the laws of God, of modesty, of decency. They are constantly exposed to the obscene interrogations, and the lewd actions of the Priests. Notwithstanding God has fixed a bar on every female mind, it is broken through by the Priests putting questions to them upon those subjects, as the scripture declares, which ought not to be named? The uncommon attractions of the young women in Convents generally indicate the greatest unchastity among them. I have known girls, sent for education to the Convent where I was, who regularly stripped themselves of every thing they could obtain from their friends; which, by the artful insinuations of the Nuns, was given to them and the Priests. The Roman priesthood may well be called a sorceress, and their doctrine 'the wine of fornication,' for nothing but the powers of darkness could work up the young female mind to receive it; unless by the subtlety of the devil, and the vile artifices of the Nuns. I shudder at the idea of young ladies going into a Convent; and also at parents who send their children to be educated in a Nunnery; where their daughters are entrapped by the Nuns into the snare of the Priests, with whom they are accomplices, and for whom the most subtle of them are decoys, whose feigned sanctity is only a cover for the satanic arts of which they are complete mistresses, and by which, through the delusions of the mother of harlots, being buried alive within the walls of a Convent, they 'drink of the wine of her fornication,' until their souls pass into the pit of destruction."—The above extract is from the seventh letter of "Correspondence between Miss M. and Mr. H." in Huntington's Works; and exposes the Nunneries in France.

George D. Emeline, who had been a Popish Priest, in his

"Eight Letters," giving an account of his "Journey into Italy," thus details the nature of the intimacy which then existed between the Priests and Nuns on the European Continent. "A young Monk at Milan, Preacher to the Benedictine Nuns, when he addressed them, added to almost every sentence in his discourse, 'my most dear and lovely sisters, whom I love from the deepest bottom of my heart.' When a monk becomes Preacher or Chaplain to a Nunnery, his days are passed in constant voluptuousness; for the Nuns will gratify their Confessor in every thing, that he may be equally indulgent to them." Emeline's Letters, p. 313.

"A regular Abbot of a Monastery in Italy, talking with me said—'Melius est habere nullam quam aliquem—It is better to have none than any woman.' I asked him what he meant; he replied, 'Because, when a person is not tied to one, he may make use of many;' and his practice was conformable to his doctrine; for he slept in the same bed with three young women every night. He was a most insatiable Exactor and Oppressor of the people who rented the lands of the Abbey, in consequence of which the Farmers complained of him to the Archbishop of the District. The Archbishop sent the Provost, the Farmers, and sixty of the serjeants at night, to seize him and his female companions. They took the Abbot in bed, and having put on him a morning-gown; and having tied his three concubines and himself back to back, placed them in a cart, and conducted them to the Archbishop's residence, in Bonnonia: who then refused to judge him; but sent him and his females to the Monastery of Saint Michael; into which, with some difficulty, he was admitted after midnight, in consequence of the Provost assuring the Friars, that if they would not receive the Abbot, they would procure his prelatical dress, and escort him and the young women in procession through the city, and back to his own Monastery the same day at noon. The females were ordered away, and the Abbot was appointed to remain in his monastery for fifteen days for penance, until the story had ceased to circulate. I was an eyewitness of that myself, when I was in the Monastery of St. Michael in the wood."—Emeline's Letters, pp. 387, 388, 389.

That the Nunneries in Portugal, as well as among those people in India who are subject to the Romish priesthood, are of the same character precisely, as Maria Monk describes the Priests and Nuns in Canada, is proved by Victorin de Faria, who had been a Brahman in India; and who afterward resided as a regular Roman Priest in the Paulist Monastery at Lisbon.

"The regular Priests in India," says Faria, "have become what the bonzes where in Japan. The Nuns were the disciples of Diana, and the nunneries seraglios for the monks; as I have proved to be

171

the case in Lisbon, by facts concerning those nuns who were more often in the family way than common women. The Jesuits in the Indies made themselves Brahmans in order to enjoy the privileges of that caste, whose idolatrous rites and superstitious practices they also externally adopted."—Among other privileges which they possessed, Faria enumerates the following, as detailed from his own prior experience as a Brahman. "Never to be put to death for any crime whatever; and to enjoy the favours of every woman who pleased them, for a Priest sanctifies the woman upon whom he bestows his attentions." That is the true Papist doctrine, as shown by Maria Monk's "Awful Disclosures;" confirmed by the Canadian carpenter in Mr. Johnson's house at Montreal; and ratified by Pope Gregory XIII. in the Decretals and Canons, in the Corpus Juris Canonici. Secrets of Nunneries disclosed by Scipio de Ricci. p. 217.

The Nunneries in Italy during the present generation are of the same description. Maria Catharine Barni, Maria Magdalen Sicini, and Victoire Benedetti, of the Nunnery called Santa Croce: all acknowledged, that they had been seduced at confession, and that they had habitually maintained criminal intercourse with a Priest called Pacchiani, who absolved his guilty companions after the commission of their crimes. Secrets of Nunneries disclosed by Scipio de Ricci. pp. 60, 61.

Six Nuns of the Convent of Catharine at Pistoia declared that the Priests who visited the Convent committed a "thousand indecorous acts. They utter the worst expressions, saying that we should look upon it as a great happiness, that we have the power of satisfying our appetites without the annoyance of children; and that we should not hesitate to take our pleasures. Men, who have contrived to get the keys, come into the Convent during the night, which they have spent in the most dissipated manner." That is the precise delineation of the Canadian Nunneries; into which other men besides Priests are admitted, if the parties are willing to pay the entrance bribe to the Chaplain.—Secrets of Nunneries, by Scipio de Ricci. pp. 80, 81.

Flavia Perraccini, Prioress of the Nunnery of Catharine of Pistoia, revealed what she knew of that and other Nunneries. All the Priests "are of the same character. They all have the same maxims and the same conduct. They are on more intimate terms with the nuns than if they were married to them. It is the same at Lucia, at Pisa, at Prato, and at Perugia. The Superiors do not know even the smallest part of the enormous wickedness that goes on between the Monks and the Nuns."—Secrets of Nunneries, by Scipio de Ricci. p. 93. That statement is so exactly conformed to Maria Monk's "Awful Disclosures," that were it not a fact that she had never seen Scipio

172

de Ricci's work it might almost be supposed that some part of her narrative had been transcribed from it.

Foggini of Rome, also wrote to Scipio de Ricci and informed him—"I know a monastery in which a Jesuit used to make the Nuns lift up their clothes, assuring them that they thereby performed an act of virtue, because they overcame a natural repugnance."— Secrets of Nunneries, p. 101. That is a very extraordinary illustration of the turpitude of the Roman Priesthood; because that doctrine is a principle which they constantly inculcate; and such is the invariable practice in the Hotel Dieu Nunnery, that the Nuns were obliged to fulfil, for the beastly gratification of the Roman Priests who visited that house, which is "the way to hell, going down to the chambers of death." Proverbs 7:27.

It is superfluous to multiply similar extracts. Scipio de Ricci was a Popish prelate, regularly commissioned by the Grand Duke of Tuscany to explore the Nunneries; and in consequence of his authentic developments, the Jesuits and Dominicans, and the dignified Papal ecclesiastics, with the two Popes, Pius VI. and Pius VII. all opposed, reviled, condemned and worried him almost to death.

One quotation more shall close this survey. Pope Paul III. maintained at Rome, forty-five thousand courtesans. Pope Sixtus IV. ordered a number of edifices to be erected expressly for the accommodation of the semi-Nuns of Rome, from whose impurity he derived a large annual revenue, under the form of a license; besides which, the prices of absolution for the different violations of the seventh commandment are as regularly fixed as the value of beads, soul-masses, blessed water, and every other article of Popish manufacture. Paolo, Hist. Council de Trent. Book I. Anno 1637.

The preceding observations, it is believed, will remove the doubts from the mind of every impartial inquirer, respecting the credibility of Maria Monk's narrative: nevertheless, a few additional remarks may not be irrelevant: especially as there is a marvellous skepticism in reference to the admission of valid testimony concerning the Roman priesthood, their system and practice. We are deafened with clamour for proof to substantiate Maria Monk's history: but that demand is tantamount to the declaration—"I will not believe."

In anticipation of speedy death, and an immediate appearance at the dread tribunal of Jehovah, Maria Monk communicated to Mr. Tappan, the Chaplain at Bellevue, one of the benevolent institutions belonging to the city of New York, the principal facts in her "Awful Disclosures." After her unexpected recovery, she personally appeared at Montreal, expressly and openly, to promulge her allegations of atrocious crimes against the chief Roman Ecclesiastics in that city, who were armed with power, and having nearly all the population her infuriated enemies. There she remained almost four weeks, constantly daring the Roman Priests and Nuns in vain. It is true, Dr. Robertson in his affidavit says, that he was willing "to take the necessary steps for a full investigation, if a direct charge were made against any particular individual of a criminal nature." Now if Maria Monk's charges are not direct, OF A CRIMINAL NATURE, and against PARTICULAR INDIVIDUALS—what charges can be so characterized? The fact is this:—Dr. Robertson would no more dare to issue a warrant for the apprehension of Lartigue, or any of the inferior Roman Priests in Montreal, than he would dare publicly to strike the Commander of the Garrison, or the Governor of Canada upon military parade. If any Papist had stated to him the same facts concerning a Protestant, or Protestant Minister, and offered to confirm them by his worthless oath, he would have issued his process at once; but Dr. Robertson knows, that in the present state of Canadian society, Roman Priests can do what they please; and no man dares to reprove, much less to "take any necessary steps for a full investigation" for their crimes. If the Jesuits and Nuns at Montreal are anxious for a full and impartial scrutiny of the Hotel Dieu Convent, Maria Monk is ready to oblige them with some facilities for that object; provided she may carry them out to all their extent and application. Mr. Ogden has one affidavit, and knows the whole matter; as can incontestably be proved by Mr. A. P. Hart, an Attorney of Montreal; and we recommend Dr. Robertson to issue his warrant for the apprehension of Lartigue, Bonin, Dufresne, and Richards, they are enough to begin with; and if Mr. Ogden will carry the facts with which he is acquainted to the Grand Jury, one witness in New York is ready to appear; and Dr. Robertson will find his hands full of employment, if he will only "take the necessary steps" to procure two or three persons who shall be pointed out to him in the Hotel Dieu Nunnery. Therefore, until Dr. Robertson commences some incipient measures as a Magistrate towards "the necessary steps for a full investigation," as he says, we shall be forced to believe, that the printer made a mistake in his affidavit, and put willing for unwilling.

The cavilling call, however, for additional evidence to be adduced by Maria Monk, is manifestly futile. That testimony is within the jurisdiction of the Priests alone who are criminated. Maria Monk reiterates her charge against the Romish Ecclesiastics of Canada and their Nuns; and she has solemnly sworn that they are true. What more can she do? Nothing, but to search the premises, to see whether the statements which she has made are correct. A

Committee of the New York Protestant Association are willing to accompany her to Montreal; to walk through the Hotel Dieu Nunnery in company with any Gentlemen of Montreal, and investigate the truth without favour or partiality, Maria Monk is willing to submit the whole affair to that short, and easy, and sensible test; in which there is no possibility of deception. It does not depend upon credibility of witnesses, conflicting evidence, personal friendship, or religions prejudices; it is reduced at once to that unerring criterion; the sight and the touch!

But, it is retorted, that will not be granted; then we repeat another proposal: let the Priest Conroy come forth girded in all the panoply of the Roman court, and appear as the champion of the Canadian Jesuits; let him institute an action, civil or criminal, or both, against the publishers of such atrocious crimes, which, as they pretend, are falsely alleged against the Roman Priests. If Lartigue and his Montreal inferior priests are implicated in the most nefarious felonies, Maria Monk has published him as a virtuous accomplice. Why does he not put her truth to the test, by subjecting her to a criminal process? Why does he not commence a suit against the Booksellers who published her "Awful Disclosures?"—Ah! if Lartigue, Bonin, Dufresne, and Richards, with their brethren, Conroy, Phelan, Kelly and Quarter, were coerced to keep Lent, and live only upon soup-maigre, until that day arrives, they would not much longer portray in their exterior, that they live upon the fat of the land; but they would vociferously whine out—"Mea culpa! O mea grandis culpa! O mea grandissima culpa! Peccava! Peccavi! Peccavi!"

APPENDIX

RECEPTION OF THE FIRST EDITIONS

I have now reached the close of what appeared in my first editions. Some of my readers may feel a wish to know what has been said of me and my book, by those whose characters or connexions it exposes. Different persons have expressed to me their fears that I should be kidnapped, stabbed or poisoned; but of this I have had but little apprehension. Others may suppose that the priests of

Montreal, and some of those in New York, against whom I have made different charges, may have appeared against me in ways of which they are ignorant, and have published facts, or used arguments of serious import, if not of decided force. For the information of my readers, I have determined, though at some inconvenience, to lay before them a fair view of what they have done.

I was well convinced before the publication of my first book, that the priests would do or say very little against me or my work; and several persons can testify, that I made declarations of this kind, with distinctness, in their presence. The reasons I gave for this opinion were these,—that they feared an investigation, and that they feared further disclosures. They must desire to keep the public mind calm, and diverted with other matters; and to avoid increasing my will.

There were individuals, I was well aware, both in and out of the nunnery, and Seminary, who, from the first notice of the appearance of my book, would be extremely disquieted, until they had ascertained the extent to which my developments reached. When they had read for themselves, I well knew, they would enjoy a temporary relief, finding that my "Disclosures" were not the most "awful" which they had reason to expect.

I also felt, that they would apprehend something further from me; and that a dread of this would probably keep them quiet, or confine them to general denials of my story. And this has been the case, even to so great a degree, that the remark has been often repeated—how feeble is their defence! Why did they not rather remain silent than do so little—that which is for them worse than nothing? The causes of this I could assign. The world does not understand them all.

Three principal grounds of opposition have been taken against me by my enemies—1st, That I had never been in the Hotel Dieu Nunnery: 2d, That my character entitled me to no confidence; 3d, That my book was copied, "word for word, and letter for letter," from an old European work, called "The Gates of Hell opened." Besides these grounds, several others have been attempted, but less seriously supported—such as that I was deranged, or subject to occasional alienation of mind; and that I was not Maria Monk, but a counterfeit of a person by that name, still in Canada, and, as some said, in the Black Nunnery.

With regard to the first of these grounds, I will here simply say, that it has been, beyond controversy, the principal one, but has recently been abandoned. The great object of the six affidavits, published in Montreal in November, 1835, and republished here soon after the publication of my book, was to prove that I had never been a nun—not even a novice. The reader may judge for himself, for those affidavits are published in full in this volume, and they are the only ones which have been published against me. The reader will also see in an extract from the New York Catholic Diary of March last that that fact is admitted; and by a later extract from it, that a Canadian priest who takes the trouble to write from Sherbrooke, has no new testimony to refer to.

As to my character, I never claimed the confidence of the American people, (as the Roman priests do,) on a pretence of a peculiar holiness of life. That would have been unreasonable in a stranger, and especially one who had been in a nunnery. My first editions, as well as the present, bear witness that I appealed to the evidence of facts which no one could controvert if once produced— an examination of the interior of my late prison. Not a lisp has yet been heard of assent to my proposition. The Protestant Association have published a challenge, for several weeks, which is on another page among the extracts—but no one has accepted it, and I will venture to say, no one will.

My publishers, on seeing the assertion made by the editor of the Boston (Roman Catholic) Pilot, that my book was a mere copy from an old European work, called "The Gates of Hell opened," published an offer of $100 for any book so resembling it—without success. If there be any volume on earth which contains the developments of any fugitive nun, whose case resembled my own, I should expect to merit such a title as the above; and I should know how to excuse the author for using so strong an expression, after struggling, as I have had to do, in giving my own narrative, with those feelings which are so apt to arise in my heart at the recollection of scenes I have passed through. The opening of the Gates of Hell, whether in a European or a Canadian Convent, may probably disclose scenes very like to each other; but if there be any resemblance between my book and any other in the world, I solemnly declare that it can be owing only to a resemblance between the things described in both, as not a sentence has been copied from any book whatever, and I defy the editor of the Boston Pilot—(not to perjure himself, as he gratuitously proposed—but to do what would be at once much more difficult and satisfactory)—produce his book, or a single page of it.

I have been charged with occasional alienation of mind—a very strong evidence, I should think, of my being a nun; for what eloped nun ever escaped that charge? Like converted Roman Catholics, run-away nuns are commonly pronounced to be out of their wits, or under the influence of evil spirits, of course, on the ground that it is proved by the fact itself.

As to my being the real Maria Monk or not, I presume the testimony of some of my old school-mates, now in New York, will pass. To these, however, it cannot be necessary to resort, otherwise the Montreal affidavits will be good for nothing.

I will now proceed to give the whole of the testimony which has been brought out against me. A few remarks, necessary to acquaint the reader with the progress of things, will be given in their place. Next to these will appear the testimony of several persons, who have voluntarily presented themselves, since the publication of my first edition, claimed acquaintance with me, and volunteered their testimony. I need not say how gratifying I have found such spontaneous marks of kindness, from friends, whose reedy and unsolicited appearance is a real favour to me, although chiefly due, as they declare, to their love of truth and justice.

Almost immediately after the appearance of my "Awful Disclosures," the following anonymous handbill was distributed through the city of New York. It was also published in the Catholic Diary, and other papers, with violent denunciations.

"Maria Monk! Villany Exposed.

"L'Amidu Peuple, a Montreal paper, gives us the denouement of the tale of scandal which the Protestant Vindicator, Christian Herald, et id genus omne, put forward a few months since, and which the Protestant Editors of three political journals in Montreal, at once indignantly repelled without knowing its origin. Instead of an eloped Nun, recounting the horrors of the Convent, the heroine of the tale is a Protestant young girl, who has been for four years past under protection of a Mr. Hoyte, once styled a Reverend Methodist Preacher, and connected with Canadian Sunday Schools. The paper quoted above, gives, at full length, the affidavits of the mother of the girl, who is also a Protestant, and of several other individuals, who had no motive to favour Catholic Institutions. The disconsolate mother testifies on oath that she had been solicited by the seducer of her child to swear that she was a Nun, and that the father of the infant was a Catholic Clergyman—that a promise had been made her of a comfortable provision for herself, and for her unfortunate child and offspring—if she would only do that. The poor woman had virtue enough to reject the base proposal; and thus, the Rev. Mr. Hoyte, who had returned from New York for this purpose, accompanied, it is stated, by the Rev. Mr. Brewster and Judge Turner, failed in the object of his visit.

"A Methodist Preacher of the place immediately disclaimed all connection of the society with Mr. Hoyte, and in a letter, published

178

in the papers, expressed his regret that any credit had been given to a foul charge, emanating from a source so polluted."—Catholic Herald.

The affidavits will be published as soon as they shall be received from Canada. Maria Monk's Book, far from injuring the Catholic religion, will promote it; for the publication is a real disclosure of the wickedness and hypocrisy of its enemies, who dare to go as far as to conceal their own crimes, by calumniating those who never did any thing against them, and have never interfered with them. Probably the author of this pious book is a minister; and, what is more remarkable, not a single one of the ministers has opposed it, or cautioned the people against it, as it is their duty to do, the calumniators being of their own congregation. However, by holding a prayer-meeting, making a few faces, and giving a few affecting turns to their voices, they certainly have already washed out the awful crime of these calumnies, because faith alone will save them, and they certainly have the true faith, which shows itself by these true fruits of charity. They are the elect, and consequently, they are not like the Catholic Priests, who are all wicked. The reader may recollect the parable of the pharisee and the publican.

* * * * *

"Granting the truth of Maria Monk's story, will it not reveal the weakness of Protestant origin? Where would Protestantism be, were it not engendered and nursed by profligate Monks and Nuns? Yes, gentlemen, profligate Monks and Nuns have been your nursing Fathers and Mothers! The chaste spouse of the Redeemer could hold no fellowship with such characters. She has flung them over the fences of the 'fold,' happy to have a sink into which to throw her filth."

As soon as my first edition appeared, several of the newspapers of New York referred to the publication in terms of unqualified condemnation. Not content with giving my motives in producing it, without having seen me, they hesitated not to pronounce it utterly false, with as much boldness as if they had really known something more of the matter than the public at large. A poor and injured female had disclosed to their countrymen facts of deep interest to all; and they, without examination, perhaps without leaving their offices to make a single inquiry, did their utmost to decry me, and used terms which they cannot but regret sooner or later.

Requests were immediately made to some of them to listen to evidence, which were not accepted. The editors of the Courier and

Enquirer were requested, in a note from the publishers, to mention in their paper what parts of my book they intended to pronounce false, and what was their evidence. But they took no notice of it, although desired to publish the note. Many other editors were invited to publish communications or extracts, but most of them refused from the first, and all the papers were soon closed against my cause.

In the country, the newspapers generally, I believe, followed the example set in this city, though in Albany, Boston, and one or two other places, a solitary one or two appeared disposed to examine the subject.

At length appeared the long-threatened Montreal affidavits, which are here inserted. They were published in several Roman Catholic, and one or two Protestant papers in New York, with this introduction—

"Maria Monk's 'Awful Disclosures.' Villany exposed!!

"Of all the curious pranks and fanatical schemes which the foes of Catholicity have been playing for some years past, there is not one that fills the mind with greater disgust than the scandalous tale given to the public by Maria Monk and her wicked associate.

"By the evidence which covers the following pages, the reader will see the man himself clearly convinced of being a base calumniator, and arch-hypocrite. He, and his associate prostitute, will be seen, with brazen impudence, attempting to fix on the virtuous Catholic Ladies and Catholic Priests of Montreal, the shameless character which belongs only to themselves."

From the Montreal Courier, Nov. 16, 1835.

"The New York Protestant Vindicator of the 4th November, reiterates its calumnies concerning the Roman Catholic Clergy and Nuns of this city. We cherished the hope that, after the simultaneous and unanimous expressions of disbelief and reprehension with which its extravagant assertions had been met by the Canadian press, both Protestant and Catholic, the conductors of that journal would have been slow to repeat, without better evidence of their truth, the same disgraceful charges. We have been deceived in our calculation. The fanatical print demands counter evidence before it will withdraw, or acknowledge the falsehood of its previous statements. We believe that counter evidence has already been adduced, of a nature far surpassing, in weight, the claims to credibility which the accusations themselves could offer. The impure fabrication trumped up by a woman of immoral character and insane mind, in conjunction with a man of equally depraved habits, can never be weighed in the balance with the testimony of

180

Protestants, living in the same community as the accused, and, therefore, possessing the means of judging of the truth or falsehood of what was advanced. By any persons of less interested credulity, and of more discriminating and moral honesty, than what the conductors of the Protestant Vindicator appear to possess, counter evidence of the above nature would have been deemed sufficient.

"There are two reasons which have mainly weighed with us, to revert to the subject of the Protestant Vindicator's charges, and to publish the subjoined lengthy documents. We consider, in the first place, our endeavours to expose falsehood as a solemn duty we owe to the defamed; and, in the second, we should regard ourselves to be degraded in the eyes of the world, did we live in a community where such abominations, as are alleged, existed, and not dare, openly and loudly, to denounce the perpetrators.

"Under these impressions, we proceed, at a considerable sacrifice of the space of our journal, to lay before our readers the following affidavits, which will sufficiently disclose the nature of the Protestant Vindicator's calumnies, their origin, and the degree of credit which can be attached to them."

(AFFIDAVIT OF DR. ROBERTSON)

"William Robertson, of Montreal, Doctor in Medicine, being duly sworn on the Holy Evangelists, deposeth and saith as follows:— On the 9th of November, 1834, three men came up to my house, having a young female in company with them, who, they said, was observed that forenoon, on the bank of the Canal, near the extremity of the St. Joseph Suburbs, acting in a manner which induced some people who saw her to think that she intended to drown herself. They took her into a house in the neighbourhood, where, after being there some hours, and interrogated as to who she was, &c., she said she was the daughter of Dr. Robertson. On receiving this information, they brought her to my house. Being from home when they came to the door, and learning from Mrs. Robertson that she had denied them, they conveyed her to the watch-house. Upon hearing this story, in company with G. Auldjo, Esq., of this city. I went to the watch-house to inquire into the affair. We found the young female, whom I have since ascertained to be Maria Monk, daughter of W. Monk, of this city, in custody. She said, that although she was not my daughter, she was the child of respectable parents, in or very near Montreal, who from some light conduct of hers, (arising from temporary insanity, to which she was at times subject from her infancy.) had kept her confined and chained in a cellar for the last four years. Upon examination, no mark or appearance indicated the wearing of manacles, or any other mode of restraint. She said, on my observing this, that her mother always took care to cover the irons with soft cloths to prevent them injuring the skin. From the appearance of her hands,[18] she evidently had not been used to work. To remove her from the watch-house, where she was confined with some of the most profligate women of the town, taken up for inebriety and disorderly conduct in the streets, as she could not give a satisfactory account of herself, I as a Justice of the Peace, sent her to jail as a vagrant. The following morning, I went to the jail for the purpose of ascertaining, if possible, who she was. After considerable persuasion, she promised to divulge her story to the Rev. H. Esson, one of the clergymen of the Church of Scotland, to whose congregation she said her parents belonged. That gentleman did call at the jail, and ascertained who she was. In the course of a few days she was released, and I did not see her again until the month of August last, when Mr. Johnston, of Griffintown, Joiner, and Mr. Cooley, of the St. Ann Suburbs, Merchant, called upon me, about ten o'clock at night, and, after some prefatory remarks, mentioned that the object of their visit was, to ask me, as a magistrate, to institute an inquiry into some very serious charges which had been made against some of the Roman Catholic Priests of that place, and the Nuns of the General Hospital, by a female, who had been a Nun in that Institution for four years, and who had divulged the horrible secrets of that establishment, such as the illicit and criminal intercourse between the Nuns and the Priests, stating particulars of such depravacy of conduct, on the part of these people, in this respect, and their murdering the offspring of these criminal connexions, as soon as they were born, to the number of from thirty to forty every year. I instantly stated, that I did not believe a word of what they told me, and that they must have been imposed upon by some evil-disposed and designing person. Upon inquiry who this Nun, their informant, was, I discovered that she answered exactly the description of Maria Monk, whom I had so much trouble about last year, and mentioned to these individuals my suspicion, and what I knew of that unfortunate girl. Mr. Cooley said to Mr. Johnston, let us go home, we are hoaxed. They told me that she was then at Mr. Johnston's house, and requested me to call there, and hear her own story. The

---

[18] Compare this with the last sentence but one in the affidavit. Why does Dr. R. not give names of persons and their affidavits? It has not yet been done—April, 1836.

next day, or the day following, I did call, and saw Maria Monk, at Mr. Johnston's house. She repeated in my presence the substance of what was mentioned to me before, relating to her having been in the Nunnery for four years; having taken the black veil; the crimes committed there; and a variety of other circumstances concerning the Priests and Nuns. A Mr. Hoyte was introduced to me, and was present during the whole of the time that I was in the house. He was represented as one of the persons who had come from New York with this young woman, for the purpose of investigating into this mysterious affair. I was asked to take her deposition, on her oath, as to the truth of what she had stated. I declined doing so, giving as reason, that, from my knowledge of her character, I considered her assertions upon oath were not entitled to more credit than her bare assertion, and that I did not believe either: intimating, at the same time, my willingness to take the necessary steps for a full investigation, if they could get any other person to corroborate any part of her solemn testimony, or if a direct charge were to be made against any particular individual of a criminal nature. During the first interview with Messrs. Johnston and Cooley, they mentioned, that Maria Monk had been found in New York in a very destitute situation by some charitable individuals, who administered to her necessities, being very sick. She expressed a wish to see a clergyman, as she had a dreadful secret which she wished to divulge before she died; a clergyman visiting her, she related to him the alleged crimes of the Priests and Nuns of the General Hospital at Montreal. After her recovery, she was visited and examined by the Mayor and some lawyers at New York, afterward at Troy, in the State of New York, on the subject; and I understood them to say, that Mr. Hoyte and two other gentlemen, one of them a lawyer, were sent to Montreal, for the purpose of examining into the truth of the accusations thus made. Although incredulous as to the truth of Maria Monk's story, I thought it incumbent upon me to make some inquiry concerning it, and have ascertained where she had been residing a great part of the time she states having been an inmate of the Nunnery. During the summer of 1832 she was at service in William Henry's; the winters of 1823-3, she passed in this neighborhood, at St. Ours and St. Denis. The accounts given of her conduct that season corroborate the opinions I had before entertained of her character.

"W. ROBERTSON.

"Sworn before me, Montreal, this 14th day of November, 1835.
"BENJ. HOLMES, J. P."

183

* * * * *

(AFFIDAVIT OF MY MOTHER)

"On this day, the twenty-fourth day of October, one thousand eight hundred and thirty-five, before me, William Robertson, one of his Majesty's Justices of the Peace for the district of Montreal, came and appeared Isabella Mills,[19] of the city of Montreal, widow of the late William Monk, who declared, that wishing to guard the public against the deception which has lately been practised in Montreal by designing men, who have taken advantage of the occasional derangement of her daughter, to make scandalous accusations against the Priests and the Nuns in Montreal, and afterward to make her pass herself for a nun, who had left the Convent. And after having made oath on the holy evangelists, (to say the truth) the said Isabella Mills declares and says, a man decently dressed (whom afterward I knew to be W. R. Hoyte, stating himself to be a minister of New York,) came to my house on or about the middle of August last, and inquired for one Mr. Mills; that Mr. Esson, a minister here, had told him I could give him some information about that man; I replied that I knew no one of that name in Montreal, but that I had a brother of that name five miles out of town. He then told me that he had lately come to Montreal, with a young woman and child of five weeks old; that the woman had absconded from him at Goodenough's tavern, where they were lodging, and left him with the child; he gave me a description of the woman: I unfortunately discovered that the description answered my daughter, and the reflection that this stranger had called upon Mr. Esson, our pastor, and inquiring for my brother, I suspected that this was planned: I asked for the child, and said that I would place it in a nunnery: to that Mr. Hoyte started every objection, in abusive language against the nuns. At last he consented to give me the child, provided I would give my writing that it should be presented when demanded. We left the house together, Mr. Hoyte requested me to walk at a distance from him, as he was a gentleman. I followed him to Mr. Goodenough's Hotel, and he directed me to room No. 17, and to demand the child; a servant maid gave it to me; Mr. Hoyte came up, and gave me the clothing. I came home with the child, and sent Mrs. Tarbert, an old acquaintance, in search of my daughter; her disposition will be seen. The next day, Mr. Hoyte came in with an elderly man, Dr. Judge Turner, decently dressed, whom he introduced to me as a Mr. Turner, of St. Alban's. They demanded to

---

[19] My mother's maiden name was Mills.

see the child, which I produced. Mr. Hoyte demanded if I had discovered the mother; I said not. She must be found, said he; she has taken away a shawl and a bonnet belonging to a servant girl at Goodenough's; he would not pay for them; she had cost him too much already; that, his things were kept at the hotel on that account. Being afraid that this might more deeply involve my daughter, I offered my own shawl to replace the one taken; Mr. Hoyte first took it but afterward returned it to me on my promise that I would pay for the shawl and bonnet. In the course of the day, Mrs. Tarbert found my daughter, but she would not come to my house; she sent the bonnet and shawl, which were returned to their owner, who had lent them to my daughter, to assist her in procuring her escape from Mr. Hoyte at the hotel. Early on the afternoon of the same day, Mr. Hoyte came to my house with the same old man, wishing me to make all my efforts to find the girl, in the meantime speaking very bitterly against the Catholics, the Priests, and the Nuns; mentioning that my daughter had been in the nunnery, where she had been ill treated. I denied that my daughter had ever been in a nunnery; that when she was about eight years of age, she went to a day-school. At that time came in two other persons, whom Mr. Hoyte introduced; one was Rev. Mr. Brewster, I do not recollect the other reverence's name. They all requested me, in the most pressing terms, to try to make it out; my daughter had been in the nunnery; and that she had some connection with the Priests of the seminary, of which nunneries and Priests she spoke in the most outrageous terms; said, that should I make that out, myself, my daughter, and child, would be protected for life. I expected to get rid of their importunities, in relating the melancholy circumstances by which my daughter was frequently deranged in her head, and told them, that when at the age of about seven years, she broke a slate pencil in her head; that since that time her mental faculties were deranged, and by times much more than at other times, but that she was far from being an idiot; that she could make the most ridiculous, but most plausible stories; and that as to the history that she had been in a nunnery, it was a fabrication, for she never was in a nunnery; that at one time I wished to obtain a place in a nunnery for her; that I had employed the influence of Mrs. De Montenach, of Dr. Nelson, and of our pastor, the Rev. Mr. Esson, but without success. I told them notwithstanding I was a Protestant and did not like the Catholic religion—like all other respectable Protestants, I held the priests of the seminary and the nuns of Montreal in veneration, as the most pious and charitable persons I ever knew. After many more solicitations to the same effect, three of them retired, but Mr. Hoyte remained, adding to the other solicitations; he was stopped, a person having rapped at the door; it was then candlelight. I opened the door, and found Doctor McDonald, who told me that my daughter Maria was at his house, in the most distressing situation; that she wished him to come and make her peace with me; I went with the Doctor to his house in M'Gill-street; she came with me to near my house, but would not come in, notwithstanding I assured her that she would be kindly treated, and that I would give her her child; she crossed the parade ground, and I went into the house, and returned for her.—Mr. Hoyte followed me. She was leaning on the west railing of the parade; we went to her: Mr. Hoyte told her, my dear Mary, I am sorry you have treated yourself and me in this manner; I hope you have not exposed what has passed between us, nevertheless; I will treat you the same as ever, and spoke to her in the most affectionate terms; took her in his arms; she at first spoke to him very cross, and refused to go with him, but at last consented and went with him, absolutely refusing to come to my house. Soon after, Mr. Hoyte came and demanded the child; I gave it to him. Next morning Mr. Hoyte returned, and was more pressing than in his former solicitation, and requested me to say that my daughter had been in the nunnery: that should I say so, it would be better than one hundred pounds to me; that I would be protected for life, and that I should leave Montreal, and that I would be better provided for elsewhere; I answered, that thousands of pounds would not induce me to perjure myself; then he got saucy and abusive to the utmost; he said he came to Montreal to detect the infamy of the Priests and the Nuns; that he could not leave my daughter destitute in the wide world as I had done: afterward said, No! she is not your daughter, she is too sensible for that, and went away—He was gone but a few minutes, when Mr. Doucet, an ancient Magistrate in Montreal, entered. That gentleman told me that Mr. Goodenough had just now called upon him, and requested him to let me know that I had a daughter in Montreal; that she had come in with a Mr. Hoyte and a child, and that she had left Mr. Hoyte and the child, but that she was still in Montreal, so as to enable me to look for her, and that I might prevent some mischief that was going on. Then I related to him partly what I have above said. When he was going, two other gentlemen came. I refused to give them any information at first, expecting that they were of the party that had so much agitated me for a few days; but being informed by Mr. Doucet, that he knew one of them, particularly Mr. Perkins, for a respectable citizen for a long time in Montreal, and the other Mr. Curry, two ministers from the United States, that if they came to obtain some information about the distressing events she related to have occurred in her family, he thought it would do no harm, and I related it to them: they appeared to be afflicted with such a circumstance; I have not seen them any more. I asked Mr. Doucet if the man Hoyte could not be put in jail; he replied that he thought not, for what he knew of the business. Then I asked if the Priests were informed of what was going on; he replied, yes, but they never take up these things; they allow their character to defend itself. A few days after, I heard that my daughter was at one Mr. Johnson's, a joiner, at Griffintown, with Mr. Hoyte; that he passed her for a nun that had escaped from the Hotel Dieu Nunnery. I went there two days successively with Mrs. Tarbert; the first day, Mrs. Johnson denied her, and said that she was gone to New York with Mr. Hoyte. As I was returning, I met Mr. Hoyte on the wharf, and I reproached him for his conduct. I told him that my daughter had been denied me at Johnson's, but that I would have a search-warrant to have her; when I returned, he had really gone with my unfortunate daughter; and I received from Mr. Johnson, his wife and a number of persons in their house, the grossest abuse, mixed with texts of the Gospel, Mr. Johnson bringing a Bible for me to swear on. I retired more deeply afflicted than ever, and further sayeth not.

"Sworn before me, this 24th of October, 1835."

* * * * *

(AFFIDAVIT OF NANCY M'GAN)

"Province of Lower Canada, District of Montreal.

"Before me, William Robertson, one of His Majesty's Justices of the Peace, for the District of Montreal, came and appeared Nancy M'Gan, of Montreal, wife of James Tarbert, who has requested me to receive this affidavit, and declared that she had been intimately acquainted with Mrs. (widow) Monk, of Montreal, a Protestant woman. I know the said Maria Monk; last spring she told me that the father of the child she then was carrying, was burned in Mr. Owsten's house. She often went away in the country, and at the request of her mother I accompanied her across the river. Last summer she came back to my lodgings, and told me that she had made out the father of the child; and that very night left me and went away. The next morning I found that she was in a house of bad fame, where I went for her, and told the woman keeping that house, that she ought not to allow that girl to remain there, for she was a girl of good and honest family. Maria Monk then told me that she would not go to him (alluding, as I understood, to the father of the child), for that he wanted her to swear an oath that would lose her soul for ever, but jestingly said, should make her a lady for ever. I then told her (Maria), do not lose your soul for money. She told me she had swapped her silk gown in the house where I had found her, for a calico one, and got some money to boot; having previously told me if she had some money she would go away, and would not go near him any more. Soon after, Mr. Hoyte and another gentleman came. Mr. Hoyte asked me where she had slept the night previous, and that he would go for the silk gown; the woman showed the gown, and told him that if he would pay three dollars he should have the gown; he went away, and came back with Maria Monk, paid the three dollars and got the gown; I was then present.

"Being at Mrs. Monk's, I saw a child which she mentioned to be her daughter Maria's child. Some time after, Mrs. Monk requested me to accompany her to Griffintown, to look for her daughter. We went, to Mr. Johnson's house, a joiner in that suburb: we met Mr. Hoyte and he spoke to Mrs. Monk; when at Mr. Johnson's, Mrs. Manly asked for her daughter; Mrs. Johnson said she was not there. I saw Mr. Hoyte at Mrs. Monk's; he was in company with three other persons, apparently Americans, earnestly engaged in conversation, but so much confused I could not make out what was said; and farther sayeth not."

"Her
"NANCY + M'GAN.
"mark.
"Sworn before me, on this 24th October, 1835.
"W. ROBERTSON, J. P."

* * * * *

(AFFIDAVIT OF ASA GOODENOUGH)

"Province of Lower Canada, District of Montreal.
"Before me, William Robertson, one of his Majesty's Justices of the Peace, for the District of Montreal, appeared Asa Goodenough, of Montreal, holder of the Exchange Coffee House, who, after having made oath upon the Holy Evangelists, declareth and sayeth, that on or about the nineteenth of August last, two gentlemen and a young female with a child, put up at the Exchange Coffee House, of which I am the owner; they were entered in the book, one under the name of Judge Turner, the other as Mr. Hoyte, a Methodist preacher, and agent or superintendent for the establishment of Sunday-schools, &c.

"Being informed by Catherine Conners, a confidential servant, that something mysterious was passing amongst the above-named,

188

which led me to call on them for an explanation, they answered in a very unsatisfactory manner. I afterward learned that the name of the young woman was Maria Monk, that her mother lived in town, that she was not married to Mr. Hoyte, and they came to Montreal with the view, as Mr. Hoyte said, to disclose the infamy of the Priests, whilst she was at the Nunnery. I thought it prudent to give information of this to a magistrate. Seeing Mr. Doucet's name on the list, I went to him, and requested him to give information to the mother of the young woman, of the circumstances in which her daughter was. He did so, and the disclosure of the design of Mr. Hoyte was the consequence.

"Montreal.

"ASA GOODENOUGH."

* * * * *

"The following affidavits have been translated from the L'Ami du Peuple, Montreal, Nov. 7, 1835."

(AFFIDAVIT OF CATHARINE CONNERS)

"Province of Lower Canada, District of Montreal.

"Before me, W. Robertson, one of His Majesty's Justices of the Peace for the District of Montreal, appeared Catherine Conners of Montreal, a servant in the hotel of Mr. Goodenough, in the city of Montreal; she having made oath on the Holy Evangelists, to say the truth and nothing but the truth, declared and said what follows:

"Towards the 19th of August last, two men and a woman came to the Exchange Coffee House; their names were written in the book, one by the name of Judge Turner, and the other as Mr. Hoyte; the name of the woman was not written in the book, in which the names of travellers are written, because I was informed that they were taking a single room with two beds. Some time after another room was given to them for their accommodation; the woman passed for the wife of Mr. Hoyte.

"The day following, when I was making the bed, I found the woman in tears; having made the remark to her that her child was a very young traveller, she replied that she had not the power to dispense with the journey, for they travelled on business of importance; she also said that she had never had a day of happiness since she had left Montreal, which was four years, with Mr. Hoyte; she expressed a wish to go and see her father. She entreated me to try and procure secretly clothes for her, for Mr. Hoyte wished to

189

dine with her in his own room, in which he was then taking care of the child. I gave her my shawl and bonnet, and conducted her secretly out by the street St Pierre; she never returned, and left the child in the hands of Mr. Hoyte. She said that her husband was a Methodist preacher, and agent of the Sunday School for Montreal, in which he had resided four months last winter; but she had not then been with him. When I returned to the room, Mr. Hoyte was still taking care of the child; he asked me if I had seen his lady; I said no. Upon this question he told me that the father of his lady was dead, that her mother yet lived in the suburbs of Quebec, and he asked me for all the clothes which I had given to wash for him, his lady and child; clothes the lady had taken from the only portmanteau which they had. Beyond that, I perceived nothing remarkable, except that Mr. Hoyte wished to conceal this woman, and to prevent her from going out. I heard the judge say to him, 'now she is yours.' Sworn before me the 2d November, 1835.

(Signed) "W. ROBERTSON."

Mary McCaffrey, also a chambermaid in the hotel of Mr. Goodenough, corroborates the preceding deposition.

(Signed) "W. ROBERTSON."

* * * * *

(AFFIDAVIT OF HENRY M'DONALD)

"Province of Lower Canada, District of Montreal.

"Before me, W. Robertson, one of His Majesty's Justices of the Peace, for the District of Montreal, appeared Henry M'Donald, physician, who, after taking an oath on the Holy Evangelists to say the truth, declared, that in the month of August last, at seven o'clock in the evening, a young woman called at his house with all the symptoms of an extraordinary agitation, and in great distress. She asked his professional advice, complaining of great pains in the breast. On questioning her, he learned that she had a young child, which she said was at Mr. Goodenough's, and that this child was taken away from her. She said that the father of the child was a Methodist Minister, and general agent of the Sunday-Schools. She told me his name, but I cannot recollect it. She told me that now and then her intellectual faculties were weakened in such a manner that she could not support herself. She told me that she would be under great obligation to me, if I would go to her mother's house, and get her child, and procure lodgings for her; that she was without means, and did not know where to go. She could not remain with her mother, because she felt that her conduct had disgraced her family. I went in quest of Mrs. Monk, her mother; she had just come in quest of her daughter, and they went away together from my house.

(Signed) "HENRY M'DONALD."

"Sworn before me the 2d November, 1835.

(Signed) "W. ROBERTSON."

* * * * *

(AFFIDAVIT OF MATTHEW RICHEY)

To the Editor of the Montreal Morning Courier.

Sir,—Among the affidavits published in your paper of to-day, relating to Mr. Hoyte and Maria Monk, I observe a deposition by Mr. Goodenough, that when Mr. Hoyte, in the month of August last, put up at the Exchange Coffee-house, he was entered on the book as a Methodist Preacher, and Agent or Superintendant of Sunday Schools, &c. It has, however, been ascertained, from an examination of the book referred too, that no official designation is appended in it to Mr. Hoyte's name. This discrepancy, Mr. Goodenough states, took place entirely through mistake, and he did not know that Mr. Hoyte was thus characterized in his affidavit till he saw it in print. But as a similar mistake has found its way into several of the depositions which have been elicited by this unhappy affair, I deem it incumbent upon me, as a regularly appointed Methodist Minister of this city, to declare that Mr. Hoyte has never had any connexion with the Methodist Society, either as a preacher or as an agent for Sunday Schools; and I would, at the same time, express my surprise and regret, that the New York Protestant Vindicator should have taken up, and industriously circulated, charges of so grave a nature against the Priests and Nuns of this city, derived from so polluted a source. From such a species of vindication, no cause can receive either honour or credit. By giving this publicity, you will confer a favour on yours, respectfully,

"MATTHEW RICHEY, Wesleyan Minister."

"Montreal, Nov. 16, 1835

* * * * *

"Although we could produce several other affidavits, of an equally unimpeachable character as the above, yet we deem the evidence advanced more than enough to show the entire, falsehood and extravagance of the fabrications in the Protestant Vindicator."

* * * * *

Here closes all the testimony that has been published or brought against me. It requires the suppression of my feelings to repeat to the world charges against myself and my companions, so unfounded, and painful to every virtuous reader. But I [illegible] to the truth to substantiate my narrative, and prefer that everything should be fairly laid before the world. That my opponents had nothing further to produce against me at that time, is proved by the following remark by the Editor of the New York Catholic Diary, to be found in very paper in which he published the preceding affidavits:—

"Here, then, is the whole!"

In a N. Y. Catholic Diary of March last, is a letter from Father McMahon, a Missionary, dated at Sherbrooke, in Canada, in which, as will be seen by the extracts given beyond, he does not even allude to any other testimony than this. Of course my readers will allow that I have reason to say—"Here, then, is the whole!"

The following extracts are given for several reasons. 1st. To prove, by the admission of my adversaries themselves, that no new testimony has been produced since the publication of the Montreal affidavits. 2d. That no disposition is shown to bring the truth to the only fair test—the opening of the Nunnery. 3d. That they are inconsistent in several respects, as, while they pretend to leave the characters of the priests and nuns to defend themselves, they labour with great zeal and acrimony to quiet public suspicion, and to discredit my testimony. 4th. Another object in giving these extracts is, to show a specimen of the style of most of the Roman Catholic writers against me. In respect to argument, temper, and scarcity of facts, Father McMahon is on a level with the editors of the Diary and Green Banner, judging from such of their papers as I have seen.

* * * * *

From Father McMahon's Letter to the editor of the N. Y. Catholic Diary of March, 1836.

"The silence by which you indulge the latent springs of a malpropense, so far from being an argument for culpability, is based upon the charitableness of a conscious innocence, and is, therefore, highly commendable. I say it is highly commendable, inasmuch as these worthy and respectable characters do not deign to answer falsehood, or turn their attention from their sacred avocations by effectually repelling allegations which all men, women, and

192

children, able to articulate a syllable, in the city of Montreal, have repeatedly pronounced to be utterly false, detestably false, and abominably scandalous.

* * * * *

"May I now call upon you, honest Americans, who, though you may differ from me in doctrinal points of religion, have, I trust, the due regard for truth and charity towards all mankind; and into whose hand that instrument of Satan's emissaries may fall, before you believe one syllable [illegible] attentively to peruse the following facts, which are [illegible] men of learning, of every persuasion, and in every country, and which you will find, by mature investigation, to serve as a sufficient key to discover the wicked falsehoods, circulated by the enemies of truth, in the work called, 'The Disclosures of Maria Monk,' but which, in consequence of the total absence of truth from the things therein contained, I have termed (and I think justly on that account), the devil's prayer-book. I beseech you to give my statements a fair, but impartial trial, weigh correctly the arguments opposed to them, according to your judgment—do not allow yourselves to be gulled by the empty or unmeaning phraseology of some of your bloated, though temperate, preachers. All I ask for the test of the following statement, is simply and solely the exercise of your common sense, without equivocation. 1st. I distinctly and unequivocally state, that the impugners of the Catholic religion and its doctrines, never dared to meet us in the fair field of argument. Never yet have they entered the lists in an eristical encounter, but to their cost. Why so? because we have reason, religion, and the impenetrable shield of true syllogistic argumentation in our favour. Witness, in support of the assertion, the stupid and besotted crew (pardon me for this expression, and find a proper term yourselves, for the politico-Theological Charlatans of England), who, not daring to encounter the Catholic Hierarchy of Ireland, in an honorable religious disputation, are forced to drag to their assistance those very apostates from Catholicity who were considered by their superiors unworthy of the situation they attempted to hold in that Church; for the purpose of propping up the staggering and debauched harlot, whose grave they are now preparing. Only remark how they are obliged to have recourse to the exploded scholastic opinion of Peter Dens, by way of showing the intolerance of the Catholics, who repudiate the doctrine of religious intolerance. Maryland, Bavaria, and the Cantons of Switzerland, prove the contrary by their universal religious toleration. Now I could mention, if I thought I had space enough on this sheet, numbers of Protestant divines, who, in their writings, have strongly inculcated the absurd doctrines of ruling our consciences by the authority of the Civil Magistrates. See then, how strange it is that they seek to condemn us for doctrines which we abhor, and which they practice, even to this day. Mark that for an argument against our doctrines.

"2dly. I assert, that notwithstanding all the persecutions, all the falsehood and defamation daily exercised against the Catholics and their religion, they are at this moment the only people on the face of the earth, who maintain amongst them the unity of the true faith, and the regular succession in the Ministry, from Christ and his Apostles.

"3dly. I assert, that the late scandalous production against the Catholic Clergy of Montreal and the Catholic institutions there, is a tissue of false, foul, designing, and scandalous misrepresentation. 1st. Because upon strict examination into all its bearings, it has been so proved upon the solemn oaths of a magistrate and others concerned. 2dly. Because it is no way consonant to reason or common sense to say that those living at a considerable distance, and avowedly hostile to the Catholics and their religion, should feel so interested in the matter? as the Catholics themselves, who are vitally concerned, and who had every facility of discovering any impropriety; who are zealous of the purity of their religion and its Ministers. 3dly. Because the loud cry of all the inhabitants of every denomination, from the well-known integrity, the extraordinary piety, the singular charity and devotedness of the Catholic Clergy, came in peals of just wrath and well-merited indignation on the heads of the degenerate monsters who basely, but ineffectually, attempted to murder the unsullied fame of those whom they deservedly held, and will hold, in the highest estimation.

"T. B. McMahon, Missionary."

Now this letter alludes to testimony legally given, as substantiating the charges against me. What testimony is intended? Any new testimony? If so, where, and what is it? I never heard of any, of any description, except what I have inserted on the preceding pages, unless I except the violent, unsupported, and inconsistent assertion in newspapers, before alluded to. Has any testimony, legally given, been produced, which neither the Catholic Diary, nor any other Catholic paper, has either inserted or alluded to? No. The Missionary, McMahon, must refer to the Montreal affidavits; and since he has expressed his opinion in relation to their credibility and weight, I request my readers to form their own opinions, as I have put the means in their power.

It may, perhaps, appear to some, an act displaying uncommon "concern" in my affairs, or those of the Convent, for Father McMahon to take the pains to write on the subject from Canada. I know more of him and his concerns than the public do; and I am glad that my book has reached him. Happy would it have been for him, if he could prove that he did not leave Sherbrooke from the day when I took the Black veil, until the day when I cast it off. There are many able to bear witness against him in that institution (if they have not been removed), and one out of it, who could easily silence him, by disclosures that he has too much reason to apprehend.

But to return—I assure my readers, then, that this book contains all the testimony that has been brought against me, so far as I can ascertain.

The extensive publication of the Montreal affidavits (for they appeared in the Roman Catholic papers, and were circulated, it is believed, very generally through New York), for a time, almost entirely closed the newspapers against me. My publishers addressed the following letter to the editor of the N. Y. Catholic Diary, and waited on him with a third person, to request its publication in his next paper, but he declined. He expressed doubts of my being in the city, and intimated a wish to see me; but when they acceded, he refused to meet me anywhere but at his own residence!

The same letter was then offered to other editors in New York, and even sent to Philadelphia for publication, but refused. It appeared on the 29th of February, in the Brooklyn Star, thus introduced:—

Extracts from the Long Island Star of Feb. 29th.

"Since the publication of our last paper, we have received a communication from Messrs. Howe and Bates, of New York, the publishers of Miss Monk's 'Awful Disclosures.' It appears that some influences have been at work in that city, adverse to the free examination of the case between her and the priests of Canada; for thus far the news papers have been almost entirely closed against every thing in her defence, while most of them have published false charges against the book, some of a preposterous nature, the contradiction of which is plain and palpable.

"Returning to New York, she then first resolved to publish her story, which she has recently done, after several intelligent and disinterested persons had satisfied themselves by much examination that it was true.

"When it became known in Canada that this was her intention, six affidavits were published in some of the newspapers, intended to destroy confidence in her character; but these were

195

found very contradictory in several important points, and others to afford undersigned confirmation of statements before made by her.

"On the publication of her book, the New York Catholic Diary, the Truth Teller, the Green Banner, and other papers, made virulent attacks upon it, and one of them proposed that the publishers should be 'Lynched.' An anonymous handbill was also circulated in New York, declaring the work a malignant libel, got up by Protestant clergymen, and promising an ample refutation of it in a few days. This was re-published in the Catholic Diary, &c. with the old Montreal affidavits which latter were also distributed through New York and Brooklyn; and on the authority of these, several Protestant newspapers denounced the work as false and malicious.

"Another charge, quite inconsistent with the rest, was also made, not only by the leading Roman Catholic papers, but by several others at second hand—viz. that it was a mere copy of an old European work. This has been promptly denied by the publishers, with the offer of $100 reward for any book at all resembling it.

"Yet, such is the resolution of some and the unbelief of others, that it is impossible for the publishers to obtain insertion for their replies in the New York papers generally, and they have been unsuccessful in an attempt in Philadelphia.

"This is the ground on which the following article has been offered to us for publication in the Star. It was offered to Mr. Schneller, a Roman priest, and editor of the Catholic Diary, for insertion in his paper of Saturday before last, but refused, although written expressly as an answer to the affidavits and charges his previous number had contained. This article has also been refused insertion in a Philadelphia daily paper, after it had been satisfactorily ascertained that there was no hope of gaining admission for it into any of the New York papers.

"It should be stated, in addition, that the authoress of the book, Maria Monk, is in New York, and stands ready to answer any questions, and submit to any inquiries, put in a proper manner, and desires nothing so strongly as an opportunity to prove before a court the truth of her story. She has already found several persons of respectability who have confirmed some of the facts, important and likely to be attested by concurrent evidence; and much testimony in her favour may be soon expected by the public.

"With these facts before them, intelligent readers will judge for themselves. She asks for investigation, while her opponents deny her every opportunity to meet the charges made against her. Mr. Schneller, after expressing a wish to see her, to the publishers, refused to meet her anywhere, unless in his own house; while Mr. Quarter, another Roman Catholic priest, called to see her, at ten o'clock, one night, accompanied by another man, without giving their names, and under the false pretence of being bearers of a letter from her brother in Montreal."

* * * * *

Reply to the Montreal Affidavits, refused publication by the Catholic Diary &c.

"To the Editor of the Catholic Diary.

"SIR—In your paper of last Saturday, you published six affidavits from Montreal, which are calculated, so far as they are believed, to discredit the truth of the 'Awful Disclosures' of Maria Monk, a book of which we are the publishers. We address the following remarks to you, with a request that you will publish them in the Catholic Diary, that your readers may have the means of judging for themselves. If the case be so plain a one as you seem to suppose, they will doubtless perceive more plainly the bearing and force of the evidence you present, when they see it brought into collision with that which it is designed to overthrow.

"First, We have to remark, that the affidavits which you publish might have been furnished you in this city, without the trouble or delay of sending to Montreal. They have been here two or three months, and were carefully examined about that period by persons who are acquainted with Maria Monk's story, and were desirous of ascertaining the truth. After obtaining further evidence from Canada these affidavits were decided to contain strong confirmation of various points in her story, then already written down, only part of which has yet been published.

"Second. It is remarkable that of these six affidavits, the first is that of Dr. Robinson, and all the rest are signed by him as Justice of the Peace; and a Justice, too, who had previously refused to take the affidavit of Maria Monk. Yet, unknown to himself, this same Dr. R., by incidents of his own stating, corroborates some very important parts of Miss Monk's statements. He says, indeed, that he has ascertained where she was part of the time when she professed to have been in the Nunnery. But his evidence on this point is merely hearsay, and he does not even favour us with that.

"Third, One of the affidavits is that of Miss Monk's mother, who claims to be a Protestant, and yet declares, that she proposed to send her infant grandchild to a Nunnery! She says her daughter has long been subject to fits of insanity, (of which, however, we can say no traces are discoverable in New York,) and has never been in a Nunnery since she was at school in one, while quite a child. She however does not mention where her daughter has spent any part of

197

the most important years of her life. A large part of her affidavit, as well as several others, is taken up with matter relating to one of the persons who accompanied Miss M. to Montreal last summer, and has no claim to be regarded as direct evidence for or against the authenticity of her book.

"Fourth, The affidavit of Nancy McGan is signed with a cross, as by one ignorant of writing; and she states that she visited a house of ill fame, (to all appearance alone,) although, as she asserts, to bring away Miss M. Her testimony, therefore, does not present the strongest claims to our confidence. Besides, it is known that she has shown great hostility, to Miss Monk, in the streets of Montreal: and she would not, it is believed, have had much influence on an intelligent court or jury, against Miss M., in that city, if the latter had been fortunate enough to obtain the legal investigation into her charges, which as Dr. R. mentions, she declared to be the express object of her visit to that city, in the last summer, and in which she failed, after nearly a month's exertion.

"Fifth, The affidavit of Mr. Goodenough is contradicted in one point by the letter of Mr. Richey, a Wesleyan minister, which you insert, and contains little else of any importance to this or any other case. * * * *

"Sixth, You copied in a conspicuous manner, from a Catholic paper in Boston, a charge against the book, the groundlessness of which has been exposed in some of the New York papers, viz. that large parts of it were, 'word for word and letter for letter.' (names only altered,) copied from a book published some years ago in Europe, under the title of 'The Gates of Hell opened.' We have not seen in your paper any correction of this aspersion, although the assertion of it has placed you in a dilemma; for, if such were the fact, as you asserted, the Montreal affidavits would have little application to the case. Besides, that book, having proceeded from Catholics, and relating, as was intimated, to scenes in European Convents, divulged by witnesses not chargeable with prejudices against them, is to be taken for true with other names; and therefore the charge of extravagance or improbability, which is so much urged against our book, is entirely nullified, without appealing to other sources of information which cannot be objected to.

"But before closing, allow us to remark, that you, who claim so strongly the confidence of your readers in the testimony of witnesses in Montreal, who speak only of things collateral to the main subject in question, must be prepared to lay extraordinary weight on evidence of a higher nature, and must realize something of the anxiety with which we, and the American public generally, we believe, stand ready to receive the evidence to be displayed to the

198

eye and to the touch, either for or against the solemn declaration of Miss Monk, whenever the great test shall be applied to which she appeals, viz. the opening of the Hotel Dieu Nunnery at Montreal. Then, sir, and not till then, will the great question be settled,—Is our book true or false? Affidavits may possibly be multiplied, although you say, 'Here, then, is the whole!' Dr. Robertson may be called again to testify, or receive testimony as Justice of the Peace,—but the question is not, what do people believe or think outside of the Convent? but, 'what has been done in it?'

"By the issue of this investigation, Miss Monk declares she is ready to stand or fall.

"You speak, sir, of the 'backwardness' of persons to appear in defence of Miss Monk's book. We promise to appear as often on the subject as you are willing to publish our communications. In one of the paragraphs you publish, our book is spoken of as one of the evils arising from a 'free press.' We think, sir, that 'a free press' is exposed to less condemnation through the 'Awful Disclosures,' than the 'close Nunneries' which it is designed to expose.

"Respectfully, &c
"New York, Feb. 22d, 1836."

* * * * *

The above was afterward copied in other papers. The following certificate appeared in the Protestant Vindicator, and other papers, in March, 1836, introducing the two first witnesses.

"The truth of Maria Monk's 'Awful Disclosures' amply certified.

"We the subscribers, having an acquaintance with Miss Maria Monk, and having considered the evidence of different kinds which has been collected in relation to her case, have no hesitation in declaring our belief in the truth of the statements she makes in her book recently published in New York, entitled 'Awful Disclosures,' &c. We at that same time declare that the assertion, originally made in the Roman Catholic newspapers of Boston, that the book was copied from a work entitled 'The Gates of Hell opened,' is wholly destitute of foundation; it being entirely new, and not copied from any thing whatsoever.

"And we further declare, that no evidence has yet been produced which discredits the statements of Miss Monk; while, on the contrary, her story has received, and continues to receive, confirmation from various sources.

"During the last week, two important witnesses spontaneously appeared, and offered to give public testimony in her favour. From them the following declarations have been received. The first is an affidavit given by Mr. William Miller, now a resident of this city. The second is a statement received from a young married woman, who, with her husband, also resides here. In the clear and repeated statements made by these two witnesses, we place entire reliance; who are ready to furnish satisfaction to any persons making reasonable inquiries on the subject.

"W. C. BROWNLEE.
"JOHN J. SLOCUM.
"ANDREW BRUCE.
"D. FANSHAW.
"AMOS BELDEN.
"DAVID WESSON.
"THOMAS HOGAN."

* * * * *

(AFFIDAVIT OF WILLIAM MILLER)

"City and County of New York, ss.
"William Miller being duly sworn, doth say—I knew Maria Monk when she was quite a child, and was acquainted with all her father's family. My father, Mr. Adam Miller, kept the government school at St. John's, Lower Canada, for some years. Captain Wm. Monk, Maria's father, lived in the garrison, a short distance from the village, and she attended the school with me for some months, probably as much as a year. Her four brothers also attended with us. Our families were on terms of intimacy, as my father had a high regard for Captain Monk; but the temper of his wife was such, even at that time, as to cause much trouble. Captain Monk died very suddenly, as was reported, in consequence of being poisoned. Mrs. Monk was then keeper of the Government House in Montreal, and received a pension, which privilege she has since enjoyed. In the summer of 1832, I left Canada, and came to this city. In about a year afterward I visited Montreal, and on the day when the Governor reviewed the troops, I believe about the end of August, I called at the Government House, where I saw Mrs. Monk and several of the family. I inquired where Maria was, and she told me that she was in the nunnery. This fact I well remember, because the information gave me great pain, as I had unfavorable opinions of the nunneries. On reading the 'Awful Disclosures,' I at once knew she was the eloped nun, but was unable to find her until a few days since, when we recognized each other immediately. I give with pleasure my testimony in her favour, as she is among strangers, and exertions

have been made against her. I declare my personal knowledge of many facts stated in her book, and my full belief in the truth of her story, which, shocking as it is, cannot appear incredible to those persons acquainted with Canada.

"WILLIAM MILLER.

"Sworn before me, this 3d day of March, 1836.

"BENJAMIN D. K. CRAIG,

"Commissioner of Deeds, &c."

* * * * *

From the Protestant Vindicator of March 9.

"The following statement has been furnished by the female witness above-mentioned; the name being reserved only from delicacy to a lady's feelings."

(TESTIMONY OF ANOTHER OLD SCHOOLMATE)

"I was born at Montreal, and resided there until within a few months, and where my friends still remain. I was educated among the Catholics, and have never separated myself from them.

"I knew Maria Monk when quite a child. We went to school together for about a year, as near as I can remember, to Mr. Workman, Sacrament-street, in Montreal. She is about one month younger than myself. We left that school at the same time, and entered the Congregational Nunnery nearly together. I could mention many things which I witnessed there, calculated to confirm some of her accounts.

"I knew of the elopement of a priest named Leclerc, who was a confessor, with a nun sent from the Congregational Nunnery to teach in a village. They were brought back, after which she gave birth to an infant, and was again employed as a teacher.

"Children were often punished in the Congregational Nunnery, by being made to stand with arms extended, to imitate Christ's posture on the cross; and when we found vermin in our soup, as was often the case, we were exhorted to overcome our repugnance to it, because Christ died for us. I have seen such belts as are mentioned in the 'Awful Disclosures,' as well as gags; but never saw them applied.

"Maria Monk left the Congregational Nunnery before I did, and became a Novice in the Hotel Dieu. I remember her entrance into the latter very well, for we had a 'jour de congé,' holiday, on that occasion.

201

"Some short time subsequently, after school hours one afternoon, while in the school-room in the second story of the Congregational Nunnery, several of the girls standing near a window exclaimed, 'There is Maria Monk.' I sprang to the window to look, and saw her with several other novices, in the yard of the Hotel Dieu, among the plants which grew there. She did not appear to notice us, but I perfectly recognised her.

"I have frequently visited the public hospital of the Hotel Dieu. It is the custom there for some of the nuns and novices to enter at three o'clock, P.M., in procession with food and delicacies for the sick. I recollect some of my visits there by circumstances attending them. For instance, I was much struck, on several occasions, by the beauty of a young novice, whose slender, graceful form, and interesting appearance, distinguished her from the rest. On inquiry, I learnt that her name was Dubois, or something like it, and the daughter of an old man who had removed from the country, and lived near the Place d'Armes. She was so generally admired for her beauty, that she was called 'la belle St. François'—St. Francis being the saint's name she had assumed in the Convent.

"I frequently went to the hospital to see two of my particular friends who were novices: and subsequently to visit one who had a sore throat, and was sick for some weeks. I saw Maria Monk there many times, in the dress of a novice, employed in different ways but we were never allowed to speak to each other.

"Towards the close of the winter of 1833-4, I visited the hospital of the Hotel Dieu very frequently, to see Miss Bourke, a friend of mine, although I was not permitted to speak with her. While there one day, at the hour of 'congé' or 'collation' which, as I before stated, was at three P.M., a procession of nuns and novices entered, and among the former I saw Maria Monk, with a black veil, &c. She perceived and recognized me; but put her finger on her lips in token of silence; and knowing how rigidly the rules were enforced, I did not speak.

"A short time afterward, I saw her again in the same place, and under similar circumstances.

"I can fix the year when this occurred, because I recollect that the nuns in the hospital stared at a red dress I wore that season; and I am certain about that time of year, because I left my galoshes at the door before I went in.

"The improper conduct of a priest was the cause of my leaving the Congregational Nunnery: for my brother saw him kissing a [illegible] one day while he was on a visit to me, and exclaimed—'O mon Dieu! what a place you are in!—If father does not take you out of it I will, if I have to tear you away.'

202

"After the last sight I had of Maria Monk in the hospital, I never saw nor heard of her, until after I had been for some time an inhabitant of New York. I then saw an extract from 'Awful Disclosures,' published in a newspaper, when I was perfectly satisfied that she was the authoress, and again at liberty. I was unable for several weeks to find her residence, but at length visited the house when she was absent. Seeing an infant among a number of persons who were strangers to me, as those present will testify, I declared that it must be the child mentioned in her book, from the striking resemblance it bears to Father Phelan, whom I well know. This declaration has also been made by others.

"When Maria Monk entered, she passed across the room, without turning towards me; but I recognised her by her gait, and when she saw me she knew me at once. I have since spent many hours with her, and am entirely convinced of the truth of her story, especially as I knew many things before which tend to confirm the statements which she makes."

["It is superfluous to add any thing to the above testimony. Let the Roman priests of Montreal open the Hotel Dieu Nunnery for our inspection, and thus confute Maria Monk: or, Mr. Conroy is again challenged to institute a criminal process against her, or a civil suit against the publishers of her volume—They dare not place the eloped nun or her booksellers in that 'Inquisition;' because they know that it would only be 'putting themselves to the torture!'"—Ed. Prot. Vind.]

* * * * *

From The Protestant Vindicator of March 16th.
"We recommend the following communications to all persons who doubt the wickedness of Nunneries. The young gentleman who sent us the letter is now in this city, and we have heard the same statements from other witnesses. That subterraneous passages from the Seminary to the Nunneries, we ourselves have seen, and close by the spot designated by our correspondent:—

(STATEMENT OF J. M.)

"Underground passage from the Jesuit Seminary to the Hotel Dieu Nunnery, Montreal.
"I have been informed that you are endeavoring to obtain facts and other incidental circumstances relative to the Black Nunnery, in Montreal, and the disclosures concerning it, made by Maria Monk, in which are many hard things, but hard as they are,

203

they are not indigestible by us Canadians; we believe that she has told but a small part of what she must know, if she was but half the time there which she says she was. Maria Monk has mentioned in her book something about the underground passage which leads from the Black Nunnery to other places in Montreal. That fact I know by ocular demonstration, and which nine tenths of the Canadians also will not deny, for it has been opened several times by the labourers, who have been digging for the purpose of laying pipes to conduct gas and water. While preparing a place for the latter I saw one of those passages; the earth being removed by the labourers, they struck upon the top of the passage, and curiosity led them to see what was beneath, for it sounded as though there was a hollow. They accordingly removed the large flat stones which formed the top of the passage. Many persons were looking on at the time, and several of them went down into it; when they returned after a few minutes, they stated that they went but a short distance, before they came to an intersection of passages, and were afraid to proceed further. Shortly after, several priests were on the spot, and prevented the people from further examining it; and had the place shut up immediately, while they stood by and guarded it until it was all done. The appearance of that part of the passage was the same as I saw while they were laying the water pipes. The floor of it in both [illegible] where I saw it was clean to appearance, with the exception of a little dirt that fell in on opening them, and of stone flagging. I have heard much about these underground passages in Montreal, in which place I have spent the most of my days. I give you my name and residence: and if you should be called upon from any quarter for the truth of this statement. I am ready to attest it upon oath; and there are others in this city who have witnessed the same things. The places where those openings were made in the underground passages were in St. Joseph street for the water pipes; and for the gas pipes in Notre-Dame street, near Sacrament street, at a short distance from the Seminary.

"W. M."

* * * * *

About the close of February last, a note was sent me from a person signing himself the man who took me to the Almshouse. Soon after I had an interview with Mr. Hilliker, whom I recognised as my first protector in New York, and to whom I owe much—indeed, as I think, my life. He kindly offered to give me his testimony, which follows:—

From the New York Journal of Commerce.

(AFFIDAVIT OF JOHN HILLIKER)

"City and County of New York, ss.

"John Hilliker, being duly sworn, doth depose and say—that one day early in the month of May, 1835, while shooting near the Third Avenue, opposite the three milestone, in company with three friends, I saw a woman sitting in a field at a short distance, who attracted our attention. On reaching her, we found her sitting with her head down, and could not make her return any answer to our questions. On raising her hat, we saw that she was weeping. She was dressed in an old calico frock, (I think of a greenish colour,) with a checked apron, and an old black bonnet. After much delay and weeping, she began to answer my questions, but not until I had got my companions to leave us, and assured her that I was a married man, and disposed to befriend her.

"She then told me that her name was Maria, that she had been a nun in a nunnery in Montreal, from which she had made her escape, on account of the treatment she had received from priests in that institution, whose licentious conduct she strongly intimated to me. She mentioned some particulars concerning the Convent and her escape. She spoke particularly of a small room where she used to attend, until the physician entered to see the sick, when she accompanied him to write down his prescriptions; and said that she escaped through a door which he sometimes entered. She added, that she exchanged her dress after leaving the nunnery, and that she came to New York in company with a man, who left her as soon as the steamboat arrived. She farther stated, that she expected soon to give birth to a child, having become pregnant in the Convent; that she had no friend, and knew not where to find one; that she thought of destroying her life; and wished me to leave her—saying, that if I should hear of a woman being found drowned in the East River, she earnestly desired me never to speak of her.

"I asked her if she had had any food that day, to which she answered, no; and I gave her money to get some at the grocery of Mr. Cox, in the neighbourhood. She left me, but I afterwards saw her in the fields, going towards the river; and after much urgency, prevailed upon her to go to a house where I thought she might be accommodated, offering to pay her expenses. Failing in this attempt, I persuaded her, with much difficulty, to go the Almshouse; and there we got her received, after I had promised to call and see her, as she said she had something of great consequence which she wished to communicate to me, and wished me to write a letter to Montreal.

"She had every appearance of telling the truth; so much so,

that I have never for a moment doubted the truth of her story, but told it to many persons of my acquaintance, with entire confidence in its truth. She seemed overwhelmed with grief, and in a very desperate state of mind. I saw her weep for two hours or more without ceasing; and appeared very feeble when attempting to walk, so that two of us supported her by the arms. We observed also, that she always folded her hands under her apron when she walked, as she has described the nuns as doing in her 'Awful Disclosures.'

"I called at the Almshouse gate several times and inquired for her; but having forgotten half her name, I could not make it understood whom I wished to see, and did not see her until the last week. When I saw some of the first extracts from her book in a newspaper, I was confident that they were parts of her story, and when I read the conclusion of the work, I had not a doubt of it. Indeed, many things in the course of the book I was prepared for from what she had told me.

"When I saw her, I recognised her immediately, although she did not know me at first, being in a very different dress. As soon as she was informed where she had seen me, she recognised me. I have not found in the book any thing inconsistent with what she had stated to me when I first saw her.

"When I first found her in May, 1835, she had evidently sought concealment. She had a letter in her hand, which she refused to let me see; and when she found I was determined to remove her, she tore it in small pieces, and threw them down. Several days after I visited the spot again and picked them up, to learn something of the contents but could find nothing intelligible, except the first part of the Signature, 'Maria.'

"Of the truth of her story I have not the slightest doubt, and I think

I never can until the Nunnery is opened and examined.

"JOHN HILLIKER.

"Sworn before me, this 14th of March, 1835.

"PETER JENKINS,

"Commissioner of Deeds."

The following challenge was published in the N. Y. Protestant Vindicator for six or seven weeks, in March and April, without a reply.

"CHALLENGE—The Roman Prelate and Priests of Montreal—Messrs. Conroy, Quarter, and Schneller, of New York—Messrs. Fenwick and Byrne of Boston—Mr. Hughes of Philadelphia—the Arch-Prelate of Baltimore, and his subordinate Priests—and Cardinal England of Charleston, with all other Roman Priests, and every Nun from Baffin's bay to the Gulf of Mexico, are hereby challenged to meet an investigation of the truth of Maria Monk's 'Awful Disclosures,' before an impartial assembly, over which shall preside seven gentlemen; three to be selected by the Roman Priests, three by the Executive Committee of the New York Protestant Association, and the Seventh as Chairman, to be chosen by the six.

"An eligible place in New York shall be appointed and the regulations for the decorum and order of the meetings, with all the other arrangements, shall be made by the above gentlemen.

"All communications upon this subject from any of the Roman Priests or Nuns, either individually, or as delegates for their superiors, addressed to the Corresponding Secretary of the New York Protestant Association, No. 142 Nassau-street, New York, will be promptly answered."

* * * * *

From the N. Y. Protestant Vindicator of April 6, 1836.

"*THE CHALLENGE.*—We have been waiting with no small degree of impatience to hear from some of the Roman priests. But neither they, nor their sisters, the nuns, nor one of their nephews or nieces, have yet ventured to come out. Our longings meet only with disappointment. Did ever any person hear of similar conduct on the part of men accused of the highest crimes, in their deepest dye? Here is a number of Roman priests, as actors, or accessories, openly denounced before the world as guilty, of the most outrageous sins against the sixth and seventh commandments. They are charged before the world with adultery, fornication, and murder! The allegations are distinctly made, the place is mentioned, the parties are named, and the time is designated; for it is lasting as the annual revolutions of the seasons. And what is most extraordinary,—the highest official authorities in Canada know that all those statements are true, and they sanction and connive at the iniquity!—The priests and nuns have been offered, for several months past, the most easy and certain mode to disprove the felonies imputed to them, and they are still as the dungeons of the Inquisition, silent as the death-like quietude of the convent cell; and as retired as if they were in the subterraneous passages between the Nunnery and Lartigue's habitation. Now, we contend, that scarcely a similar instance of disregard for the opinions of mankind, can be found since the Reformation, at least, in a Protestant country. Whatever disregard for the judgment of others, the Romish priests may have felt, where the Inquisition at their command, and the civil power was their Jackal and their Hyena: they have been obliged to pay some little regard to the opinion of protestants, and to the dread of exposure.

We therefore repeat the solemn indubitable truth—that the facts which are stated by Maria Monk, respecting the Hotel Dieu Nunnery at Montreal, are true as the existence of the priests and nuns,—that the character, principles, and practices of the Jesuits and Nuns in Canada are most accurately delineated—that popish priests, and sisters of charity in the United States, are their faithful and exact counterparts—that many female schools in the United States, kept by the papist teachers, are nothing more than places of decoy through which young women, at the most delicate age, are ensnared into the power of the Roman priests—and that the toleration of the monastic system in the United States and Britain, the only two countries in the world, in which that unnatural abomination is now extending its withering influence, is high treason against God and mankind. If American citizens and British Christians, after the appalling developments which have been made, permit the continuance of that prodigious wickedness which is inseparable from nunneries and the celibacy of popish priests, they will ere long experience that divine castigation which is justly due to transgressors, who wilfully trample upon all the appointments of God, and who subvert the foundation of national concord, and extinguish the comforts of domestic society. Listen to the challenge again! All the papers with which the Protestant Vindicator exchanges, are requested to give the challenge one or two insertions." (Here it was repeated.)

* * * * *

Testimony of a friend in the hospital

Statement made by a respectable woman, who had the charge of me during a part of my stay in the Bellevue Hospital, in New York. She is ready to substantiate it. It is now first published.

"I was employed as an occasional assistant in the Bellevue Hospital, in New York, in the spring of the year 1835. My department was in the Middle House and the pantry. I was present one day in the room of Mrs. Johnston, the Matron, when a man came in with a young woman, and gave a note to Mrs. J., (which I understood was from Col. Fish.) the Superintendent, Mr. Stevens, being out. The female was dressed in a light blue calico frock, a salmon-coloured shawl, and a black bonnet, under which was a plain cap, something like a night-cap, which I afterward understood was a nun's cap. Being occupied at that time, I paid no attention to the conversation which took place between her and the Matron; but I soon heard that she was a nun who had escaped from a convent in Canada, who had been found in a destitute condition, by some

208

persons shooting in the fields, and that she was in such a situation as to demand comforts and careful treatment.

"She was placed in room No. 33, where most of the inmates were aged American women; but as she appeared depressed and melancholy, the next day Mr. Stevens brought her into No. 26, and put her under my particular charge, as he said the women in that room were younger. They were, however, almost all Roman Catholics as there are many in the institution generally.

"I told her she might confide in me, as I felt for her friendless and unhappy situation; and finding her ignorant of the Bible, and entertaining some superstitious views, I gave her one, and advised her to read the scriptures, and judge for herself. We had very little opportunity to converse in private; and although she several times said she wished she could tell me something, no opportunity offered, as I was with her only now and then, when I could step into the room for a few minutes. I discouraged her from talking, because those around appeared to be constantly listening, and some told her not to mind 'that heretic.'

"Seeing her unhappy state of mind, it was several times proposed to her to see Mr. Tappan; and, after a week or two, as I should judge, he visited her, advised her to read the Bible, and judge for herself of her duty.

"One Sabbath I invited her to attend service, and we went to hear Mr. Tappan preach; but after her return, some of the Irish women told her to go no more, but mind her own religion. This produced an impression upon her, for she seemed like a child of tender feeling, gentle, and disposed to yield. She bound herself round my heart a good deal, she was of so affectionate a turn. The rudeness with which she was treated by several of the women, when they dared, would sometimes overcome her. A large and rather old woman, named Welsh, one of the inmates, entered the room one day, very abruptly, saying, 'I want to see this virtuous nun;' and abused her with most shameful language, so that I had to return to her, and complain of her to the Superintendent, who was shocked at such impudence in a foreign pauper, so that she was put into another room. Maria was washing her hands at the time Mrs. Welsh came in, and was so much agitated, that she did not raise her head, and almost fainted, so that I had to lift her upon a bed.

"Before this occurrence, the women would often speak to Maria while I was away and, as I had every reason to believe, endeavoured to persuade her to go to the priests. I told them that they ought rather to protect her, as she had come to the same country where they had sought protection.

"Mr. Conroy, a Roman priest, used to be regularly at the

209

institution two or three times a week, from about 10 till 1 o'clock, both before and after Maria Monk became an inmate of it. No. 10 was his confession-room. He baptised children in the square-ward, and sometimes visited the sick Catholics in other rooms. Sometimes he went up in the afternoon also.

"I heard it said, that Mr. Conroy had asked to speak with Maria: and that an offer was made to him that he might see her before others, but not otherwise, to which Mr. Conroy did not consent.

"Sometimes Maria was much disturbed in her sleep, starting suddenly, with every appearance of terror. Some nights she did not sleep at all, and often told me, what I had no doubt was the fact, that she was too much agitated by the recollection of what she had seen in the Nunnery. She would sometimes say in the morning, 'O, if I could tell you! You think you have had trouble, but I have had more than ever you did.'

"Her distressing state of mind, with the trials caused by those around her, kept me constantly thinking of Maria, so that when employed at a distance from her, I would often run to her room, to see how she was for a moment, and back again. Fortunately, the women around held me somewhat in fear, because they found my reports of the interference of some were attended to; and this kept them more at a distance; yet they would take advantage of my absence sometimes. One day, on coming to No. 23. I found Maria all in a tremour, and she told me that Mrs. ——, one of the Roman Catholic nurses, had informed her that Mr. Conroy was in the institution, and wished to see her. 'And what shall I do?' she inquired of me, in great distress.

"I told her not to be afraid, and that she should be protected, as she was among friends, and endeavoured to quiet her fears all I could; but it was very difficult to do so. One of the women in the house, I know, told Maria, in my presence, one day, that Mr. Conroy was waiting in the passage to see her. The present Superintendent (another Mr. Stevens) succeeded the former while Maria and I were in the Hospital. Abby Welsh (not the Mrs. Welsh mentioned before) got very angry with me one day, because, as usual on the days when Mr. Conroy came, I was watchful to prevent his having an interview with Maria. Another person, for a time, used to employ her in sewing in her room on those days, for she also protected her, as well in this way, as by reproving those who troubled her. Abby Welsh, finding me closely watching Maria on the day I was speaking of, told me, in a passion, that I might watch her as closely as I pleased—Mr. Conroy would have her. Not long after this, I saw Abby Welsh talking earnestly with Mr. Conroy, in the yard, under one of the

210

windows of the Middle House, and heard her say, 'the nun,' and afterward, 'she's hid.'

"A Roman Catholic woman, who supposed that Maria had been seen in St. Mary's Church, expressed a wish that she could have caught her there; and said, she would never again have made her appearance. I inquired whether there was any place where she could have been confined. She replied, in a reserved, but significant manner, 'There is at least one cell there for her.'

"New York, March 23d, 1836."

It would be a natural question, if my readers should ask, "What said the Roman Catholics to such testimonials? They laid great stress on affidavits sent for to Montreal; what do they think of affidavits spontaneously given in New York?"

So far as I know, they have republished but one, and that is Mr. Miller's!

The New York Catholic Diary of March 19th, said—

"We take the following overwhelming testimony from the Brooklyn American Citizen of the 11th instant:

"The following affidavits, &c., are copied from the last No. of the 'Protestant Vindicator,' and prove, it seems to us, taken with other corroborating circumstances, the falsehood and irrelevancy of the testimony against Miss Monk, and therefore establish the truth of her narrative:"

(Here it inserted Mr. Miller's affidavit, and then added:)

"What is the weight of the affidavit? Of ponderous import? I inquired where Maria was, and she told me she was in the Nunnery? Therefore she is an eloped Nun. Marvellous logical affidavit! We may say, that when an inquiry is made after the editor of this paper, and the answer is, that he was in Protestant Church, therefore he is a Protestant minister."

The Rev. Mr. Schneller, (for a Catholic priest is the editor of that paper,) thus tries to slide over the important testimony of Mr. Miller, and in doing it, admits that I was in the Hotel Dieu Nunnery in the summer of 1832. Of course, he admits then, that Dr. Robertson's testimony to the contrary it false, and gives up the great point which the Montreal affidavits were intended to settle, viz. that I had not been in any Nunnery—at least, not since I was a child.

But another thing is worthy of remark. The Diary says, "We take the following overwhelming testimony from the Brooklyn American Citizen," yet he really leaves out the greater part of the testimony which that paper contained, viz. the certificate beginning on page 251. Let any one turn to that, and ask whether the editor had not some reason to wish to keep it from his readers? Did he not

211

get rid of it very ingeniously, when he inserted the following remarks instead of it?

"The following statement has been furnished by the female witness above mentioned; the name being reserved only from delicacy to a lady's feelings."

"Excellent! 'delicacy to a lady's feelings!!' we are absorbed in an exclamation of wonder; the delicate name, in a matter of such vast importance, as that which affects the truth of the slanderous tale, cannot be mentioned!

"Therefore, 'we, the subscribers,' 'Brownlee, Slocum, Brace, Fanshaw, Belden, Wesson, and Hogan,' rest the weight of their authority upon the 'delicacy' of a nameless 'lady's feelings.'"

Now here Mr. Shellner pretends that the witness was not accessible, and leaves it in doubt, whether the subscribers, (men of known character and unimpeachable veracity.) knew any thing of her. Yet it was expressly stated by them that she was known, and that any reasonable inquiries would be readily answered.

I have no intention of attempting to enforce the evidence presented in the testimonials just given. I shall leave every reader to form his own conclusions independently and dispassionately. I could easily say things likely to excite the feelings of every one who peruses these pages—but I prefer to persist in the course I have thus far pursued, and abstain from all exciting expressions. The things I declare are sober realities, and nothing is necessary to have them so received, but that the evidence be calmly laid before the public.

I will make one or two suggestions here, for the purpose of directing attention to points of importance, though one or two of them have been already touched upon.

1st. One of the six affidavits was given by Dr. Robertson, and the remaining five were sworn to before him.

2d. The witnesses speak of interviews with me, on two of the most distressing days of my life. Now let the reader refer to those affidavits and then say, whether any expressions which they may have misunderstood, or any which may have been fabricated for me, (as I strongly suspect must have been the fact with some,) ought to destroy my character for credibility; especially when I appeal to evidence so incontestible as an inspection of the nunnery, and my opponents shrink from it. Let the reader observe also, that in the interviews spoken of in the affidavits, no third person is commonly spoken of as present; while those who are named are most of them inimical to me.

3d. All the testimony in the affidavits is aimed to destroy my character, and to prevent me from receiving any credit as a witness. Not a bit of it meets the charges I make against the priests and

212

nuns. If they had proved that I never was in the nunnery, that, indeed would set aside my testimony: but failing to do [illegible], the attempt goes far to set their own aside.

Having now fairly shown my readers what reception my first edition met with, both from enemies and friends, I proceed to the "Sequel" of my narrative.

THE END

THE END